Welcome to

Pearson Math Makes Sense 6

Math helps you understand what you see and do every day.

You will use this book to learn about the math around you. Here's how.

In each Unit:

- A scene from the world around you reminds you of some of the math you already know.

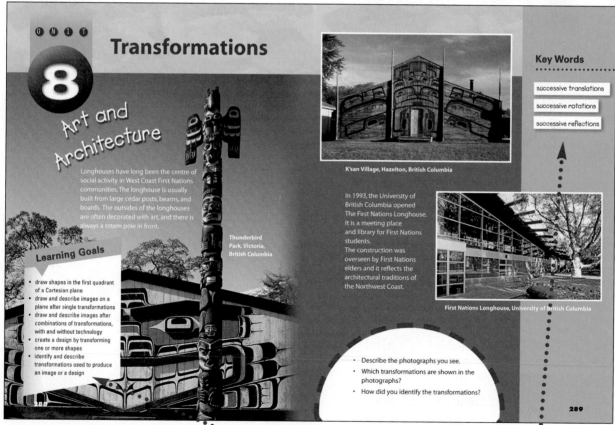

U N I T

8
Art and Architecture

Transformations

Longhouses have long been the centre of social activity in West Coast First Nations communities. The longhouse is usually built from large cedar posts, beams, and boards. The outsides of the longhouses are often decorated with art, and there is always a totem pole in front.

Thunderbird Park, Victoria, British Columbia

K'san Village, Hazelton, British Columbia

In 1993, the University of British Columbia opened The First Nations Longhouse. It is a meeting place and library for First Nations students. The construction was overseen by First Nations elders and it reflects the architectural traditions of the Northwest Coast.

First Nations Longhouse, University of British Columbia

Key Words

successive translations

successive rotations

successive reflections

Learning Goals

- draw shapes in the first quadrant of a Cartesian plane
- draw and describe images on a plane after single transformations
- draw and describe images after combinations of transformations, with and without technology
- create a design by transforming one or more shapes
- identify and describe transformations used to produce an image or a design

- Describe the photographs you see.
- Which transformations are shown in the photographs?
- How did you identify the transformations?

289

Find out what you will learn in the **Learning Goals** and important **Key Words**.

In each Lesson:

You **Explore** an idea or problem, usually with a partner. You often use materials.

Connect summarizes the math. It often shows a solution, or multiple solutions, to a question.

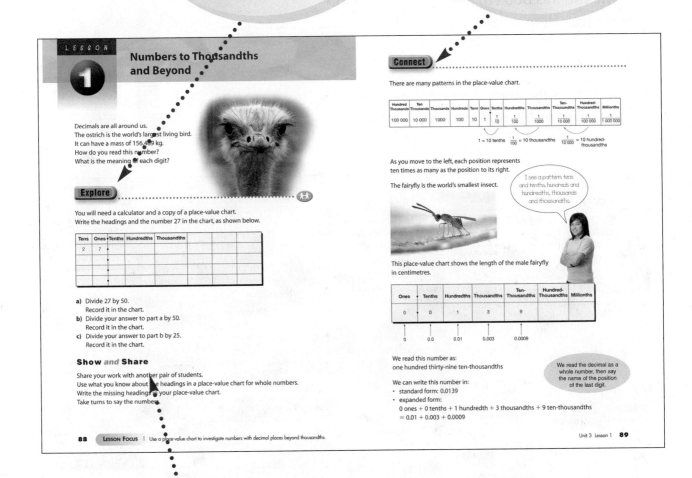

Then you **Show and Share** your results with other students.

Practice questions help you to use and remember the math.

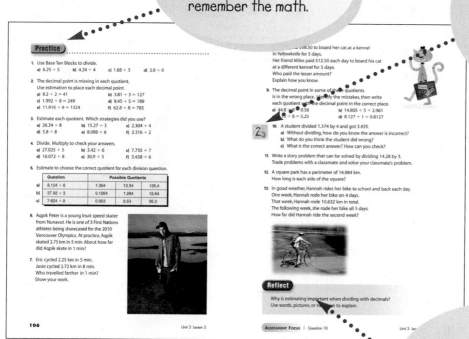

Practice

1. Use Base Ten Blocks to divide.
   a) $6.25 \div 5$ b) $4.24 \div 4$ c) $1.68 \div 3$ d) $3.9 \div 6$

2. The decimal point is missing in each quotient. Use estimation to place each decimal point.
   a) $8.2 \div 2 = 41$ b) $3.81 \div 3 = 127$
   c) $1.992 \div 8 = 249$ d) $9.45 \div 5 = 189$
   e) $11.916 \div 9 = 1324$ f) $62.8 \div 8 = 785$

3. Estimate each quotient. Which strategies did you use?
   a) $26.34 \div 8$ b) $15.27 \div 3$ c) $2.304 \div 4$
   d) $5.8 \div 8$ e) $8.088 \div 6$ f) $2.316 \div 2$

4. Divide. Multiply to check your answers.
   a) $27.025 \div 5$ b) $3.42 \div 6$ c) $7.735 \div 7$
   d) $16.072 \div 8$ e) $30.9 \div 5$ f) $3.438 \div 6$

5. Estimate to choose the correct quotient for each division question.

	Question		Possible Quotients	
a)	$8.124 \div 6$	1.354	13.54	135.4
b)	$37.92 \div 3$	0.1264	1.264	12.64
c)	$7.624 \div 8$	0.953	9.53	95.3

6. Aqpik Peter is a young Inuit speed skater from Nunavut. He is one of 3 First Nations athletes being showcased for the 2010 Vancouver Olympics. At practice, Aqpik skated 2.75 km in 5 min. About how far did Aqpik skate in 1 min?

7. Eric cycled 2.25 km in 5 min. Josie cycled 2.72 km in 8 min. Who travelled farther in 1 min? Show your work.

... $58.50 to board her cat at a kennel in Yellowknife for 5 days. Her friend Miles paid $12.50 each day to board his cat at a different kennel for 5 days. Who paid the lesser amount? Explain how you know.

9. The decimal point in some of these quotients is in the wrong place. Identify the mistakes, then write each quotient with the decimal point in the correct place.
   a) $44.8 \div 8 = 0.56$ b) $14.805 \div 5 = 2.961$
   c) $6 \div 6 = 5.25$ d) $8.127 \div 1 = 0.8127$

10. A student divided 1.374 by 4 and got 3.435.
    a) Without dividing, how do you know the answer is incorrect?
    b) What do you think the student did wrong?
    c) What is the correct answer? How can you check?

11. Write a story problem that can be solved by dividing 14.28 by 3. Trade problems with a classmate and solve your classmate's problem.

12. A square park has a perimeter of 14.984 km. How long is each side of the square?

13. In good weather, Hannah rides her bike to school and back each day. One week, Hannah rode her bike on 4 days. That week, Hannah rode 10.832 km in total. The following week, she rode her bike all 5 days. How far did Hannah ride the second week?

Reflect

Why is estimating important when dividing with decimals? Use words, pictures, or numbers to explain.

106 — Unit 3 Lesson 5

ASSESSMENT FOCUS | Question 10 — Unit 3 Les...

reminds you to use pictures, words, or numbers in your answers.

In **Reflect**, think about the big ideas of the lesson and about your learning style.

• Learn about strategies to help you solve problems in each **Strategies Toolkit** lesson.

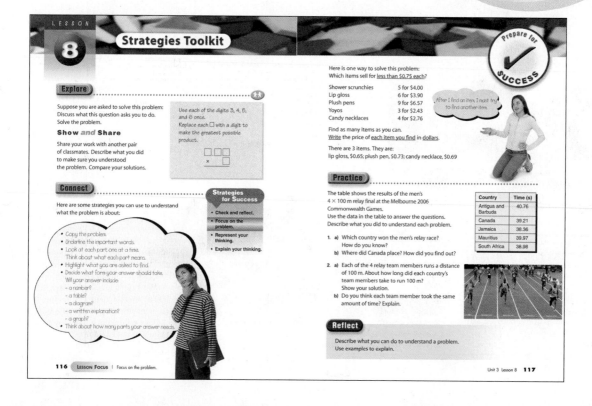

LESSON

8

Strategies Toolkit

Explore

Suppose you are asked to solve this problem: Discuss what this question asks you to do. Solve the problem.

Show and Share

Share your work with another pair of classmates. Describe what you did to make sure you understood the problem. Compare your solutions.

Use each of the digits 3, 4, 5, and 6 once. Replace each □ with a digit to make the greatest possible product.

□.□□
× □

Connect

Here are some strategies you can use to understand what the problem is about:

• Copy the problem.
• Underline the important words.
• Look at each part, one at a time. Think about what each part means.
• Highlight what you are asked to find.
• Decide what form your answer should take. Will your answer include:
  – a number?
  – a table?
  – a diagram?
  – a written explanation?
  – a graph?
• Think about how many parts your answer needs.

Strategies for Success

• Check and reflect.
• Focus on the problem.
• Represent your thinking.
• Explain your thinking.

Here is one way to solve this problem: Which items sell for less than $0.75 each?

Shower scrunchies 5 for $4.00
Lip gloss 6 for $3.90
Plush pens 9 for $6.57
Yoyos 3 for $2.43
Candy necklaces 4 for $2.76

Find as many items as you can. Write the price of each item you find in dollars.

There are 3 items. They are:
lip gloss, $0.65; plush pen, $0.73; candy necklace, $0.69

After I find an item, I must try to find another item.

Practice

The table shows the results of the men's 4×100 m relay final at the Melbourne 2006 Commonwealth Games. Use the data in the table to answer the questions. Describe what you did to understand each problem.

1. a) Which country won the men's relay race? How do you know?
   b) Where did Canada place? How did you find out?

2. a) Each of the 4 relay team members runs a distance of 100 m. About how long did each country's team members take to run 100 m? Show your solution.
   b) Do you think each team member took the same amount of time? Explain.

Country	Time (s)
Antigua and Barbuda	40.76
Canada	39.21
Jamaica	38.36
Mauritius	39.97
South Africa	38.98

Reflect

Describe what you can do to understand a problem. Use examples to explain.

116 LESSON FOCUS | Focus on the problem.

Unit 3 Lesson 8 **117**

xiii

- Check up on your learning in **Show What You Know** and **Cumulative Review**.

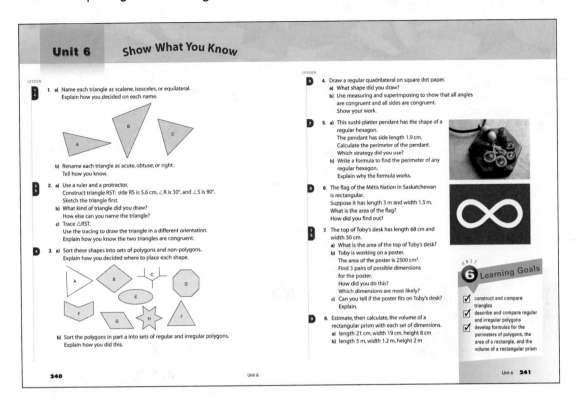

- The **Unit Problem** returns to the opening scene.

  It presents a problem to solve or a project to do using the math of the unit.

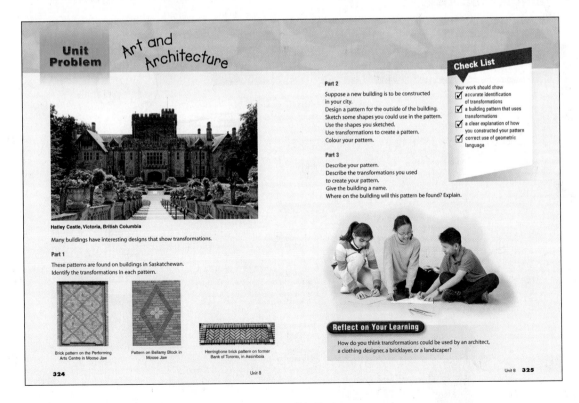

- Explore some interesting math when you do the **Investigations**.

- Use **Technology.** Follow the instructions for using a calculator or computer to do math.

  Look for 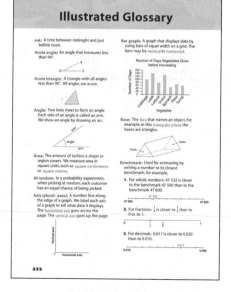 and .

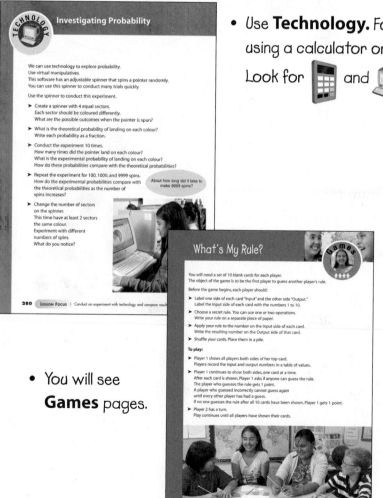

- You will see **Games** pages.

- The **Glossary** is an illustrated dictionary of important math words.

Investigation

Palindromes

You will need a hundred chart and coloured pencils.

A **palindrome** is a word, a phrase, or a number
that reads the same from both directions.
Here are some examples of palindromes:

- mom
- never odd or even
- level
- 3663

Many numbers, such as 7, 11, and 232, are palindromes.
If a number is not a palindrome, follow these steps
to make it a palindrome:

Reverse the digits.
Add the reverse number to
the original number.

$$\begin{array}{r} 67 \\ + \ 76 \\ \hline 143 \end{array}$$

Continue to reverse and add
until the sum is a palindrome.

$$\begin{array}{r} 143 \\ + \ 341 \\ \hline 484 \end{array}$$

If you follow these steps, all the numbers from
1 to 100 will eventually become palindromes.

Sixty-seven
becomes a palindrome in
2 steps. I had to reverse
the digits and add
two times.

Part 1

➤ Use a hundred chart.
   Shade the numbers that are palindromes yellow.
   For the numbers that are not palindromes, reverse the digits
   and add to make palindromes.
   Shade the numbers that become palindromes:
   – in 1 step blue
   – in 2 steps orange
   – in 3 steps green
   – in 4 steps red
   – in more than 4 steps purple

➤ How are the numbers that became palindromes in 1 step related?
In 2 steps? In 3 steps? In 4 steps?
Describe any patterns you found.

Part 2

➤ A decimal such as 63.36 is a palindrome.
Why is a decimal such as 8.48 not a palindrome?

➤ Use the method from Part 1 to make palindrome decimals
from these decimals.
7.1   6.5   4.7   3.65   4.81
How do the results for 6.5 and 4.7 compare to the results
for 65 and 47?

Display Your Work

Create a summary of your work.
Use pictures, numbers, and words.

Take It Further

The years 1991 and 2002 are palindromes.
They are 11 years apart.
What is the next pair of palindrome years
that are 11 years apart? What was the previous pair?
How far apart are palindrome years usually?

Patterns and

Crack the Code!

Learning Goals

- describe patterns and relationships using graphs and tables
- use equations to represent number relationships
- use relationships within tables of values to solve problems
- identify and plot points in a Cartesian plane
- demonstrate the preservation of equality

Guglielmo Marconi received the first transatlantic wireless communication on December 12, 1901.
Morse code for the letter "s" was sent from Poldhu, Cornwall, England to Signal Hill, St. John's, Newfoundland.

Equations

One reason for coding messages was to be able to communicate without using a spoken language.

Morse code was developed by Samuel Morse almost 175 years ago.
It uses dots and dashes to represent letters, numbers, and punctuation.

Number	International Morse Code
0	— — — — —
1	• — — — —
2	• • — — —
3	• • • — —
4	• • • • —
5	• • • • •
6	— • • • •
7	— — • • •
8	— — — • •
9	— — — — •

Key Words

Input/Output machine

coordinate grid

Cartesian plane

origin

coordinates

ordered pair

horizontal axis

vertical axis

commutative property of addition

commutative property of multiplication

preservation of equality

equivalent form of an equation

- What other reasons might there be for coding a message?
- What patterns do you see in the Morse code for numbers?
- How would you write the number 503 in Morse code?

5

Input/Output Machines

Look at this **Input/Output machine**.
Any number that is put into this
machine is multiplied by 5.
When you input 6, the output is 30.
Suppose you input 9.
What will the output be?

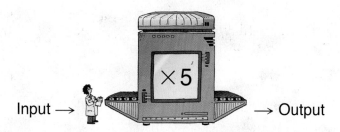

Input →   → Output

Explore

➤ Draw your own Input/Output machine.
   Choose a number to go inside your machine.
   Choose an operation.
   Use your machine to create a number pattern.

> An *operation* is add,
> subtract, multiply, or
> divide.

➤ Copy and complete this table of values for your pattern.
   Write the pattern rule for the output numbers.

Input	Output
1	
2	
3	

Show and Share

Share your machine and table of values
with another pair of classmates.
Use your classmates' machine
to extend their number pattern.

   LESSON FOCUS | Explore the pattern within each column of a table of values.

We can use an Input/Output machine to make a growing pattern.

➤ This machine adds 8 to each input to get the output.

The pattern rule that relates the input to the output is: Add 8 to the input.

When each input increases by 1, the output increases by 1.
The pattern rule for the input is: Start at 1. Add 1 each time.
The pattern rule for the output is: Start at 9. Add 1 each time.

Input	Output
1	9
2	10
3	11
4	12

➤ This Input/Output machine doubles each input, then adds 6.

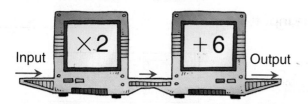

Input ×2 +6 Output

The pattern rule that relates the input to the output is: Multiply the input by 2, then add 6.

Input	Output
2	10
4	14
6	18
8	22

The pattern rule for the input is: Start at 2. Add 2 each time.
The pattern rule for the output is: Start at 10. Add 4 each time.

When each input increases by 2, the output increases by 4.

1. For each Input/Output machine:
   - Copy and complete the table.
   - Write the pattern rule that relates the input to the output.
   - Write the pattern rule for the input.
   - Write the pattern rule for the output.

Input	Output
1	9
2	18
3	27
4	36
5	20

   a)

   Input ⟶ ×9 ⟶ Output

   b)

   Input ⟶ +12 ⟶ Output

2. For each Input/Output machine:
   - Copy and complete the table.
   - Write the pattern rule that relates the input to the output.
   - Write the pattern rule for the input.
   - Write the pattern rule for the output.

Input	Output
2	14
4	16
6	18
8	20
10	22

   a)

   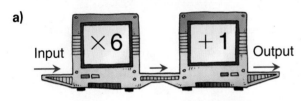

   Input ⟶ ×6 ⟶ +1 ⟶ Output

   b)

   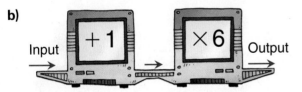

   Input ⟶ +1 ⟶ ×6 ⟶ Output

3. Look at question 2 and your tables.
   a) How are the Input/Output machines the same? How are they different?
   b) How do the output numbers from the two machines compare? Explain.
   c) Is it possible to get more than one output number for each input? How do you know?

4. Copy and complete this table.
The pattern rule that relates the input to the
output is:
Divide the input by 6.
a) Write the pattern rule for the input.
b) Write the pattern rule for the output.

Input	Output
36	6
42	7
48	8
54	9
60	10

5. Copy and complete this table.
The pattern rule that relates the input to the
output is:
Divide the input by 3, then subtract 2.
a) Write the pattern rule for the input.
b) Write the pattern rule for the output.

Input	Output
30	8
60	18
90	28
120	38
150	48

6. The pattern rule that relates the input
to the output is:
Add 4 to the input. Then divide by 2.
Check the data in the Input/Output table.
Identify any output numbers that are incorrect.
How do you know they are incorrect?
Show your work.

Input	Output
4	2
8	4
16	10
26	15
30	19

7. The pattern rule that relates the input to the
output is:
Divide the input by 6, then add 5.
a) Check the data in the Input/Output table.
Identify any output numbers that are
incorrect. How do you know they are
incorrect?
b) Correct the table.
c) Write 3 more input and output numbers for
this pattern rule.
Show your work.

Input	Output
6	6
12	7
30	10
42	2
54	15

8. The pattern rule that relates the input to the output is:
   Multiply the input by 4. Then subtract 3.
   Find the missing numbers in the table.
   How can you check your answers?

Input	Output
3	9
6	?
9	?
12	45
15	?

9. The pattern rule that relates the input to the output is:
   Add 5 to the input. Then multiply by 3.
   Find the missing numbers in the table.
   What strategies did you use?

Input	Output
2	21
5	?
?	39
11	?
?	57
?	66

10. a) Draw an Input/Output machine with two operations.
       Choose two numbers and two operations for your machine.
    b) Choose 5 input numbers.
       Find the output numbers.
    c) Erase 2 input numbers and 2 output numbers.
       Each row must have at least one number.
       Trade tables with a classmate.
       Trade pattern rules that relate the input to the output.
       Find your classmate's missing numbers.

Reflect

Suppose you want to make an Input/Output machine to convert
millimetres to metres.
Describe what your machine would look like.

Patterns from Tables

How does this pattern of squares represent the table of values?

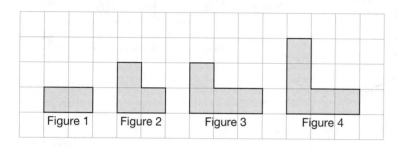

Figure 1   Figure 2   Figure 3   Figure 4

Input	Output
1	2
2	3
3	4
4	5

Explore

You will need toothpicks and dot paper.

➤ Build 5 figures to represent the pattern in this table. Make sure the figures show a pattern.

➤ Draw each figure in the pattern on dot paper.

➤ What patterns do you see in the figures? In the table?

➤ Write a pattern rule that relates each figure number to the number of toothpicks. Predict the number of toothpicks needed to build the 7th figure. Use toothpicks to check.

Figure	Number of Toothpicks
1	3
2	5
3	7
4	9
5	11

Show *and* Share

Compare your patterns and drawings with those of another pair of classmates.
Are your drawings the same or different?
If they are different, do both sets of drawings represent the table of values? Explain.
What Input/Output machine could you use to represent the table?

➤ We can draw pictures to show the relationship in a table of values.

Input	Output	
1	1	
2	4	} 3
3	7	} 3
4	10	} 3
5	13	} 3

In this table:
The input increases by 1 each time.
The output increases by 3 each time.

We could draw a pattern of triangles on triangular dot paper.
The figure number is the input.
The number of triangles in each figure is the output.

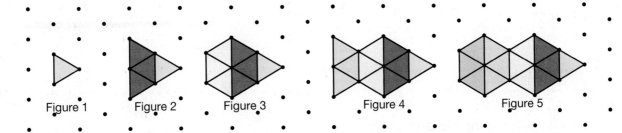

Figure 1   Figure 2   Figure 3   Figure 4   Figure 5

➤ We can use a pattern rule to describe the relationship between the 2 columns in a table of values.
This pattern rule tells us the numbers and operations in the corresponding Input/Output machine.

The table shows the input and output for this two-operation machine.

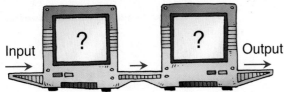

Input → ?   ? → Output

Input	Output	
1	1	
2	5	) 4
3	9	) 4
4	13	) 4
5	17	) 4

To identify the numbers and operations in the machine:

Think:

When the output increases by 4, that is a clue about what to do.

The pattern rule for the output is:

Start at 1. Add 4 each time.

This suggests that the input numbers are multiplied by 4.

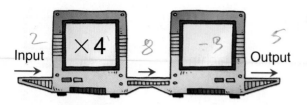

Input   Output

The output increases by 4. Each input must be multiplied by 4.

Look at the input 2.
Multiply by 4.
$2 \times 4 = 8$
But, the output is 5.

Think:

I have 8. To get 5, I subtract 3.
So, −3 goes into the second part of the machine.
$8 - 3 = 5$

I check all the inputs to make sure I have found the correct numbers and the correct operations.

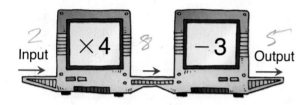

Input   Output

This Input/Output machine multiplies each input by 4, then subtracts 3.
The pattern rule that relates the input to the output is:
Multiply the input by 4.
Then subtract 3.

We can use this rule to predict the output for any input.
For an input of 8, the output should be:
$8 \times 4 - 3 = 29$

We can check this by extending the table.
Add 1 to each input and 4 to each output.

Input	Output	
1	1	4
2	5	4
3	9	4
4	13	4
5	17	4
6	21	4
7	25	4
8	29	4

1. Each table shows the input and output from a machine with one operation. For each table:
   - Identify the number and the operation in the machine.
   - Continue the patterns.
     Write the next 4 input and output numbers.
   - Write the pattern rule that relates the input to the output.

a)

Input	Output
1	7
2	14
3	21
4	28

b)

Input	Output
50	39
49	38
48	37
47	36

c)

Input	Output
2	20
4	40
6	60
8	80

d)

Input	Output
500	485
450	435
400	385
350	335

2. Each table shows the input and output from a machine with two operations. For each table:
   - Identify the numbers and the operations in the machine.
   - Choose 4 different input numbers. Find the output for each input.
   - Predict the output when the input is 10. Check your prediction.

a)

Input	Output
1	2
2	5
3	8
4	11

b)

Input	Output
1	9
2	14
3	19
4	24

c)

Input	Output
3	3
4	5
5	7
6	9

d)

Input	Output
4	17
5	21
6	25
7	29

3. Use the table of values in question 2a.
   Draw pictures to show the relationship in the table.

4. Each table shows the input and output from a machine with two operations.
   - Find the pattern rule that relates the input to the output.
   - Use the pattern rule to find the missing numbers in the table.
   - Use the patterns in the columns to check your answers.
   - Predict the output when the input is 40. Check your prediction.

a)

Input	Output
5	21
6	24
7	27
?	30
9	?
10	?

b)

Input	Output
0	1
5	2
10	3
?	4
20	?
25	?

5. You may need Colour Tiles or counters, and dot paper.
   a) Use tiles, counters, or pictures to show the relationship in this table. Record your work.
   b) Write a pattern rule that relates the input to the output.
   c) Predict the output when the input is 9. Extend your pictures to check.
   d) Which input has an output of 28? Describe the strategy you used to find out.

Input	Output
1	6
2	8
3	10
4	12

6. a) Draw an Input/Output machine with two operations. Choose two numbers and two operations for your machine.
   b) Choose 5 input numbers. Find the output numbers.
   c) Trade tables with a classmate.
      Find the pattern rule that relates the input to the output.
      Use this pattern to write the next 4 input and output numbers.

Reflect

When you look at an Input/Output table, what strategies do you use to identify the numbers and operations in the machine?

Strategies Toolkit

Explore ·

Abi made an Input/Output machine
that uses two operations.

Here is a table for Abi's machine.

Find out what the machine does
to each input number.

Input ? → ? Output

Input	Output
15	6
5	4
20	7
25	8
10	5

Show and Share

Explain the strategy you used to solve the problem.

Connect ·

Ben made an Input/Output
machine that uses two operations.
Here is a table for Ben's machine.
What does Ben's machine do
to each input number?

Input	Output
2	13
4	23
6	33
8	43
10	53

Strategies

- **Make a table.**
- **Solve a simpler problem.**
- **Guess and test.**
- **Make an organized list.**
- **Use a pattern.**

What do you know?
- The machine uses two operations on
  an input number.

Think of a strategy to help you solve the problem.
- You can **use a pattern**.
- Analyse the pattern in the *Output* column to find out what
  the machine does to each input number.

The output numbers increase by 10.
This suggests the input numbers are
multiplied by 10. Look at input 2.
Multiply by 10: $2 \times 10 = 20$
But the output is 13.
We subtract 7 from 20 to get 13.

Check: Look at input 4.
Multiply by 10: $4 \times 10 = 40$
Subtract 7: $40 - 7 = 33$
The output should be 23.
This pattern rule does not work.

Try a different pattern.
When the input increases by 2,
the output increases by 10.
So, when the input increases by 1,
the output increases by $10 \div 2 = 5$.
This suggests the pattern involves multiples of 5.
Which two operations does Ben's machine use?

Input	Output
2	13
3	18
4	23
5	28
6	33

Use the operations in the machine to extend
the pattern of the output numbers.
Check that the rule is correct.

Practice

Choose one of the

Strategies

1. Design an Input/Output machine for each table below.
   How did you decide which operations to use?

a)

Input	Output
2	7
4	15
6	23
8	31

b)

Input	Output
3	10
6	19
9	28
12	37

Reflect

Choose one part of question 1.
Explain how you used a pattern to solve it.

What's My Rule?

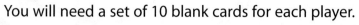

You will need a set of 10 blank cards for each player.
The object of the game is to be the first player to guess another player's rule.

Before the game begins, each player should:

➤ Label one side of each card "Input" and the other side "Output."
Label the Input side of each card with the numbers 1 to 10.

➤ Choose a secret rule. You can use one or two operations.
Write your rule on a separate piece of paper.

➤ Apply your rule to the number on the Input side of each card.
Write the resulting number on the Output side of that card.

➤ Shuffle your cards. Place them in a pile.

To play:

➤ Player 1 shows all players both sides of her top card.
Players record the input and output numbers in a table of values.

➤ Player 1 continues to show both sides, one card at a time.
After each card is shown, Player 1 asks if anyone can guess the rule.
The player who guesses the rule gets 1 point.
A player who guessed incorrectly cannot guess again
until every other player has had a guess.
If no one guesses the rule after all 10 cards have been shown, Player 1 gets 1 point.

➤ Player 2 has a turn.
Play continues until all players have shown their cards.

Publisher
Mike Czukar

Research and Communications Manager
Barbara Vogt

Publishing Team
Enid Haley
Claire Burnett
Lesley Haynes
Alison Rieger
Ioana Gagea
Lynne Gulliver
Ruth Peckover
Annette Darby
Stephanie Cox
Jane Schell
Karen Alley
Judy Wilson

Photo Research
Maria DeCambra
Monika Schurmann

Design and Art Direction
Word & Image Design Studio Inc.

Composition
Integra Software Services Pvt. Ltd.
Lapiz Digital Services, India

The information and activities presented in this book have been carefully edited and reviewed. However, the publisher shall not be liable for any damages resulting, in whole or in part, from the reader's use of this material.

Brand names that appear in photographs of products in this textbook are intended to provide students with a sense of the real-world applications of mathematics and are in no way intended to endorse specific products.

The publisher wishes to thank the staff and students of Greenway School and Roberta Bondar Public School for their assistance with photography.

PEARSON

ISBN-13   978-0-321-49844-1
ISBN-10   0-321-49844-5

Printed and bound in the United States.

14 15 16 17 18   CKV   19 18 17 16 15

PEARSON

Math
Makes Sense

6

Author Team

Ray Appel

Lissa D'Amour

Sandra Glanville Maurer

Cynthia Pratt Nicolson

Trevor Brown

Sharon Jeroski

Peggy Morrow

Gay Sul

With Contributions from

Nora Alexander

Angela D'Alessandro

Jason Johnston

Antonietta Lenjosek

Steve Thomas

Ralph Connelly

Mary Doucette

Don Jones

Carole Saundry

Michael Davis

Lalie Harcourt

Bryn Keyes

Jeananne Thomas

Ricki Wortzman

PEARSON

Table of Contents

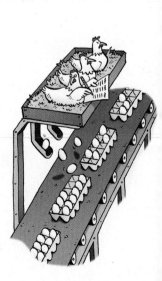

Advisers and Reviewers

Pearson Education thanks its advisers and reviewers, who helped shape the vision for *Pearson Mathematics Makes Sense* through discussions and reviews of prototype materials and manuscript.

Alberta

Joanne Adomeit
Calgary Board of Education

Bob Berglind
Calgary Board of Education

Jason Binding
Calgary Arts Academy Charter School

Jacquie Bouck
Lloydminster Public School Division 99

Auriana Burns
Edmonton Public School Board

Daryl Chichak
Edmonton Catholic School District

Lissa D'Amour
Medicine Hat School District 76

Greg Forsyth
Edmonton Public School Board

Florence Glanfield
University of Alberta

Wendy Jensen
Calgary Catholic

Jodi Mackie
Edmonton Public School Board

Melody M. Moon
Northern Gateway Public Schools

Jeffrey Tang
Calgary R.C.S.S.D. 1

British Columbia

Sandra Ball
School District 36 (Surrey)

Lorraine Baron
School District 23 (Central Okanagan)

Donna Beaumont
School District 41 (Burnaby)

Bob Belcher
School District 62 (Sooke)

Jennifer York Ewart
School Dictrict 83 (North Okanagan Shuswap)

Denise Flick
School District 20 (Kootenay-Columbia)

Marc Garneau
School District 36 (Surrey)

Blair Lloyd
School District 73 (Kamloops)

Selina Millar
School District 36 (Surrey)

Lenora Milliken
School District 70 (Alberni)

Sandy Sheppard
Vancouver School Board

Chris Van Bergeyk
School District 23 (Central Okanagan)

Denise Vuignier
School District 41 (Burnaby)

Mignonne Wood
Formerly School District 41 (Burnaby)

Judy Zacharias
School District 52 (Prince Rupert)

Consultants, Advisers, and Reviewers

Series Consultants

Trevor Brown
Maggie Martin Connell
Craig Featherstone
John A. Van de Walle
Mignonne Wood

Assessment Consultant
Sharon Jeroski

Aboriginal Content Consultant
Rhonda Elser
Calgary Catholic Separate School District

Using Variables to Describe Patterns

Which expression below represents this number pattern?
34, 35, 36, 37, 38, . . .
$33 + t$ $33 - t$ $34 + t$

Explore

A Grade 6 class plans to go to
the Winnipeg Planetarium.
The cost to rent the school bus is $75.
The cost of admission is $5 per student.

➤ Make a table of values to show the total
cost for 1, 2, 3, 4, 5, and 6 students.

Number of Students	Total Cost ($)
1	
2	

➤ What patterns do you see in the table?
Write a pattern rule that relates the number
of students to the total cost.

➤ Use the pattern rule to find the cost for 25 students.

➤ Suppose the total cost was $180.
How many students would be on the trip?
How did you find out?

Show *and* Share

Share your pattern rule and answers with another pair of classmates.
How did the patterns in the table help you solve the problem?
If your pattern rules are the same, work together to use a variable to write
an expression to represent the pattern.

➤ To find the pattern rule that relates the input
to the output:

The pattern rule for the output is:
Start at 7. Add 4 each time.
This suggests the input numbers are multiplied by 4.
Look at input 2.
Multiply by 4: $2 \times 4 = 8$
To get output 11, add 3.

Input	Output
1	7
2	11
3	15
4	19
5	23

The pattern rule that relates the input
to the output is:
Multiply the input by 4. Then add 3.
We can use a variable in an expression to
represent this rule.
Let the letter n represent any input number.

Then, the expression $4n + 3$ relates
the input to the output.

$4n$ is the same as $4 \times n$.

Input	Output
1	$4 \times 1 + 3 = 7$
2	$4 \times 2 + 3 = 11$
3	$4 \times 3 + 3 = 15$
4	$4 \times 4 + 3 = 19$
5	$4 \times 5 + 3 = 23$
⋮	⋮
n	$4 \times n + 3$

➤ We can use a pattern to solve a problem.

Minowa works at a fishing camp in the Yukon.
Minowa earns $25 a day, plus $8 for each fishing net she repairs.
On Saturday, Minowa repaired 9 nets. How much money did she earn?

Fishing Camp, Ten Mile Lake, Yukon

Here are two strategies to find out.

- Make a table of values.
  Use the patterns in the columns.
  When we add 1 to the number of nets,
  we add $8 to the amount earned.

  The pattern in the number of nets is:
  Start at 0. Add 1 each time.
  The pattern in the amount earned is:
  Start at 25. Add 8 each time.

  We can use these patterns to extend the table.
  Minowa earned $97 for repairing 9 nets.

Number of Fishing Nets	Amount Earned ($)
0	25
1	33
2	41
3	49
4	57
5	65
6	73
7	81
8	89
9	97

) 8
) 8
) 8
) 8
) 8
) 8
) 8
) 8
) 8

- Use a variable in an expression.
  Minowa earns $25 even when there are
  no nets to be repaired.
  For each net Minowa repairs, she earns $8.

  For 0 nets, she earns: $8 \times 0 + 25 = 25$
  For 1 net, she earns: $8 \times 1 + 25 = 33$
  For 2 nets, she earns: $8 \times 2 + 25 = 41$
  For 3 nets, she earns: $8 \times 3 + 25 = 49$
  This pattern continues.

We can use an expression to write the pattern rule.
We use the letter n to represent any number of nets.
Then, the amount earned in dollars for repairing n nets is:
$8 \times n + 25$, or $8n + 25$

To check that this expression is correct,
substitute $n = 3$.
$$8n + 25 = 8 \times 3 + 25$$
$$= 49$$

This is the same as the amount earned
for 3 nets in the list above.

To find the amount earned for repairing 9 nets,
substitute $n = 9$ into the expression:
$$8n + 25 = 8 \times 9 + 25$$
$$= 72 + 25$$
$$= 97$$

Minowa earned $97 for repairing 9 nets.

1. Kilee builds model cars.
   She needs 4 plastic wheels for each car she builds.
   a) Make a table to show the number of wheels
      needed for 1, 2, 3, 4, and 5 cars.
   b) Write a pattern rule that relates the number
      of cars to the number of wheels.
   c) Write an expression to represent the pattern.
   d) Find the number of wheels needed to build 11 cars.
      How can you check your answer?

2. For each table of values, write an expression that relates the input to the output.

a)

Input	Output
1	0
2	2
3	4
4	6
5	8

b)

Input	Output
1	5
2	8
3	11
4	14
5	17

c)

Input	Output
1	2
2	6
3	10
4	14
5	18

3. Here is a pattern of squares on grid paper.

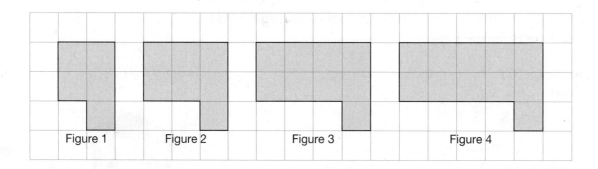

Figure 1   Figure 2   Figure 3   Figure 4

a) Make a table to show the numbers of squares in the first 4 figures.
b) Write a pattern rule that relates the figure number to the
   number of squares.
c) Write an expression to represent the pattern.
d) Find the number of squares in the 7th figure.
   Which strategy did you use?
   Continue the pattern to check your answer.

4. The Grade 6 class held a dance-a-thon to raise money to buy a new computer for the class. Tyson's friend, Alana, pledged $10, plus $2 for each hour Tyson danced.
   a) Make a table to show the amount Alana pledged for 1, 2, 3, 4, and 5 hours danced.
   b) Write a pattern rule that relates the amount pledged to the number of hours danced. Show your work.
   c) Write an expression to represent the pattern.
   d) Find how much Alana pledged when Tyson danced 9 h. What strategy did you use?
   e) Suppose Alana pledged $34. How many hours did Tyson dance? How did you find out?

5. The pattern in this table continues.
   a) Write a pattern rule that relates the number to the amount.
   b) Write an expression to represent the pattern.
   c) Write a story problem you could solve using the pattern. Solve your problem.

Number	Amount ($)
0	5
1	11
2	17
3	23
4	29

6. Skylar wants to adopt a whale through the BC Wild Killer Whale Adoption Program. The cost of a 1-year adoption is $59. Skylar walks his neighbour's dog to raise the money. He gets $3 for each walk.
   a) Make a table to show the amount left to raise after 1, 2, 3, 4, and 5 walks.
   b) Write a pattern rule that relates the number of walks to the amount left to raise.
   c) Write an expression to represent the pattern.
   d) Find the amount left to raise after 15 walks.
   e) After how many walks will Skylar have raised enough money? How do you know?

Reflect

What is one advantage of using a variable to represent a pattern?
How does this help you solve a problem?

Plotting Points on a Coordinate Grid

How could Hannah describe where her great-grandmother is in this family photo?

In math, we illustrate ideas whenever we can. To find a way to illustrate Input/Output tables, we need a way to describe the position of a point on a grid.

Explore

Each of you will need two 10 by 10 grids and a ruler.

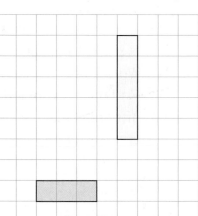

➤ Draw a horizontal and a vertical rectangle on your grid.
Use the grid to the right as an example.
Place your rectangles where you like.
Do not show your partner your grid.

➤ Think of a way to describe the locations of the rectangles to your partner.

➤ Take turns. Use your method to describe the locations of your rectangles to your partner.
Your partner uses your description to draw the rectangles on a blank grid. Compare grids. Do they match?
If not, try to improve your descriptions of the locations.

Show and Share

Share your descriptions with another pair of students.
Did you use the same method to describe the locations of the rectangles?
If your answer is no, do both methods work?

Connect

René Descartes was a French mathematician who lived
from 1596 to 1650.
He developed the **coordinate grid** system shown below.
In his honour, it is called the **Cartesian plane**.

➤ Two perpendicular number lines intersect at 0.
The point of intersection, O, is called the **origin**.
To describe the position of a point on a coordinate grid,
we use two numbers.
The numbers locate a point in relation to the origin, O.

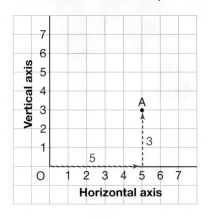

> The first number tells
> how far you move right.
> The second number tells how
> far you move up.

From O, to reach point A, we move 5 units right
and 3 units up.
We write these numbers in brackets: (5, 3)
These numbers are called **coordinates**.
Because the coordinates are always written in the
same order, the numbers are also called an **ordered pair**.

> We move right along the
> **horizontal axis**.
> We use the **vertical axis**
> to count the units up.

We say: A has coordinates (5, 3).
We write: A(5, 3)

The point O has coordinates (0, 0) because you do not move
anywhere to plot a point at O.

➤ When the numbers in an ordered pair are large,
we use a scale on the coordinate grid.
On this coordinate grid, 1 square represents 5 units.

"Coordinates" is another name for "ordered pair."

To plot point B(10, 30):
Start at O.
Move 2 squares right.
Move 6 squares up.

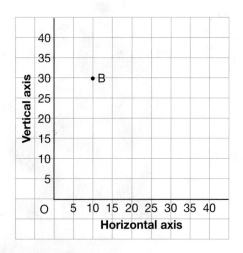

Practice

1. Match each ordered pair with a letter on the coordinate grid.
   a) (1, 5)
   b) (5, 1)
   c) (0, 7)
   d) (7, 0)

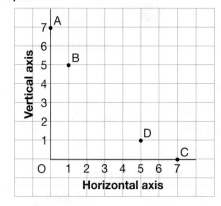

2. Draw and label a coordinate grid.
   Plot each ordered pair.
   Explain how you moved to do this.
   a) V(5, 9)   b) W(0, 9)   c) X(5, 7)   d) Y(8, 0)

3. Draw and label a coordinate grid.
   Plot each point on the grid.
   a) P(2, 7)   b) Q(6, 5)   c) R(1, 4)   d) S(0, 3)   e) O(0, 0)

Unit 1 Lesson 5

4. Mr. Kelp's class went to the Vancouver Aquarium.
Angel drew this map of the aquarium site.

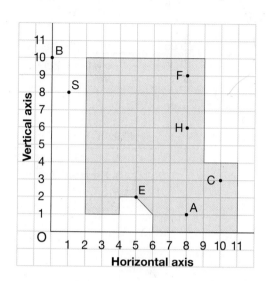

Write the ordered pair for each place.
a) Amazon Jungle Area: A
b) Beluga Whales: B
c) Carmen the Reptile: C
d) Entrance: E
e) Frogs: F
f) Sea Otters: S
g) Sharks: H

5. Use the map in question 4.
a) To get to the Pacific Canada Pavilion at point P:
You move 1 square left and 3 squares up from the entrance, E.
What are the coordinates of P?
b) To get to the Clam Shell Gift Shop at point G:
You move 5 squares left and 4 squares down from the sharks, H.
What are the coordinates of G?

6. Draw and label a coordinate grid.
Plot each point on the grid.
How did you decide which scale to use on the axes?
a) A(10, 40) **b)** B(10, 0) **c)** C(20, 20) **d)** D(0, 30) **e)** E(50, 60)

7. Draw and label a coordinate grid.
Plot each point on the grid.
How did you decide which scale to use on the axes?
a) J(14, 20) **b)** K(6, 12) **c)** L(0, 18) **d)** M(8, 4) **e)** N(16, 0)

8. A student plotted 6 points on a coordinate grid, then labelled each point with its coordinates. The student has made some mistakes.
For each point that has been labelled incorrectly:
a) Explain the mistake.
b) Write the coordinates that correctly describe the location of the point.

9. Draw and label a coordinate grid. Use a scale of 1 square represents 5 units. Plot 5 points on the grid. Use an ordered pair to describe the location of each point.

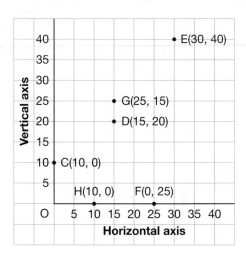

10. a) The first number in the ordered pair for Point A is 0. What does this tell you about Point A?
b) The second number in the ordered pair for Point B is 0. What does this tell you about Point B?

Math Link

Agriculture

To maximize crop yield, farmers test the soil in their fields for nutrients. The results help farmers to decide on the amount and type of fertilizer to use. Grid soil sampling is one method of collecting samples. The field is divided into a grid. A soil sample is taken from the centre of each grid cell.

At Home

Reflect

How is plotting a point on a coordinate grid similar to plotting a point on a number line?
How is it different?

Look at a map of your neighbourhood. Suppose a delivery truck is trying to find your home. How would you use the map to describe the location of your home to the driver?

Drawing the Graph of a Pattern

How are these patterns alike?
How are they different?

Describe Figure 5 for each pattern.

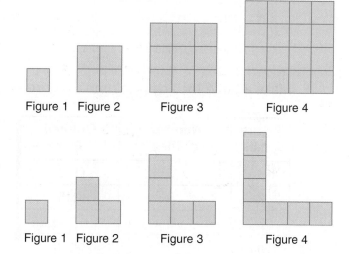

Figure 1   Figure 2   Figure 3   Figure 4

Figure 1   Figure 2   Figure 3   Figure 4

Explore

You will need Colour Tiles or congruent squares, and grid paper.

➤ Use Colour Tiles.
   Build the first 4 figures of a growing pattern.
   Record your pattern on grid paper.

➤ Make a table.
   Record each figure number and
   its number of tiles.
   Write these numbers as an ordered pair.

➤ Plot each ordered pair on a coordinate grid.
   Describe the graph formed by the points.

Show *and* Share

Share your work with another pair of students.
Compare your graphs.
If they are different, try to find out why.

Figure Number	Number of Tiles in a Figure	Ordered Pair
1		

➤ Here are some different ways to represent a pattern.

• Model the pattern with tiles or on grid paper.

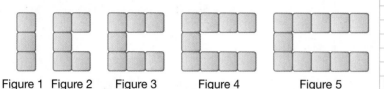

Figure 1   Figure 2   Figure 3   Figure 4   Figure 5

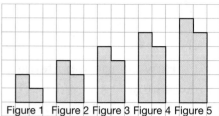

Figure 1   Figure 2 Figure 3 Figure 4 Figure 5

• Make a table. Include a column for ordered pairs.

Figure Number	Number of Tiles	Ordered Pair
1	3	(1, 3)
2	5	(2, 5)
3	7	(3, 7)
4	9	(4, 9)
5	11	(5, 11)
6	13	(6, 13)
7	15	(7, 15)

The figure number is the first coordinate. The number of tiles in a figure is the second coordinate.

We have extended the table to find the number of tiles in the 7th figure.

• Draw a graph.
Draw and label a coordinate grid.

We label the axes with the column headings.

Plot the ordered pairs.
Mark points at (1, 3), (2, 5), (3, 7), (4, 9), and (5, 11).

From the graph, we see that each time the figure number increases by 1, the number of tiles increases by 2.

From (3, 7), move 1 to the right and 2 up to reach (4, 9).

To get from one point to the next, move 1 to the right and 2 up.

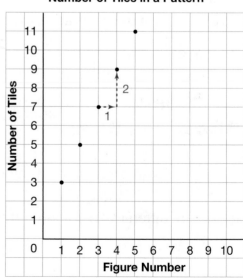

Number of Tiles in a Pattern

➤ We can graph the relationship shown in an Input/Output table.

Input	Output
1	5
2	8
3	11
4	14

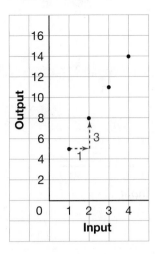

As the input increases by 1,
the output increases by 3.

Practice

1. Record each pattern in a table. Then draw a graph to represent the pattern.
   Explain how the graph represents the pattern.

   a)

   b)

   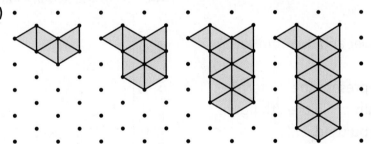

   c)

2. Use grid paper. Graph each table.
   Describe the relationship shown on the graph.

   a)

Input	Output
1	3
2	6
3	9
4	12

   b)

Input	Output
1	5
2	6
3	7
4	8

3. For each graph, make an Input/Output table.

a)

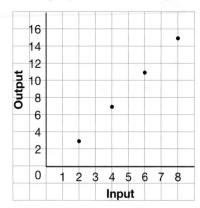

b)

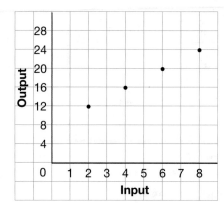

4. Use grid paper.
   a) Graph the data in the table.
   b) Describe the relationship shown on the graph.
   c) Write an expression to represent the pattern.
   d) Find the number of shapes in the 8th figure.
      What strategy did you use?
      Could you use the same strategy to find
      the number of shapes in the 18th figure?
      Explain.

Figure Number	Number of Shapes
1	1
2	6
3	11
4	16
5	21

5. Use grid paper.
   a) Make a table.
      Record the figure number and the number of
      counters in a figure.
   b) How does the graph represent the pattern?
   c) Find the number of counters in the 7th figure.
      Describe the strategy you used.
   d) How many counters are in the 23rd figure?
      Describe the strategy you used to find out.

Number of Counters in a Pattern

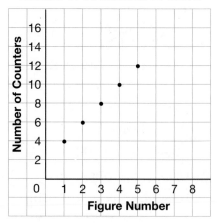

Reflect

Describe some of the different ways you can represent a pattern.
Which way do you prefer? Why?

Understanding Equality

Suppose the boy puts on his backpack.
What will happen?

Explore

You will need balance scales, counters, and drawings of balance scales.

➤ Choose 2 expressions from the box at the right.
On a drawing of balance scales, write one expression
in each pan.

➤ Suppose you were using real balance scales and
counters for the numbers.
Would the scales tilt to the left, to the right,
or would they balance?
How do you know?
Use balance scales and counters to check.

➤ Repeat the steps above with different pairs
of expressions. Find as many pairs of
expressions as you can that balance.

Expressions	
4 + 5	8 + 3
3 × 5	2 × 4
17 − 10	4 × 2
18 ÷ 6	24 ÷ 4
15 − 8	30 ÷ 5
21 − 10	5 + 4
27 ÷ 9	5 × 3

Show and Share

Share your work with another pair of classmates.
What strategies did you use to decide whether the scales balance or tilt?
What did you notice about the expressions 4 + 5 and 5 + 4, and 2 × 4 and 4 × 2?
What does it mean when the scales balance?

Each of the scales below are balanced.
For each balance scales, the expression in one pan is equal to the expression in the other pan.
We use the equals sign to show that the two expressions are equal.

$$36 \div 6 = 6 \quad \text{and}$$
$$15 - 9 = 6$$
So, $36 \div 6 = 15 - 9$

$$12 + 5 = 17 \quad \text{and}$$
$$5 + 12 = 17$$
So, $12 + 5 = 5 + 12$

$$3 \times 7 = 21 \quad \text{and}$$
$$7 \times 3 = 21$$
So, $3 \times 7 = 7 \times 3$

➤ When we add 2 numbers, their order does not affect the sum.
The scales always balance.
This is called the **commutative property of addition**.
For example,
$$3 + 2 = 2 + 3$$
$$114 + 35 = 35 + 114$$

We can use variables to show this property for any pair of numbers we add:
$$a + b = b + a$$

➤ Multiplication is also *commutative*.
When we multiply two numbers, their order does not affect the product.
For example,
$$3 \times 2 = 2 \times 3$$
$$55 \times 8 = 8 \times 55$$

We can use variables to show this property
for any pair of numbers we multiply:
$$a \times b = b \times a$$

This illustrates the
**commutative property
of multiplication**.

1. Suppose you were using real balance scales.
   Which scales below would balance?
   How did you find out?

   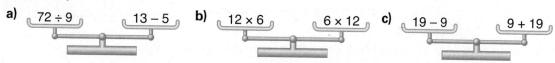

   a) 72 ÷ 9   13 − 5   **b)** 12 × 6   6 × 12   **c)** 19 − 9   9 + 19

2. **a)** Write an expression with 2 numbers and one operation.
   b) Write 5 different expressions that equal your expression in part a.
   What strategy did you use to find the expressions?
   c) Suppose you used real balance scales.
   You put counters to represent 3 of the expressions in the left pan and
   3 in the right pan. What would happen? How do you know?

3. Rewrite each expression using a commutative property.
   a) $5 + 8$ **b)** 6×9 **c)** 11×7
   d) $12 + 21$ **e)** $134 + 72$ **f)** 36×9

4. **a)** Are these scales balanced?

   36 + 27 − 50   4 × 3

   b) If your answer is yes, why do you think so?
   If your answer is no, what could you do to balance the scales?
   Why would this work?

5. **a)** Addition and subtraction are inverse operations.
   Addition is commutative. Is subtraction commutative?
   Use an example to show your answer.
   b) Multiplication and division are inverse operations.
   Multiplication is commutative. Is division commutative?
   Use an example to show your answer.

Reflect

Are subtractions and division commutative operations?
Explain why or why not.

Keeping Equations Balanced

Each of these tug-of-war teams has the same total mass.
Suppose a girl with mass 48 kg joins Team A.
What could be done to keep the match fair?

Explore

You will need counters.
Each group member chooses a different expression.

➤ Write a different expression that is equal to
the expression you chose.
Use the expressions to write an equation.

➤ Model the equation with counters.
How do the counters show the expressions are balanced?

➤ Find 4 different ways to adjust the original equation
so that it remains balanced.
Use counters to model what you did each time.
Use symbols to record your work.

Expressions	
3×6	$17 - 5$
$3 + 5$	$24 \div 4$

Show *and* Share

Share your work with another group of students.
What strategies did you use to keep the equation balanced?
Were you able to use each of the 4 operations?
If not, work together to try the operations that you did not use.

➤ Max started with this equation each time:
$2 + 4 = 3 \times 2$
He modelled it using counters.
Each side has 6 counters.

First, Max subtracted 4 from each side.
$6 - 4 = 6 - 4$
Each side now has 2 counters.

Second, Max added 2 to each side.
$6 + 2 = 6 + 2$
Each side now has 8 counters.

Third, Max multiplied each side by 2.
$6 \times 2 = 6 \times 2$
Each side now has 12 counters.

Fourth, Max divided each side into
2 equal groups.
$6 \div 2 = 6 \div 2$
Each group has 3 counters.

Whatever Max did to one side of the equation, he did to the other side, too.
Each time, the numbers of counters on both sides remained equal.
So, the equation remained balanced.

When each side of the equation is changed in the same way,
the values remain equal.
This is called the **preservation of equality**.
The same is true if one side of the equation is an expression containing a variable.

➤ Suppose we know $6 = 3t$.
We can model this equation with paper strips.

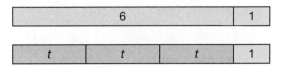

To preserve the equality, we can:
• Add the same number to each side.
So, $6 + 1 = 3t + 1$

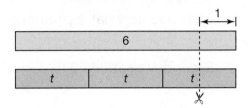

• Subtract the same number from each side.
So, $6 - 1 = 3t - 1$

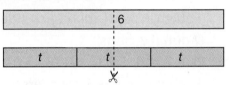

• Multiply each side by the same number.
So, $2 \times 6 = 2 \times 3t$

6	6

t	t	t	t	t	t

• Divide each side by the same number.
So, $6 \div 2 = 3t \div 2$

When we do the same to each side of an equation,
we produce an **equivalent form of the equation**.

So, $6 + 1 = 3t + 1$
$\quad 6 - 1 = 3t - 1$ are all equivalent forms of the equation $6 = 3t$.
$\quad 2 \times 6 = 2 \times 3t$
$\quad 6 \div 2 = 3t \div 2$

Practice

1. For each equation below:
   • Model the equation with counters.
   • Use counters to model the preservation of equality for addition.
   • Draw a diagram to record your work.
   • Use symbols to record your work.

   a) $9 + 6 = 15$ b) $14 - 8 = 6$

   c) $2 \times 5 = 10$ d) $15 \div 3 = 9 - 4$

2. For each equation below:
   - Model the equation with counters.
   - Use counters to model the preservation of equality for subtraction.
   - Draw a diagram to record your work.
   - Use symbols to record your work.

   a) $7 + 8 = 15$ b) $12 - 7 = 5$
   c) $3 \times 4 = 12$ d) $10 \div 5 = 9 - 7$

3. For each equation below:
   - Model the equation with counters.
   - Use counters to model the preservation of equality for multiplication.
   - Draw a diagram to record your work.
   - Use symbols to record your work.

   a) $2 + 3 = 5$ b) $9 - 6 = 3$
   c) $2 \times 4 = 8$ d) $12 \div 4 = 2 + 1$

4. For each equation below:
   - Model the equation with counters.
   - Use counters to model the preservation of equality for division.
   - Draw a diagram to record your work.
   - Use symbols to record your work.

   a) $5 + 1 = 6$ b) $8 - 4 = 4$
   c) $5 \times 2 = 10$ d) $16 \div 2 = 2 \times 4$

5. For each equation below:
   - Apply the preservation of equality.
     Write an equivalent form of the equation.
   - Use paper strips to check that equality has been preserved.

   Try to use a different operation for each part.

   a) $3b = 12$ b) $2t = 8$
   c) $16 = 4s$ d) $15 = 5s$

   How do you know that equality has been preserved each time?

Reflect

Talk to a partner. Tell your partner what you think
the preservation of equality means. Describe how you
could model the preservation of equality for each
of the 4 operations.

LESSON

1

1. The pattern rule that relates the input to the output is:
   Divide the input by 5, then subtract 1.

Input	Output
5	0
10	2
15	3
30	7
45	8
50	11

   a) Check the data in the table.
      Identify any output numbers that are incorrect.
      How do you know they are incorrect?
   b) Write the pattern rule for the input.
   c) Write the pattern rule for the corrected output.
   d) The pattern continues.
      Write the next 4 input and output numbers.

2

2. The table shows the input and output for this machine.

   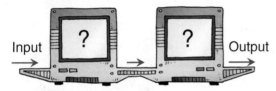

   Input → ? → ? → Output

Input	Output
1	0
2	2
3	4
4	6
5	8
6	10
7	12

   a) Identify the numbers and operations in the machine.
   b) Write a pattern rule that relates the input to the output.
   c) Choose 4 different input numbers.
      Find the output for each input.
   d) Predict the output when the input is 11. Check your prediction.

4

3. In a dogsled race, teams of 6 dogs race to the finish.

   a) Make a table to show the numbers of dogs in a race when 2, 3, 4, 5, and 6 teams are entered.
   b) Write a pattern rule that relates the number of dogs to the number of teams entered.
   c) Write an expression to represent this pattern.
   d) Use the expression to find the number of dogs when 13 teams are entered.
      How can you check your answer?

5

4. Draw and label a coordinate grid.
   Plot each point on the grid.
   How did you decide which scale to use on the axes?
   a) A(10, 5)   b) B(0, 20)   c) C(20, 30)   d) D(0, 0)   e) E(30, 0)

5. Use dot paper.

a) Draw a pattern to model the data in the table. Extend the pattern to Figure 6.

b) Graph the data in the table.

c) Describe the relationship shown on the graph.

d) Write an expression to represent the pattern.

e) Find the number of shapes in the 21st figure. Which strategy did you use? Why?

Figure Number	Number of Shapes
1	4
2	8
3	12
4	16

6. Rewrite each expression using a commutative property.

a) 24×3 b) $121 + 27$

c) $46 + 15$ d) 9×12

e) 11×8 f) $37 + 93$

7. For each equation below:

• Model the equation with counters.

• Use counters to model the preservation of equality. Use a different operation for each equation.

• Draw diagrams to record your work.

• Use symbols to record your work.

a) $11 - 3 = 8$

b) $3 \times 1 = 5 - 2$

c) $3 + 4 = 7$

d) $12 \div 6 = 9 - 7$

8. For each equation below:

• Apply the preservation of equality. Write an equivalent form of the equation.

• Use paper strips to check that equality has been preserved.

Try to use a different operation for each part.

a) $4b = 8$

b) $t = 3$

c) $12 = 6s$

d) $4 = 2s$

How do you know that equality has been preserved each time?

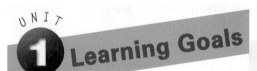

UNIT
1 Learning Goals

☑ describe patterns and relationships using graphs and tables

☑ use equations to represent number relationships

☑ use relationships within tables of values to solve problems

☑ identify and plot points in a Cartesian plane

☑ demonstrate the preservation of equality

Crack the Code!

Jen and Rodrigo are planning a surprise skating party for their friend Lacy. They use a secret code to send messages to each other.

To create their code, Jen and Rodrigo wrote the position number of each letter in the alphabet.

A	B	C	D	E	F	G	H	I	J	K	L	M	N	O	P	Q	R	S	T	U	V	W	X	Y	Z
1	2	3	4	5	6	7	8	9	10	11	12	13	14	15	16	17	18	19	20	21	22	23	24	25	26

They applied a secret pattern rule to each number. Then, each letter is represented by a code number.

Jen's copy of their code went through the washing machine. Here is what was left of the code.

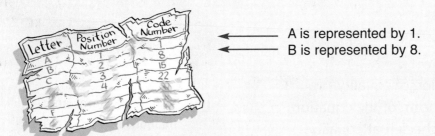

→ A is represented by 1.
→ B is represented by 8.

Step 1 Copy and complete the table for the first 8 letters of the alphabet.
- Write the pattern rule for the position number.
- Write the pattern rule for the code number.
- Write the pattern rule that relates the position number to the code number. Write the rule in words and using symbols.
- Which code number represents the letter "Y" in a message? Can you find this code number without completing the table for the entire alphabet? Explain.

Step 2   Here is a coded message that Jen received from Rodrigo. What does it say?

155 50 1 134   134 57 85 29

155 57 78 78   134 50 29

106 1 120 134 169   127 134 1 120 134?

Check List

Your work should show
- ☑ completed tables
- ☑ pattern rules represented in words and in symbols
- ☑ the decoded message
- ☑ a graph that represents your code
- ☑ clear descriptions using math language

Step 3   Jen replies to Rodrigo with a mystery picture.
To see Jen's reply, draw and label
a 10 by 10 coordinate grid.
Plot these points on the grid.
Join the points in order. Then join the last
point to the first point.
(3, 7), (6, 7), (6, 2), (3, 2), (3, 3), (5, 3), (5, 4), (4, 4),
(4, 5), (5, 5), (5, 6), (3, 6)

Step 4   Work with a partner. Make up your own code
for the letters of the alphabet.
➤ Make a table to show the code for the
first 5 letters of the alphabet.
➤ Describe the pattern rules for the position
number and code number.
➤ Describe the pattern rule that relates
the position number to the code number.
➤ Write an expression to represent the pattern.
➤ Represent the pattern on a graph.
Describe how the graph represents the pattern.
➤ Write messages to each other using your code.

Reflect on Your Learning

What did you find easy about working with patterns?
What was difficult for you?
Give examples to show your answers.

Understanding

At the Apiary

HONEY

Learning Goals

- use place value to represent whole numbers greater than one million
- solve problems involving large numbers, using technology
- determine multiples and factors of numbers less than 100
- solve problems involving multiples
- identify composite and prime numbers
- apply the order of operations to solve multi-step problems, with or without technology
- demonstrate an understanding of integers

Number

Honeybees have been producing honey for more than 150 million years. Honeybees gather nectar from flowers. They convert the nectar to honey and store it as food in the beehive. A colony of honeybees produces more honey than it needs. For 6000 years, beekeepers have harvested honey for people to eat.

Key Words
. . . .

billion

trillion

common multiples

prime number

composite number

common factors

order of operations

expression

integer

positive integer

negative integer

opposite integers

- Lesley has 20 hives.
  Each hive has about 75 000 honeybees.
  How could you find out about how many honeybees Lesley has?

- A honeybee travels about 195 km in 50 round trips to collect enough nectar to make 1 g of honey. About what distance does a honeybee travel in one round trip? How do you know?

- What else do you know about Lesley's honeybees?

Exploring Large Numbers

The world's all-time best-selling copyright book is *Guinness World Records*. From October 1955 to June 2002, 94 767 083 copies were sold.

Suppose the number is written in this place-value chart. Where will the digits 9 and 4 appear?

Hundred Millions	Ten Millions	Millions	Hundred Thousands	Ten Thousands	Thousands	Hundreds	Tens	Ones

Explore

Here are some of the world records reported in the *Guinness World Records 2008*.

- The largest bag of cookies was made in Veenendaal, Netherlands. It contained 207 860 cookies.
- The greatest attendance at an Olympic Games was 5 797 923, in Los Angeles in 1984.
- The most dominoes toppled by a group was 4 079 381, out of a possible 4 400 000. This took place at Domino Day 2006 in Leeuwarden, Netherlands.
- The longest gum-wrapper chain contains 1 192 492 wrappers. The maker of the chain has been working on it since 1965.

➤ Take turns reading the records aloud.

➤ Each of you chooses 2 numbers from the records. Show each number in as many ways as you can.

Show *and* Share

Share your work with another pair of students.
Talk about the different ways you showed your numbers.

Connect

➤ These patterns in the place-value system may help you read and write large whole numbers.

- From right to left, each group of 3 place values is called a *period*.

- Within each period, the digits of a number are read as hundreds, tens, and ones.

- Each position represents ten times as many as the position to its right. For example, 2 hundreds = 20 tens   and   4 ten thousands = 40 thousands

This place-value chart shows the number of items in the world's largest collection of matchbook covers, 3 159 119.

Millions Period			Thousands Period			Units Period		
Hundreds	Tens	Ones	Hundreds	Tens	Ones	Hundreds	Tens	Ones
		3	1	5	9	1	1	9

3 000 000   100 000   50 000   9000   100   10   9

We read this number as:
three *million* one hundred fifty-nine *thousand* one hundred nineteen

> When we read large numbers, we say the period name after each period except the units period.

> We leave a space between the periods when we write a number with 5 or more digits.

We can write this number in:

- standard form: 3 159 119

- expanded form: 3 000 000 + 100 000 + 50 000 + 9000 + 100 + 10 + 9

- number-word form: 3 million 159 thousand 119

➤ The place-value chart can be extended to the left to show greater whole numbers. This place-value chart shows the approximate number of cells in the human body.

One thousand million is one **billion**.
One thousand billion is one **trillion**.

Trillions			Billions			Millions			Thousands			Units		
H	T	O	H	T	O	H	T	O	H	T	O	H	T	O
	5	0	0	0	0	1	0	0	0	0	0	0	0	0

We write: 50 000 100 000 000
We say: fifty trillion one hundred million

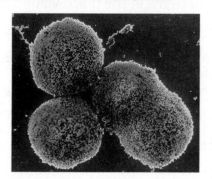

Practice

1. Write each number in standard form.
   a) 20 000 000 + 4 000 000 + 300 000 + 40 000 + 2000 + 500 + 80 + 4
   b) 6 million 276 thousand 89
   c) two billion four hundred sixty million sixty-nine thousand eighteen

2. How many times as great as one thousand is one million?
   Use a calculator to check your answer.

3. Write each number in expanded form.
   a) 75 308 403   b) 64 308 470 204   c) 99 300 327

4. Write the value of each underlined digit.
   a) 6<u>2</u>7 384   b) 5<u>4</u> 286 473   c) 41 <u>9</u>62 014   d) 2<u>5</u> 041 304 000

5. Write the number that is:
   a) 10 000 more than 881 462   b) 100 000 less than 2 183 486
   c) 1 000 000 more than 746 000   d) one million less than 624 327 207
   Tell how you know.

6. China is the most populated country in the world. In 2007, it had an estimated population of one billion three hundred twenty-one million eight hundred fifty-one thousand eight hundred eighty-eight.
   Write this number in standard form and in expanded form.

7. The largest known prehistoric insect is a species of dragonfly.
   It lived about 280 000 000 years ago.
   Write this number in words.

8. North America's largest shopping centre is in Edmonton, Alberta.
   It covers an area of 492 386 m² and cost about $1 200 000 000 to build.
   Write these numbers in a place-value chart.

9. A student read 3 000 146 as "three thousand one hundred forty-six."
   How would you explain the student's error?

10. I am a number between 7 000 000 and 8 000 000.
    All my digits are odd.
    All the digits in my thousands period are the same.
    All the digits in my units period are the same.
    The sum of all my digits is 31.
    What number am I?
    Give as many answers as you can.
    What strategies did you use to find the
    mystery number?

11. In November, 2005, six-year-old
    Brianna Hunt found a fossilized squid
    near her home on the Blood Reserve,
    outside Lethbridge, Alberta.
    The fossil is believed to be about
    73 million years old.
    Write this number in standard form.

12. The table shows estimates of the populations of some cities in 2015.
Order the cities from least to greatest expected population.

City	Expected Population in 2015
Dhaka (Bangladesh)	22 766 000
Mumbai (India)	22 577 000
Tokyo (Japan)	27 190 000

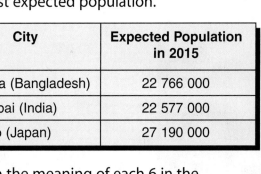

13. Explain the meaning of each 6 in the number 763 465 284 132.

14. Describe three examples where large numbers are used outside the classroom.

15. How do the patterns in the place-value system help you to read and write large numbers?

Math Link

Number Sense

A googol is a number represented by 1 followed by 100 zeros. The word *googol* was created in 1920 by an American mathematician, Edward Kasner, on the basis of his 9-year-old nephew's word for a very large number.

What patterns are there in a place-value chart? How can you use these patterns to read a number such as 5 487 302?

At Home

Search the Internet, or look through magazines. Find examples where large numbers are used. How are the numbers written?

Numbers All Around Us

We add, subtract, multiply, or divide with numbers to solve problems.
Addition, subtraction, multiplication, and division are *operations*.
We use numbers to understand and describe our world.

Saturday, August 23, 2003

Southern BC Fires Approach City

KELOWNA, BC – Police with bullhorns ordered a staggering 20,000 Kelowna residents to evacuate their homes as fast-moving wildfires moved closer.
Thick smoke choked Kelowna's 100,000 residents and at times clouded the view of nearby Okanagan Lake.
The fire prompted the closure of Route 97, between Okanagan Falls and Penticton, and brought the total number of evacuees driven out by the fire to 30,000.
More than 3,000 firefighters from British Columbia and elsewhere in Canada are battling over 825 fires in the province.

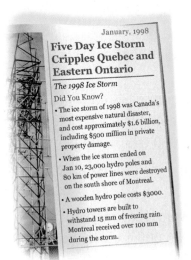

January, 1998

Five Day Ice Storm Cripples Quebec and Eastern Ontario

The 1998 Ice Storm
Did You Know?

• The ice storm of 1998 was Canada's most expensive natural disaster, and cost approximately $1.6 billion, including $500 million in private property damage.

• When the ice storm ended on Jan 10, 23,000 hydro poles and 80 km of power lines were destroyed on the south shore of Montreal.

• A wooden hydro pole costs $3000.

• Hydro towers are built to withstand 15 mm of freezing rain. Montreal received over 100 mm during the storm.

June, 2002

Canadian Prairies Prepare For Grasshopper Plague

Reuters--Winnipeg, MB. – Western Canadian farmers are readying for battle against swarms of voracious grasshoppers that are poised to destroy millions of dollars worth of crops. The government of Alberta recently announced a $10.3 million pre-emptive strike against the grasshoppers. If left uncontrolled, the province said grasshopper damage could cost between $80 million and $100 million this year.

Read the articles above.

➤ Use the numbers in the articles.
Write a problem you would solve using each operation:
  • addition   • subtraction
  • multiplication   • division

➤ Estimate first. Then solve your problems.
Use a calculator when you need to.

➤ Trade problems with another pair of students.
Solve your classmates' problems.

Show *and* Share

How did you decide which operation to use to solve each of your classmates' problems?
How did you decide whether to use a calculator?
How do you know your answers are reasonable?

The population of Canada was about 32 980 000 in July 2007.
Data show that there were about 497 cellular phones per 1000 people in that year.
How many cellular phones were there in Canada in 2007?

➤ First, find how many groups of 1000
there are in 32 980 000.
To find how many equal groups,
divide: 32 980 000 ÷ 1000 = 32 980

This is a 2-step problem.

➤ There are about 497 cellular phones
for one group of 1000.
To find how many cellular phones for
32 980 groups of 1000, multiply:
32 980 × 497 = 16 391 060

The numbers in this problem are large, so I use a calculator.

There were about 16 391 060 cellular phones in Canada in 2007.

Estimate to check the answer is reasonable.

Use benchmarks:
• 32 980 000 is closer to 30 000 000 than to 40 000 000.
30 000 000 ÷ 1000 = 30 000
• 497 is closer to 500 than to 400.
30 000 × 500 = 15 000 000

16 391 060 is close to 15 000 000.
So, 16 391 060 is a reasonable answer.

Practice •

Use a calculator when you need to.

1. The ticket agent sold
357 adult tickets and
662 student tickets for a
concert. How much money
did the ticket agent take in?
Explain how you know your
answer is reasonable.

THE **Arythematics** in **Concert**
Adults — $28
Students — $24
with the New Merrick Chorus

2. The table shows the populations of the western provinces and territories in 2006.

   a) Find the total population of the 4 western provinces.

   b) How many more people live in Saskatchewan than in Nunavut?

   c) Make up your own problem about these data. Solve it.

Provinces and Territories	Population
British Columbia	4 113 487
Alberta	3 290 350
Saskatchewan	968 157
Manitoba	1 148 401
Yukon Territory	30 372
Northwest Territories	41 464
Nunavut	29 474

3. The total population of Canada was 30 007 094 in 2001 and 31 612 897 in 2006. By how much did the population increase from 2001 to 2006?

4. Monarch butterflies migrate from Canada to Mexico every fall. It is estimated that the butterfly travels about 82 km each day. Suppose the butterfly travels from Edmonton to El Rosario. This is a distance of about 3936 km. How many days does it take? How did you decide which operation to use?

5. The Fairview High School community of 1854 students and 58 teachers attended a special performance of a play at a local theatre. The theatre has 49 rows, with 48 seats in each row.

   a) Were any seats empty? How do you know?

   b) If your answer to part a is yes, find the number of empty seats.

6. This table shows the number of participants at the 2002 and 2006 North American Indigenous Games.

Year	Athletes	Coaches, Managers, and Chaperones
2002 (Winnipeg)	6136	1233
2006 (Denver)	7415	1360

Opening Ceremonies, 2002 North American Indigenous Games, Winnipeg

   a) What was the total number of participants in 2002?

   b) How many more athletes participated in 2006 than in 2002?

   c) About how many times as many athletes participated in 2002 as coaches, managers, and chaperones?

   How did you decide which operation to use each time?

7. The food bank received 325 cases of 24 cans of soup, and 227 cases of 48 cans of soup. Estimate first. Then find how many cases of 12 cans of soup can be made.

8. Ms. Talby's hens laid 257 dozen eggs last month.
   a) About how many eggs is that?
      Explain your estimation strategy.
   b) Exactly how many eggs is that?
      How do you know your answer is reasonable?

9. The owner of a building renovated 18 apartments. Painting cost $5580 and new lights cost $3186.
   a) Which operation or operations will you use to find the cost for each apartment? Explain.
   b) Estimate this cost. Explain the strategy you used.
   c) Find the exact cost.

10. A newspaper prints 8762 papers, each with 16 pages. A roll of newsprint can be used to print 6150 pages. About how many rolls of newsprint are required? Show your work. How do you know your answer is reasonable?

11. The world's longest novel, *À la recherche du temps perdu* by Marcel Proust of France, contains about 9 609 000 letters.
    a) Suppose each page contains about 2400 letters. About how many pages does the novel contain?
    b) Suppose it took Jacques 85 days to read the novel. He read the same number of pages per day. About how many pages did Jacques read each day?
    How do you know your answers are reasonable?

Reflect

When you read a problem, how do you decide which operation you need to use to solve the problem? Use examples from this lesson to explain your answer.

Exploring Multiples

Explore

On Thursday morning, the local radio station held a call-in contest.

• Every third caller won a T-shirt.
• Every seventh caller won a baseball cap.

In 50 calls, which callers won a T-shirt? A baseball cap?
Both prizes?

Use any materials you like to solve this problem.
Show how you used materials to solve this problem.

Sorry, you are caller number 10.

Show and Share

Share your answers with another pair of students.
What strategies did you use to solve the problem?
Discuss how using materials helped.
Describe any patterns you noticed.

Connect

To find the multiples of a number, start at that number and count on by the number.
You can use a hundred chart to find the multiples of a number.

The multiples of 4 are:
4, 8, 12, 16, 20, 24, 28, 32, 36, 40, …

The multiples of 6 are:
6, 12, 18, 24, 30, 36, …

1	2	3	4	5	6	7	8	9	10
11	12	13	14	15	16	17	18	19	20
21	22	23	24	25	26	27	28	29	30
31	32	33	34	35	36	37	38	39	40

12, 24, and 36 appear in both lists.
They are multiples of 4 and of 6.
They are **common multiples** of 4 and 6.
12 is the *least common multiple* of 4 and 6.

Each common multiple of 4 and 6 is divisible
by 4 and by 6.

The least common multiple
is the first common multiple.

We can use multiples to solve some problems.

Wieners are sold in packages of 12.
Hot dog buns are sold in packages of 8.
Suppose you plan to sell about 75 hot dogs
to raise money for charity.
You do not want any wieners or buns left over.
How many packages of each should you buy?

You can use number lines to find the multiples of 8 and 12.
To find the multiples of 8, start at 0 and skip count by 8.

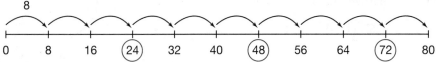

To find the multiples of 12, start at 0 and skip count by 12.

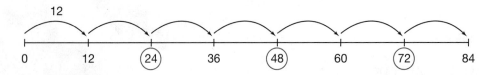

Circle the common multiples: 24, 48, 72
Since 72 is close to 75, you should buy 72 wieners and 72 buns.
You skip counted by eight 9 times to reach 72, so buy 9 packages of buns.
You skip counted by twelve 6 times to reach 72, so buy 6 packages of wieners.

Practice

You may use a hundred chart or number lines to model your solutions.

1. List the first 10 multiples of each number.
   a) 2   b) 5   c) 8   d) 7

2. List the first 6 multiples of each number.
   a) 12   b) 11   c) 16   d) 15

3. Which numbers below are multiples of 6?
   What strategy did you use to find out?
   36   70   66   42   54   27   120   81

4. Which of the numbers 21, 24, 45, 30, 42, 60, and 84 are multiples of:
   a) 3?   b) 12?   c) 7?   d) 15?

5. Find the first 3 common multiples of each pair of numbers.
    a) 4 and 5   b) 7 and 4   c) 3 and 9   d) 10 and 15

6. Find the first 3 common multiples of each set of numbers.
    Which is the least common multiple? Explain your work.
    a) 3, 4, and 6   b) 2, 3, and 4   c) 4, 5, and 10

7. Find all the common multiples of 8 and 9 that are less than 100.

8. Two TV movies start at 8:00 P.M.
    One channel airs commercials every 6 min.
    The other channel airs commercials every 9 min.
    When will the two channels start commercial breaks at the same time?

9. A spider has 8 legs. An ant has 6 legs.
    There are a group of spiders and a group
    of ants.
    The groups have equal numbers of legs.
    What is the least number of spiders and
    ants in each group? Show your work.

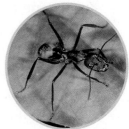

10. Make a large copy of this Venn diagram.
    Sort these numbers.
    45, 24, 52, 30, 66, 15, 85, 90, 72, 60, 20, 38
    What can you say about the numbers in the overlap?

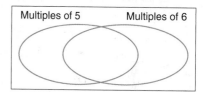

Multiples of 5   Multiples of 6

11. Taho plays shinny every 2 days. He plays lacrosse every 3 days.
    Suppose Taho plays shinny and plays lacrosse on October 1.
    What are the next 3 dates on which he will play shinny
    and play lacrosse? Explain how you know.

12. Find the first 2 common multiples of 36 and 48.

13. Which numbers are common multiples of 8 and 3?
How did you find out?
a) 32   **b)** 72   **c)** 48
d) 54   **e)** 66   **f)** 96

14. Veggie patties are sold in packages of 5.
Buns are sold in packages of 8.
You need about 125 veggie burgers for a school barbecue.
You do not want any patties or buns left over.
How many packages of each should you buy?
What strategy did you use to find out?

15. Kevin, Yone, and Miroki work part-time at the YMCA in Kamloops.
Kevin works every second day.
Yone works every third day.
Miroki works every fourth day.
Today, they worked together.
When will they work together again?
Explain how you know.

16. a) A group of friends get together to make
friendship bracelets. A package of embroidery
floss can be shared equally among 3, 5, or 6 friends
with no strands left over. What is the least number
of strands the package can contain?
b) Suppose the package in part a could also
be shared equally between 2 friends. Does this
change your answer to part a? Why or why not?

17. A common multiple of two numbers is 64.
a) How could you find the two numbers?
b) Is there more than one possible answer?
c) If your answer to part b is yes, find as many pairs of numbers as you can.

Reflect

Write your own problem you could solve using multiples.
Solve your problem.

Prime and Composite Numbers

Numbers multiplied to form a product are factors of the product.

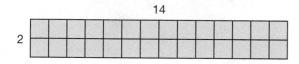

14

2

$$2 \times 14 = 28$$

factor   factor   product

2 and 14 are factors of 28.
What are other factors of 28? How do you know?

Explore

You will need Colour Tiles or
congruent squares and grid paper.

➤ Find all the different rectangles you
can make using each number
of tiles from 2 to 20.
Draw each rectangle on grid paper.
Write a multiplication sentence that
describes the number of tiles in
each rectangle.

➤ For which numbers of tiles could
you make only 1 rectangle?
For which numbers of tiles could
you make 2 rectangles?
3 rectangles?

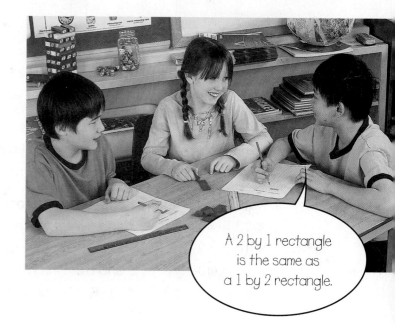

A 2 by 1 rectangle
is the same as
a 1 by 2 rectangle.

Show and Share

Share your work with another group of students.
What are the factors of 2? Of 3?
What are the factors of 16? Of 20?
How could you find the factors of a number without making rectangles?

➤ Suppose you have 23 Colour Tiles.
You can make only 1 rectangle with all 23 tiles.

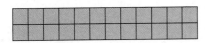

23 has 2 factors: 1 and 23
A number with exactly 2 factors,
1 and itself, is a **prime number**.
23 is a prime number.

> A prime number is a number greater than 1 that is divisible only by 1 and itself.

➤ Suppose you have 24 Colour Tiles.
You can make 4 different rectangles with 24 tiles.

 $1 \times 24 = 24$

$2 \times 12 = 24$

$3 \times 8 = 24$  $4 \times 6 = 24$

24 has 8 factors: 1, 2, 3, 4, 6, 8, 12, and 24
The factors that are prime numbers are 2 and 3.

Here are 2 different strategies students used to find factors.
• Yao used multiplication facts to find all the factors of 40.
  She looked for whole numbers whose product is 40.

$1 \times 40 = 40$	1 and 40 are factors of 40.
$2 \times 20 = 40$	2 and 20 are factors of 40.
$4 \times 10 = 40$	4 and 10 are factors of 40.
$5 \times 8 = 40$	5 and 8 are factors of 40.

40 has 8 factors: 1, 2, 4, 5, 8, 10, 20, and 40
The factors that are prime numbers are 2 and 5.

• Maddie used arrays to find all the factors of 18.

 $1 \times 18 = 18$

$2 \times 9 = 18$ $3 \times 6 = 18$

The factors of 18 are: 1, 2, 3, 6, 9, and 18
The factors that are prime numbers are 2 and 3.
Every number has at least 2 factors: 1 and the number itself
A number with more than 2 factors is a **composite number**.

Practice

You may use Colour Tiles or counters to model your solutions.

1. List all the factors of each number.
   a) 6   b) 9   c) 25   d) 30   e) 12
   f) 50   g) 28   h) 98   i) 20   j) 63

2. a) Name a prime number.
      Explain how you know it is a prime number.
   b) Name a composite number.
      Explain how you know it is a composite number.

3. Which numbers below are factors of 80?
   How do you know?
   a) 2   b) 3   c) 4   d) 5
   e) 6   f) 8   g) 9   h) 10

4. Which of the numbers 2, 3, 4, 5, 6, 8, 9, 12, 15, 17, and 19 are factors of:
   a) 24?   b) 38?   c) 45?   d) 51?
   What strategy did you use to find out?

5. Eggs are packaged in cartons of 12.
   Which of these numbers of eggs can be packaged
   in full cartons? How do you know?
   a) 96   b) 56   c) 60   d) 74

6. Write 3 numbers between 30 and 50 that have:
   a) exactly 2 factors each   b) more than 2 factors each

7. Write 3 numbers less than 100 that have exactly 4 factors each.

8. Sort these numbers as prime or composite.
   How did you decide where to place each number?
   59   93   97   87   73   45

9. Between 20 and 28 students signed up for the chess club.
   The students could not be divided exactly
   into groups of 2, 3, 4, or 5.
   How many students signed up for the chess club?
   Show your work.

10. How many numbers between 70 and 80 are prime numbers?
    What numbers are they?
    Explain how you know they are prime numbers.

11. How many days in September
    have a prime number date?
    How many have a composite
    number date?
    Show how you know.

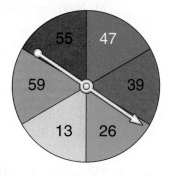

12. How can you tell that 32 and 95 are not prime numbers
    without finding their factors?

13. Brigitte and Stéphane play a game with this spinner.
    Brigitte gets a point if the pointer lands on a prime number.
    Stéphane gets a point if the pointer lands on a composite number.
    The first person to get 20 points wins. Who is more likely to win?
    How do you know?

14. A student said, "All prime numbers except for the number 2 are odd.
    So, all odd numbers must be prime numbers."
    Do you agree with the student? Explain.

15. Copy this Carroll diagram.

	Prime	Composite
Even		
Odd		

Sort the numbers from 2 to 30.

Reflect

Both 0 and 1 are neither prime nor composite.
Explain why.

Investigating Factors

The factors of 6 are 1, 2, 3, and 6.
A number is *perfect* when all its factors, other than the number itself, add up to the number.
$1 + 2 + 3 = 6$
So, 6 is a perfect number.

Explore

➤ There are 50 people practising martial arts in Kinsman Park, Saskatoon.
  Is 50 a perfect number? Explain how you know.
➤ How many students are in your class?
  Is it a perfect number?
  If not, how many more or fewer students would you need to make a perfect number? Show your work.

Kinsman Park, Saskatoon

Show *and* Share

Share your work with another pair of students.
What strategies did you use to find the factors of each number?
How do you know you found all the factors?

Connect

You used factors to find perfect numbers.
➤ When we find the same factors for 2 numbers, we find **common factors**.

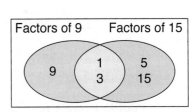

We can show the factors of 9 and 15 in a Venn diagram.
The factors of 9 are: 1, 3, 9
The factors of 15 are: 1, 3, 5, 15

The common factors of 9 and 15 are in the overlapping region.
The common factors of 9 and 15 are 1 and 3.

➤ Every composite number can be written as a product of its factors.

- We can use division facts to find all the factors of 45.
  For example, $45 \div 1 = 45$; $45 \div 3 = 15$; $45 \div 5 = 9$
  We can record the factors as a "rainbow."

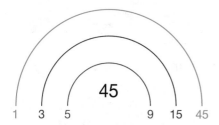

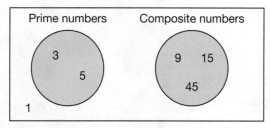

If you are systematic, you are less likely to make errors.

There are no numbers between 5 and 9 that are factors of 45.
So, we know we have found all the factors.

The factors of 45 are: 1, 3, 5, 9, 15, 45
Some of the factors are prime numbers.
We can sort the factors:

Prime numbers
3
5
1

Composite numbers
9   15
45

Here are two ways to find the factors of 45 that are prime.

- Draw a factor tree.

  Write 45 as the product of 2 factors.
  9 and 5 are factors of 45.
  9 is a composite number, so we can factor again.

  So, 3 and 5 are the factors of 45 that are prime numbers.

- Use repeated division by prime numbers.

  Begin by dividing 45 by the least prime number
  that is a factor: 3

  Divide by this prime number until it is no longer a factor.

  Continue to divide each quotient by a prime number
  until the quotient is 1.

  The factors of 45 that are prime numbers are 3 and 5.

$$\begin{array}{r} 15 \\ 3\overline{)45} \end{array}$$
$$\begin{array}{r} 5 \\ 3\overline{)15} \end{array}$$
$$\begin{array}{r} 1 \\ 5\overline{)5} \end{array}$$

Practice

1. Use a Venn diagram. Show the factors of 18 and 24.
   What are the common factors of 18 and 24?

2. Find the common factors of each pair of numbers.
   a) 15, 25   b) 16, 40   c) 18, 42   d) 35, 60

3. Find all the factors of each number.
   Record the factors as a "rainbow."
   a) 48   b) 50   c) 78   d) 62

4. List all the factors of each number.
   How do you know you have found all the factors?
   Sort the factors into prime numbers and composite numbers.
   What do you notice?
   a) 34   b) 40   c) 72   d) 94

5. Draw a factor tree to find the factors of each number
   that are prime.
   a) 64   b) 85   c) 90   d) 76

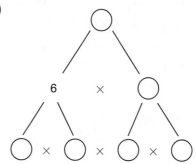

6. Use division to find the factors of each number
   that are prime.
   a) 18   b) 35   c) 36   d) 50

7. Use mental math to find the factors of each number
   that are prime.
   a) 15   b) 6   c) 21   d) 33

8. Copy and complete each factor tree in as many different ways as you can.

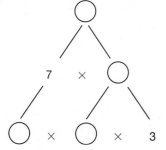

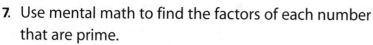

9. Patan uses a bead loom to make a bracelet.
   She wants to use all 84 beads, and to put the beads
   in rows of equal length.
   Patan also wants the number of beads in each row
   to be a factor of 84 that is a prime number.
   How many beads could Patan put in each row?
   Give as many answers as you can.
   Explain how you found the numbers.

Bead Loom

10. Julia and Sandhu bought packages of granola bars.
    Each package has the same number of bars.
    a) Julia and Sandhu each had a total of 12 bars.
       How many bars could there be in one package?
    b) Suppose Julia had 24 bars and Sandhu had 18 bars.
       How many bars could there be in one package?
       Draw a picture to show your thinking.

11. Choose any 2-digit number.
    Write clues to help a classmate guess your number.
    One or more of your clues should be about factors.

12. a) Draw 2 different factor trees for each number.
       i) 56   ii) 32   iii) 90   iv) 75
    b) Why is it possible to draw 2 different factor trees for each number in part a?
    c) Name 2 composite numbers for which you can draw only one factor tree.
       Explain why this is so.
    d) How many factor trees can you draw for the number 67? Explain.

13. Is your age a perfect number?
    If it is not, when will your age be a perfect number?

14. A number is *almost perfect* when all its factors, other than the number itself,
    add up to one less than the number.
    There are two numbers between 5 and 20 that are almost perfect.
    Find these numbers.

Reflect

Which method for finding factors do you prefer?
Explain your choice.

The Factor Game

Play with a partner.
You will need one game board and 2 coloured markers.
The object of the game is to circle the factors of a number.
Decide who will be Player A and Player B.

➤ Player A circles a number on the game board and scores that number.
Player B uses a different colour to circle all the factors of that number not already circled. She scores the sum of the numbers she circles.

For example, suppose Player A circles 18.
Player B circles 1, 2, 3, 6, and 9 (18 is already circled)
to score 1 + 2 + 3 + 6 + 9 = 21 points

➤ Player B circles a new number.
Player A circles all the factors of that number not already circled. Record the scores.

➤ Continue playing.
If a player chooses a number with no factors left to circle, the number is crossed out. The player loses her or his turn, and scores no points.

For example, if player A circled 16, but 1, 2, 4, and 8 have already been circled, he would lose his turn and score no points.

1	2	3	4	5	6	7	8
9	10	11	12	13	14	15	16
17	18	19	20	21	22	23	24
25	26	27	28	29	30	31	32
33	34	35	36	37	38	39	40
41	42	43	44	45	46	47	48
49	50	51	52	53	54	55	56
57	58	59	60	61	62	63	64

➤ The game continues until all numbers have been circled or crossed out.
The player with the higher score wins.

Strategies Toolkit

Explore

Tarra has 10 clown fish and 15 snails.
She wants to place all of them in fish tanks so
each tank has the same number of fish and
the same number of snails.
What is the greatest number of tanks
Tarra can set up?

You may use any materials to model your solution.
Record your solution.

Show *and* Share

Describe the strategy you used to solve the problem.

Connect

Twenty-four girls and 18 boys are forming teams.
All the children are on a team.
Teams must have equal numbers of girls
and equal numbers of boys.
What is the greatest number of teams that can be formed?

Strategies

- **Make a table.**
- **Solve a simpler problem.**
- **Guess and test.**
- **Make an organized list.**
- **Use a pattern.**

Understand

What do you know?
- There are 24 girls and 18 boys.
- Boys and girls should be divided equally among the teams.

Plan

Think of a strategy to help you solve the problem.
- You can **make an organized list**.
- How many girls and how many boys are on each of 2 teams? 3 teams?

Can you make 4 teams? 5 teams? 6 teams?
Explain.
What is the greatest possible number of teams?
How many girls and how many boys
will be on each team?

Check your work.
Did you find the greatest number of teams?
Does each team have the same number of girls
and the same number of boys?
How could you have used common factors
to solve this problem?

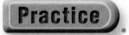
Practice

Choose one of the
Strategies

1. Keshav is making party bags for his mystery party.
   He has 40 notepads, 32 plastic magnifying glasses, and
   16 fingerprinting kits.
   Keshav wants to make as many party bags as possible.
   He wants all the bags to be the same.
   a) How many party bags can Keshav make?
   b) How many notepads, magnifying glasses, and
      fingerprinting kits will be in each bag?
      How do you know?

2. Macie has 36 photos of Kakinga, her favourite gorilla
   at the Calgary Zoo.
   She wants to arrange the photos in groups that have
   equal numbers of rows and columns.
   How many different arrangements can Macie make?
   Show your work.

Kakinga, Calgary Zoo

Reflect

Explain how an organized list can help you solve a problem.

Order of Operations

Which operations would you use to find the answer to this question?
$18 - 6 \div 3 = ?$

Explore

To win a contest, Harry's dad must answer this skill-testing question:

$$9 + 3 \times 6 - 4 = \underline{\hspace{1.5cm}}$$

➤ Find the answer in as many ways as you can.
➤ Record the strategy you use for each method.
➤ The correct answer is 23.
   Which strategy gives this answer?

Show and Share

Share your work with another student.
Discuss how to rewrite the question so the only possible answer is 23.

Connect

When you solve a problem that uses more than one operation,
the answer depends on the order in which you perform the operations.

Evaluate the expression: $3 + 6 \times 4$
If you add first, you get: $9 \times 4 = 36$
If you multiply first, you get: $3 + 24 = 27$

> An **expression** is a mathematical statement with numbers and operations. When we calculate the answer, we *evaluate* the expression.

To avoid getting two answers, there is a rule
that multiplication is done before addition.

So, $3 + 6 \times 4 = 3 + 24$
$\qquad\qquad\quad = 27$, which is the correct answer

We use brackets if we want certain operations carried out first.
To make sure everyone gets the same answer when evaluating
an expression, we use this order of operations:

- Do the operations in brackets.
- Multiply and divide, in order, from left to right.
- Then add and subtract, in order, from left to right.

➤ Evaluate: $16 - 14 \div 2$

$$16 - 14 \div 2$$
$$= 16 - 7$$
$$= 9$$

Divide first: $14 \div 2 = 7$
Then subtract: $16 - 7 = 9$

➤ Evaluate: $18 - 10 + 6$

$$18 - 10 + 6$$
$$= 8 + 6$$
$$= 14$$

Subtract first: $18 - 10 = 8$
Then add: $8 + 6 = 14$

➤ Evaluate: $7 \times (4 + 8)$

$$7 \times (4 + 8)$$
$$= 7 \times 12$$
$$= 84$$

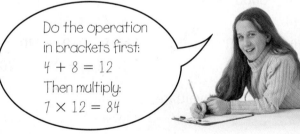

Do the operation
in brackets first:
$4 + 8 = 12$
Then multiply:
$7 \times 12 = 84$

The order of operations is :
Brackets
Multiply and Divide
Add and Subtract

Some calculators follow the order of operations.
Others do not.
Check to see how your calculator works.

Practice

1. Evaluate each expression.
   Use the order of operations.
   a) $18 + 4 \times 2$ b) $25 - 12 \div 3$ c) $24 + 36 \div 9$
   d) $12 - 8 - 4$ e) $50 - 7 \times 6$ f) $7 \times (2 + 9)$
   g) $81 \div 9 - 6$ h) $25 \div (9 - 4)$ i) $13 - 6 + 8$
   j) $(9 + 6) \div 3$ k) $19 + 56 \div 8$ l) $8 \times (12 - 5)$

2. Does your calculator follow the order of operations?
   Press: $9 \boxed{+} 6 \boxed{\times} 3 \boxed{=}$
   Explain how you know.

3. Bianca entered $52 \boxed{+} 8 \boxed{\times} 2 \boxed{=}$ in her calculator.
   She got the answer 120.
   In what order did Bianca's calculator perform the operations?
   How do you know?

4. Use a calculator to evaluate each expression.
   a) $332 - 294 \div 49$ b) $209 \times 12 \div 4$
   c) $312 \times 426 - 212 \times 158$ d) $2205 + 93 \div 3 - 1241$
   e) $156 \times 283 + 215 \times 132$ f) $245 \times 138 \div (7 + 23)$
   g) $(148 + 216) \times (351 - 173)$ h) $1258 + 341 \times 28 - 2357$

5. Use mental math to evaluate.
   a) $20\,000 - 4000 \times 2$ b) $6 + 125 \div 25$
   c) $(1000 + 6000) \times 3$ d) $60 \times 3 \div 9$
   e) $5 \times (4 + 11)$ f) $50 + 50 \div 50$
   g) $(50 + 50) \div 50$ h) $9 \times 10 - (30 + 30)$
   i) $16 \div 2 \times 9$ j) $200 - 200 \div 20$

6. Use mental math to evaluate.
   a) $4 \times 7 - 2 + 1$ b) $4 \times (7 - 2) + 1$
   c) $4 \times 7 - (2 - 1)$ d) $4 \times (7 - 2 + 1)$
   e) $(4 \times 7 - 2) + 1$ f) $4 \times 7 - (2 + 1)$
   Which expressions give the greatest answer?
   The least answer?

7. How many different answers can you get by inserting
   one pair of brackets in this expression?
   $10 + 20 - 12 \div 2 \times 3$
   Write each expression, then evaluate it.

8. Use the numbers 2, 3, and 4 and any operations or brackets.
   Write an expression that equals each number below.
   Try to do this more than one way.
   a) 9   **b)** 10   **c)** 14   **d)** 20   **e)** 6

9. Alexi bought 5 T-shirts for $12 each
   and 3 pairs of socks for $2 a pair.
   Which expression shows how much
   Alexi spent in dollars? How do you know?
   a) $5 \times 12 \times 3 \times 2$
   b) $5 \times 12 + 3 \times 2$
   c) $(5 + 3) \times (12 + 2)$

10. Choose mental math, a calculator,
    or paper and pencil to evaluate.
    For each question, how did you decide
    which method to use?
    a) $238 - (2 \times 73)$ **b)** $47 \times (16 \times 18)$
    c) $(36 + 14) \div 10$ **d)** $36 \times (48 \times 8)$
    e) $60 \times (4 \div 2)$ **f)** $(200 + 50) \times (9 \div 3)$

11. Monsieur Lefèvre bought 2 boxes of fruit bars
    for his 3 children.
    Each box has 6 fruit bars.
    The children shared the fruit bars equally.
    How many fruit bars did each child get?
    Write an expression to show
    the order of operations you used.

12. Copy each number sentence.
    Use brackets to make each number sentence true.
    a) $36 \div 4 \times 3 = 3$
    b) $20 \div 5 \times 2 + 3 = 5$
    c) $10 - 4 \div 2 - 1 = 6$
    d) $6 \times 2 + 8 \div 4 = 15$

Reflect

Why do we need rules for the order in which we perform operations?
Give examples to support your answer.

What Is an Integer?

Temperature is measured in degrees Celsius (°C).
Water freezes at 0°C.

On a typical summer day in La Ronge, Saskatchewan, the temperature might be 24 degrees Celsius above zero.

On a typical winter day in La Ronge, the temperature might be 18 degrees Celsius below zero.

A temperature greater than 0°C is positive.
We write: +24°C
We say: twenty-four degrees Celsius

A temperature less than 0°C is negative.
We write: −18°C
We say: minus eighteen degrees Celsius

 **Explore**

Use a positive or negative number to represent each situation.
- eight degrees above zero
- ten degrees below zero
- parking three levels below ground level
- twenty-three metres above sea level in Victoria, BC
- a loss of sixteen dollars
- taking four steps backward

Suppose you change the sign of each number.
What situation would each number now represent?

Butchart Gardens, Victoria

Show and Share

Compare your answers with those of another pair of students.
For each situation, how did you decide whether to use a positive number or a negative number?

Numbers such as +24 and −18 are **integers**.
The + sign in front of a number tells that it is a **positive integer**.
The − sign in front of a number tells that it is a **negative integer**.

➤ We can use coloured tiles to represent integers.

One yellow tile represents +1.

One red tile represents −1.

To model +6, we use 6 yellow tiles.

To model −5, we use 5 red tiles.

➤ We can show integers on a horizontal or vertical number line.

You have used horizontal number lines
with whole numbers.
We extend the number line to the left of 0
to show *negative integers*.

A thermometer is
a vertical number line.

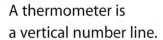

The arrow on the number line represents −3.
−3 is a negative integer. We say, "Negative 3."

➤ **Opposite integers** are the same distance from 0 but are on opposite sides of 0.
For example, +2 and −2 are opposite integers.
They are the same distance from 0 and are on opposite sides of 0.

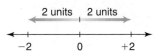

+4 and −4 are also opposite integers, as are −21 and +21.

➤ We use integers to represent quantities that have both size and direction.
  • Mark saved $25.
    This can be represented as +$25, or $25.

  • A scuba diver swam to a depth of 50 m.
    This can be represented as −50 m.

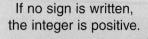
If no sign is written, the integer is positive.

Practice

1. Write the integer modelled by each set of tiles.

   a)    b) ▢

   c) ▢ ▢ ▢ ▢   d) ■ ■ ■

2. Use yellow or red tiles to model each integer. Draw the tiles.
   a) −6   b) +8   c) +5   d) −2
   e) +11   f) −4   g) +2   h) −9

3. Mark these integers on a number line.
   Tell how you knew where to place each integer.
   a) +1   b) −5   c) −2   d) +9

4. Write the opposite of each integer.
   Mark each pair of integers on a number line.
   Describe any patterns you see.
   a) +3   b) −1   c) −19   d) +10

5. Write an integer to represent each situation.
   a) Sascha dug a hole 1 m deep.
   b) Vincent deposited $50 in his bank account.
   c) A plane flies at an altitude of 11 000 m.
   d) A submarine travels at a depth of 400 m.

6. Use an integer to represent each situation.
   Then use yellow or red tiles to model each integer. Draw the tiles.
   a) 12°C below zero
   b) 10 m above sea level
   c) 9 s before take-off
   d) a drop of $2 in the price of a movie ticket
   e) a parking spot 5 levels below ground level

7. Describe a situation that could be represented by each integer.
   a) 125
   b) −22
   c) −900
   d) 42 000
   e) 4

8. Describe two situations in which you might use negative and positive integers. Write integers for your situations.

9. We measure time in hours.
   Suppose 12 noon is represented by the integer 0.
   a) Which integer represents 1 P.M. the same day?
   b) Which integer represents 10 A.M. the same day?
   c) Which integer represents 12 midnight the same day?
   d) Which integer represents 10 P.M. the previous day?
   Describe the strategy you used to find the integers.

Clock Tower, Calgary's Old City Hall

10. Statistics Canada reported these data about Canada's population.

Years	Births	Deaths	Immigration	Emigration
1961–1966	2 249 000	731 000	539 000	280 000
1996–2001	1 705 000	1 089 000	1 217 000	376 000

a) Which numbers can be represented by positive integers? By negative integers? Explain your choices.
b) Choose one time period. Use a number line to explain the relationship between births and deaths.

Reflect

Suppose you read about a situation that can be described with integers.
What clues do you look for to help you decide whether to use
a positive integer or a negative integer?
Use examples in your explanation.

Comparing and Ordering Integers

Elevation is the height above or below sea level. Elevation influences climate and how people live. For example, crops will not grow at elevations above 5300 m.

```
5000 m
4000 m
3000 m
2000 m
1000 m
   0 m
-1000 m
-2000 m
-3000 m
-4000 m
-5000 m
```

Explore

You will need an atlas or Internet access.
Here are some examples of extreme elevations around the world.

Place	Elevation
Vinson Massif, Antarctica	4897 m above sea level
Dead Sea, Israel/Jordan	411 m below sea level
Bottom of Great Slave Lake, Canada	458 m below sea level
Mt. Nowshak, Afghanistan	7485 m above sea level
Challenger Deep, Pacific Ocean	10 924 m below sea level

Find at least 4 more extreme elevations.
Two should be above sea level, and two should be below sea level.
At least one elevation should be in Canada.

Order *all* the elevations from least to greatest.

Great Slave Lake, NWT

Show *and* Share

What strategies did you use to order the elevations? What other ways could you display these data to show the different elevations?

We can use a number line to order integers.

➤ We use the symbols > and < to show order.
The symbol points to the lesser number.

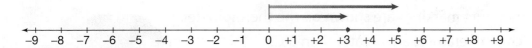

+5 is to the right of +3 on a number line.
+5 is greater than +3, so we write: +5 > +3
+3 is less than +5, so we write: +3 < +5

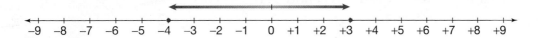

+3 is to the right of −4 on a number line.
+3 is greater than −4, so we write: +3 > −4
−4 is less than +3, so we write: −4 < +3

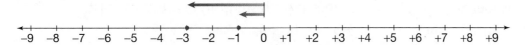

−3 is to the left of −1 on a number line.
−3 is less than −1, so we write: −3 < −1
−1 is greater than −3, so we write: −1 > −3

➤ To order the integers 0, +1, −2, +3, and −5,
draw a number line from −6 to +6.
Mark each integer on the number line.

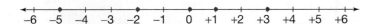

The integers increase from left to right.
So, the integers from least to greatest are:
−5, −2, 0, +1, +3

1. Copy each number line. Fill in the missing integers.

   a)
   −4   −2   0 +1 +2   +4

   b)
        −7   −5   −3   −1   +1

2. Six temperature markings are shown on the thermometer.

   a) Which temperatures are greater than 0°C?

   b) Which temperatures are less than 0°C?

   c) Which temperatures are opposite integers?
       How do you know?

3. Which integer is greater? How did you find out?

   a) +4, +3   **b)** +4, −3   **c)** −4, +3   **d)** −4, −3

4. Mark each set of integers on a number line.
   Use the number line to order the integers from least to greatest.

   a) +5, +13, +1   **b)** −3, −5, −4   **c)** +4, −2, +3

5. Use a number line. Order the integers in each set from greatest to least.

   a) +4, +1, +8   **b)** −7, −5, −3   **c)** 0, +4, −4

6. This table shows the coldest temperatures ever
   recorded in 6 provinces and territories.

   a) Draw a thermometer like the one shown.
       Mark each temperature on it.

Province/ Territory	Coldest Temperature (°C)
Alberta	−61
Manitoba	−53
Nova Scotia	−47
Nunavut	−64
Ontario	−58
Quebec	−54

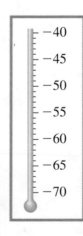

Dog Sledding in Nunavut

   b) Order the temperatures in part a from least to greatest.
       How can you use your thermometer to do this?

7. Copy and complete by placing $<$, $>$, or $=$ between the integers. Then, use a number line to verify your answer.
   a) $+5 \, \square \, +10$ b) $-5 \, \square \, -10$ c) $+5 \, \square \, 5$ d) $-6 \, \square \, 0$
   e) $-5 \, \square \, -4$ f) $10 \, \square \, -11$ g) $-8 \, \square \, -4$ h) $-8 \, \square \, -8$

8. Look at the integers in the box.
   a) Which integers are:
      i) greater than 0?
      ii) between -3 and $+3$?
      iii) greater than -10 and less than -5?
      iv) less than $+1$?
   b) What other questions can you ask about these integers? Write down your questions and answer them.

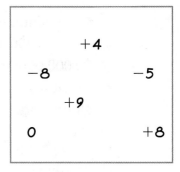

9. Order the integers in each set from least to greatest.
   a) $+5, -5, +4, +2, -2$ b) $-8, -12, +10, 0, -10$
   c) $+41, -39, -41, -15, -25$ d) $+1, -1, +2, -2, +3$

10. Order the integers in each set from greatest to least.
    a) $-7, +8, -9, +10, -11$ b) $-18, 16, -11, -4, +6$
    c) $0, +1, +2, -1, -2$ d) $+14, -25, -30, +3, -10$

11. On January 16, 2008, these temperatures were recorded in Canada.

Place	Temperature	Place	Temperature
Lethbridge, AB	–16°C	Iqaluit, NU	–29°C
La Ronge, SK	–27°C	Dawson City, YT	–26°C
Hay River, NWT	–29°C	Prince George, BC	–6°C
Campbell River, BC	0°C	Ste. Rose du Lac, MB	–17°C

Which place was the warmest? The coldest? How did you find out?

12. a) Which of these integers are greater than -6? How do you know?
       $-3, +2, -7, -5$
    b) Which of these integers are less than -3? How do you know?
       $+2, -11, +3, -2, -4$

13. You know that 8 is greater than 3. Explain why -8 is less than -3.

Reflect

When two integers have different signs, how can you tell which is greater?
When two integers have the same sign, how can you tell which is greater?

LESSON

1

1. Write each number in standard form.
   a) 3 billion 400 thousand 7 hundred
   b) 20 000 000 + 3 000 000 + 60 000 + 4000 + 900 + 7
   c) twenty-seven trillion fifty-seven million three hundred twenty-four thousand eighty-three

2. Write each number in expanded form.
   a) 86 209 402   b) 23 854 265 001

2

3. Mrs. Wisely has $635 000 in the bank.
   How much more money does she need before she can call herself a millionaire?
   How did you decide which operation to use?

4. Top Tickets sells tickets for the Olympic Figure
   Skating Gala Exhibition, where all the medal-winning
   skaters perform. Use the table below.

2006 Olympic Figure Skating Gala

Tickets Sold by Top Tickets		
Seating Level	Price	Number Sold
A	$525	126
B	$325	348
C	$175	1235

   a) How much money did Top Tickets take in?
   b) Suppose Top Tickets wants to take in $700 000.
      How much more money do they need to take in?
   c) Suppose Top Tickets sold $284 725 worth of Level C tickets.
      How many Level C tickets did they sell?

3

5. Which numbers below are multiples of 7?
   How did you find out?
   24   35   42   27   63   96   84

6. Find a common multiple of 4, 5, and 6.
   Explain how you know the number you found is a common multiple.

4

7. Tell if each number is prime or composite. How do you know?
   a) 18   **b)** 21   **c)** 48   **d)** 37

8. Only one prime number is even.
   Which number is it? How do you know it is a prime number?

5

9. List all the factors of each number.
   Sort the factors into prime numbers and composite numbers.
   a) 52   **b)** 28   **c)** 63   **d)** 76

10. Find the common factors of each pair of numbers.
   a) 16, 32   **b)** 18, 27   **c)** 30, 75

11. Draw a factor tree to find the factors of each number that are prime.
   a) 18   **b)** 48   **c)** 21   **d)** 75

7

12. Evaluate each expression.
   a) $35 - 16 \div 4$ **b)** $8 \times (6 + 4)$ **c)** $86 - 9 \times 9$

13. Evaluate each expression.
   a) $16\ 974 - (18 \times 45)$ **b)** $8537 + 4825 \div 25$

8

14. Draw a number line. Mark each integer on the line.
   How did you know where to place each integer?
   $+3, -5, +1, -2, 0$

15. Use an integer to represent each situation.
   a) Sandha skated backward 100 m.
   b) Karl earned $140 mowing lawns.
   c) The temperature in Alida, SK, was 12°C
      below zero.
   d) The elevator went up 7 floors.

9

16. Use a number line.
   Order the integers in each set from least
   to greatest.
   a) $+4, -3, -2, +1, -4$
   b) $+8, +5, 0, -5, -17$
   c) $+10, -9, +8, -7, +6$

UNIT

2 Learning Goals

☑ use place value to represent whole numbers greater than one million
☑ solve problems involving large numbers, using technology
☑ determine multiples and factors of numbers less than 100
☑ solve problems involving multiples
☑ identify composite and prime numbers
☑ apply the order of operations to solve multi-step problems, with or without technology
☑ demonstrate an understanding of integers

Unit Problem

At the Apiary

Honeybees have 4 wings that beat about 11 400 times per minute.

The ideal temperature of a hive is 32°C. In winter, when the temperature can be −20°C, honeybees beat their wings to generate heat to keep the queen and her hive from freezing.

A honeybee flies an average of 22 km each hour.

A honeybee visits about 4400 flowers to gather enough nectar to make 10 g of honey.

During her busy season, the queen bee lays about 1500 eggs in 24 h.

In 2000, there were 603 828 hives in Canada. The average number of hives per beekeeper was 61, and the average yield of honey per hive was 52 kg.

Solve questions 1 to 3.
Use a calculator when you need to.
Check your solutions. Show all your work.

1. During her busy season, about how many eggs does the queen bee lay each hour? Each minute?

2. Each day, the queen bee eats 80 times her mass in food.
   Suppose a cat needed to eat 80 times its mass each day.
   How many kilograms of food would a cat eat each day? Each month?

3. The typical Canadian eats about 880 g of honey each year.
   Millicent is 12 years old.
   She estimates she has eaten about 11 kg of honey in her lifetime.
   Is Millicent a typical Canadian honey eater? Explain.

4. Use some of the honeybee data on page 84 or use data you can find about honeybees.
   Write a story problem.
   Solve the problem.
   Describe your strategy.

Reflect on Your Learning

Write about some of the things you have learned about numbers in this unit.

Decimals

Harnessing the Wind

Wind is a clean, renewable source of energy used to produce electricity. It does not pollute or contribute to global warming.

Learning Goals

- use place value to represent numbers less than one thousandth
- multiply decimals by a 1-digit number
- divide decimals by a 1-digit number

86

Weather Dancer is a 72-m wind turbine in southern Alberta. It generates 2.96 gigawatt hours of electricity each year. Weather Dancer supplies electricity to 460 homes.

Electrical power is measured in units called watts.

1000 watts = 1 kilowatt
1 000 000 watts = 1 megawatt
1 000 000 000 watts = 1 gigawatt

The amount of electricity generated or consumed is measured in watt hours. One kilowatt hour means 1 kilowatt of electricity is used in 1 h.

CANADIAN ENVIRONMENT AWARDS · PRIX CANADIENS DE L'ENVIRONNEMENT 2004

The winner of the Canadian Environment Award in 2004 was William Big Bull, a member of the Piikani First Nation. Through his efforts, Weather Dancer was built.

- How are kilowatts, megawatts, and gigawatts related?
- About how many gigawatt hours of electricity will Weather Dancer generate in 5 years?
- How could you find how many megawatt hours of electricity Weather Dancer generates in 1 year?
- A typical Alberta household uses about 21.37 kilowatt hours of electricity each day. About how much is used in 1 week?

87

Numbers to Thousandths and Beyond

Decimals are all around us.
The ostrich is the world's largest living bird.
It can have a mass of 156.489 kg.
How do you read this number?
What is the meaning of each digit?

Explore

You will need a calculator and a copy of a place-value chart.
Write the headings and the number 27 in the chart, as shown below.

Tens	Ones	Tenths	Hundredths	Thousandths			
2	7						

a) Divide 27 by 50.
   Record it in the chart.
b) Divide your answer to part a by 50.
   Record it in the chart.
c) Divide your answer to part b by 25.
   Record it in the chart.

Show *and* Share

Share your work with another pair of students.
Use what you know about the headings in a place-value chart for whole numbers.
Write the missing headings in your place-value chart.
Take turns to say the numbers.

There are many patterns in the place-value chart.

Hundred Thousands	Ten Thousands	Thousands	Hundreds	Tens	Ones	Tenths	Hundredths	Thousandths	Ten-Thousandths	Hundred-Thousandths	Millionths
100 000	10 000	1000	100	10	1	$\frac{1}{10}$	$\frac{1}{100}$	$\frac{1}{1000}$	$\frac{1}{10\ 000}$	$\frac{1}{100\ 000}$	$\frac{1}{1\ 000\ 000}$

$1 = 10$ tenths $\frac{1}{100} = 10$ thousandths $\frac{1}{10\ 000} = 10$ hundred-thousandths

As you move to the left, each position represents ten times as many as the position to its right.

The fairyfly is the world's smallest insect.

> I see a pattern: tens and tenths, hundreds and hundredths, thousands and thousandths.

This place-value chart shows the length of the male fairyfly in centimetres.

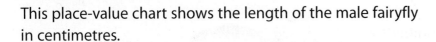

Ones	Tenths	Hundredths	Thousandths	Ten-Thousandths	Hundred-Thousandths	Millionths
0	0	1	3	9		

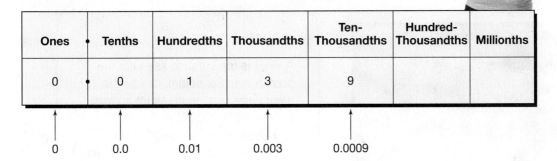

0   0.0   0.01   0.003   0.0009

We read this number as:
one hundred thirty-nine ten-thousandths

> We read the decimal as a whole number, then say the name of the position of the last digit.

We can write this number in:
• standard form: 0.0139
• expanded form:
  0 ones + 0 tenths + 1 hundredth + 3 thousandths + 9 ten-thousandths
  $= 0.01 + 0.003 + 0.0009$

In expanded form, we write 3.268 579 as:

3 ones + 2 tenths + 6 hundredths + 8 thousandths +
5 ten-thousandths + 7 hundred-thousandths + 9 millionths
= 3 + 0.2 + 0.06 + 0.008 + 0.0005 + 0.000 07 + 0.000 009

We leave a space after each group of 3 digits when the number has more than 4 decimal places.

We read this decimal as: three and two hundred sixty-eight thousandths, five hundred seventy-nine millionths

Small decimals are often used in science. For example:

A garden snail moves very slowly. In 1 h, it travels 0.0483 km. We read this number as: four hundred eighty-three ten-thousandths

Sound travels very fast. It would take 0.0046 min for sound to travel from one end of a football field to the other. We read this number as: forty-six ten-thousandths

The diameter of a human hair is 0.000 025 m. We read this number as: twenty-five millionths

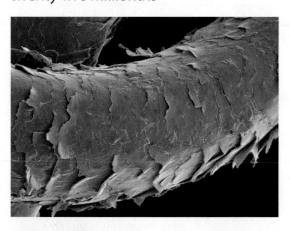

Math Link

Science

A virus is too small to see with the human eye. So, scientists use the nanometre (nm) to measure a virus.
1 nm = 0.000 000 001 m
The Ebola virus has length 0.000 02 cm, or 200 nm. As a comparison, the head of a pin has diameter 0.2 cm.

Practice

1. Use a place-value chart to show each number.
   a) 2.3425　　　b) 0.142 86　　　c) 0.0007　　　d) 0.000 298

2. Use the numbers in the table.
   Write the number that has a 5 in:
   a) the ten-thousandths position
   b) the millionths position
   c) the thousandths position
   d) the hundred-thousandths position
   e) the tenths position

   | 0.635 734 |
   | 0.506 312 |
   | 1.003 825 |
   | 3.702 456 |
   | 2.184 592 |

3. Describe the meaning of each digit in 4.524 371.

4. Write each number in standard form.
   a) 8 and 26 ten-thousandths
   b) 24 millionths
   c) 3 hundred-thousandths
   d) 4 and 374 millionths

5. Write each number in expanded form.
   a) 0.0056
   b) 0.000 49
   c) 3.000 023
   d) 0.348 619

6. Write a decimal that is between:
   a) 2.153 and 2.154
   b) 0.6534 and 0.6535

7. Find two examples of very small numbers in the media. Write each number in a place-value chart. Explain how you use the patterns in the chart to read these numbers.

8. How are the values of the red digits in each number related?
   a) 5.000 05
   b) 2.1433
   c) 0.677 56
   d) 4.234 654

9. Write the number in each fact in as many different forms as you can.
   a) A strand of silk in the web of a garden spider has a diameter of about 0.000 003 m.
   b) The diameter of one red blood cell is about 0.000 762 cm.
   c) The mass of a grain of rice is about 0.000 02 kg.

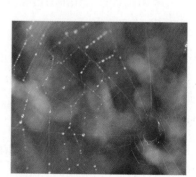

10. Use any or all of these digits: 1, 0, 2, 0, 4, 0, 5, 0
    a) Write 5 numbers less than one thousandth.
    b) Which of your numbers is the least? How do you know?
    c) Which of your numbers is the greatest? How do you know?

Reflect

How do the patterns in a place-value chart help you read and write decimals less than one thousandth?

Estimating Products and Quotients

Bernie needs 1.15 m of string to make a
beaded sunglass cord.
He wants to make 6 cords.
About how much string does Bernie
need altogether?
How can he use decimal benchmarks
to help him estimate?

Explore

For each problem below:
• Estimate the answer.
• Record your strategy and your estimate.
Show your work.

➤ A nickel has a mass of 3.95 g.
   What is the approximate mass of 7 nickels?

➤ Nine bags of dog food have
   a mass of 134.55 kg.
   What is the approximate mass of one bag?

Show and Share

Share your estimates with another pair of students.
Discuss the strategies you used to estimate.
How could you use decimal benchmarks to estimate?
Did you get the same estimates?
If your answer is no, is one estimate closer than the other? Explain.

Connect

➤ A ping-pong ball has a mass of 2.73 g.
Estimate the mass of 8 ping-pong balls.

Here are two strategies students used to estimate: 2.73×8
- Lara used front-end estimation.
  She wrote 2.73 as 2.
  Then multiplied: $2 \times 8 = 16$

> In *front-end estimation*, we use the place value of the front digits of a number.

The mass of 8 ping-pong balls is about 16 g.
This is an underestimate because 2 is less than 2.73.

- Hal used decimal benchmarks.
  Since 2.73 is closer to 3 than to 2,
  he wrote 2.73 as 3.
  Hal multiplied: $3 \times 8 = 24$

The mass of 8 ping-pong balls is about 24 g.
This is an overestimate because 3 is greater than 2.73.

➤ Four baseballs have a total mass of 575.94 g.
Estimate the mass of 1 baseball.

Here are two strategies students used to estimate: $575.94 \div 4$
- Aki used front-end estimation.
  He wrote 575.94 as 500.
  Then divided: $500 \div 4 = 125$

The mass of 1 baseball is about 125 g.
This is an underestimate because 500 is less than 575.94.

- Adele looked for compatible numbers.
  Since 575.94 is close to 600,
  she divided: $600 \div 4 = 150$

> *Compatible numbers* are numbers that are easy to use mentally.

The mass of 1 baseball is about 150 g.
This is an overestimate because 600 is greater than 575.94.

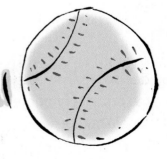

Practice

1. Estimate each product or quotient. Which strategies did you use?
   Tell if your estimate is an overestimate or an underestimate.
   a) 7.01×9 b) 3.8×7 c) 11.85×5 d) 19.925×4
   e) $9.8 \div 5$ f) $12.31 \div 2$ g) $56.093 \div 7$ h) $225.3 \div 5$

2. Waldo paid $29.85 for 3 admission tickets to the Calgary Tower.
   Estimate the cost of one admission ticket.

3. A pair of ice cleats for ice fishing costs $14.89.
   About how much will 6 pairs of ice cleats cost?
   How did you find out?

4. Estimate the perimeter of each square.
   Tell if your estimate is an overestimate or an underestimate.
   How do you know?
   a)

   1.3 cm
   b)

   2.1 cm
   c)

   2.6 cm

5. Estimate the side length of a square with perimeter:
   a) 24.2 cm   b) 29.8 cm   c) 35.6 cm

6. a) Is 9.47×5 greater than, or less than, 45?
      How can you estimate to find out?
   b) Is $23.86 \div 4$ greater than, or less than, 6?
      How can you estimate to find out?
   Show your work.

7. Copy and complete. Write $>$, $<$, or $=$.
   How did you decide which symbol to use?
   a) $5.6 \times 2 \; \square \; 1.4 \times 4$ b) $4.8 \div 2 \; \square \; 15.5 \div 5$

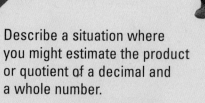

At Home

Reflect

Describe how you decide which strategy
to use to estimate the product or quotient
of a decimal and a whole number.

Describe a situation where
you might estimate the product
or quotient of a decimal and
a whole number.

Multiplying Decimals by a Whole Number

Many Canadians love the thrill of
riding a roller coaster.
The longer the ride, the greater the thrill.

Explore

This table shows the lengths of some of
the world's top roller coasters.
Choose 3 roller coasters you would like
to ride.
Suppose you rode each of them 8 times.
Estimate how far you would travel
on each roller coaster.
Then calculate the actual distance.

Roller Coaster	Country	Length (km)
The Beast	USA	2.243
The Steel Dragon	Japan	2.479
The Corkscrew	Canada	0.732
The Dragon Khan	Spain	1.269
The Mighty Canadian Minebuster	Canada	1.167
The Ultimate	England	2.268

Show and Share

Share your results with another pair of classmates.
Discuss the strategies you used to estimate and to calculate.
How do you know your answers are reasonable?

LESSON FOCUS | Multiply decimals by a whole number.

95

➤ The Superman Ride of Steel roller coaster is 1.646 km long.
Beth and Ujjal rode this roller coaster 3 times.
How far did Beth and Ujjal travel on the Superman Ride of Steel?

Multiply: 1.646 × 3
Here are two different strategies students used to calculate 1.646 × 3.

• Jiri used Base Ten Blocks on a place-value mat.
He modelled 3 groups of 1.646.
Jiri then traded 10 thousandths for 1 hundredth,
10 hundredths for 1 tenth, and 10 tenths for 1 one.

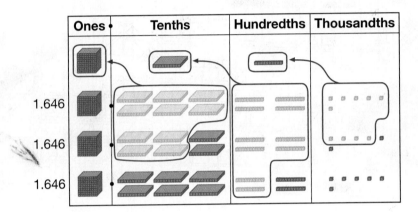

Jiri then counted the blocks.
4 ones + 9 tenths + 3 hundredths + 8 thousandths = 4.938
So, 1.646 × 3 = 4.938

• Hanna used the strategy for multiplying 2 whole numbers,
then estimated to place the decimal point.

The closest whole-number benchmark to 1.646 is 2.
2 × 3 = 6
Hanna placed the decimal point in the product so the
whole number part is a number close to 6; that is: 4.938

```
  1646
 ×   3
─────────
    18
   120
  1800
  3000
─────────
  4938
```

So, 1.646 × 3 = 4.938

Beth and Ujjal travelled 4.938 km on the Superman Ride of Steel.

1. Use Base Ten Blocks to multiply.

   a) 2.3
   × 2

   b) 1.8
   × 4

   c) 1.23
   × 5

   d) 2.42
   × 3

2. The decimal point is missing in each product.
   Use front-end estimation to place each decimal point.

   a) 7.1 × 5 = 355

   b) 3.12 × 6 = 1872

   c) 15.466 × 3 = 46398

   d) 1.408 × 5 = 7040

   e) 2.005 × 8 = 1604

   f) 8.25 × 4 = 330

3. Use benchmarks to estimate each product.

   a) 2.4 × 6

   b) 4.38 × 4

   c) 1.499 × 6

   d) 6.721 × 2

   e) 3.983 × 3

   f) 7.3225 × 5

4. Multiply.

   a) 8.2 × 4

   b) 1.02 × 6

   c) 5.9 × 2

   d) 6.112 × 3

   e) 3.525 × 7

   f) 5.354 × 6

5. Estimate to choose the correct product for each multiplication question.

	Question	Possible Products		
a)	2.85 × 3	855	85.5	8.55
b)	12.36 × 4	494.4	49.44	4.944
c)	148.73 × 5	7.4365	74.365	743.65

6. Elisa works in a hospital lab in Brandon, Manitoba.
   In 1 h, she tested 7 tubes of blood.
   Each tube contained 12.25 mL of blood.
   How much blood did Elisa test?
   How did you find out?

7. Naja saved $14.75 each week for 8 weeks.
   She had just enough money to buy a family membership
   to the Vancouver Aquarium. About how much was
   the cost of the membership?

8. Tianna has saved $9.75 each week for 7 weeks.
   She wants to buy a snowboard that costs $80.45, including tax.

   a) Does Tianna have enough money? How do you know?

   b) If your answer to part a is no, how much more money does Tianna need?

9. The decimal point in some of these products is in the wrong place. Identify the mistakes, then write each product with the decimal point in the correct place.
a) 4.01 × 5 = 200.5
b) 7.893 × 3 = 23.679
c) 89.85 × 4 = 35.94
d) 1.98 × 3 = 0.594

10. a) Akuna sold three 1.375-L bottles of birch syrup to raise money for his school in Hay River.
Did Akuna sell more or less than 4 L of syrup?
How much more or less? Explain how you know.
b) Akuna sold each bottle of syrup for $74.79.
How much money did he raise?

11. The Townsend's big-eared bat lives in river valleys in southern British Columbia. It has a mass of 8.812 g. What is the combined mass of 6 of these tiny bats?

12. Write a story problem that can be solved by multiplying 4.026 by 7.
Trade problems with a classmate and solve your classmate's problem.

13. You can estimate how tall a child will be as an adult by doubling her height at 2 years of age.
Serena is 2 years old and 81.4 cm tall.
About how tall will Serena be as an adult?

14. The Three Dog Bakery in Vancouver sells bags of all-natural chicken-flavoured dog food for $7.95 each.
Saima buys 3 bags.
a) Saima gives the cashier $25.00.
How much change should she receive?
b) Each bag has a mass of 2.268 kg.
Does Saima have more or less than 7 kg of dog food altogether? How do you know?

Reflect

Explain how you decide where to place the decimal point in the product 7.146 × 7.

Multiplying a Decimal Less than 1 by a Whole Number

Iron is a part of our blood.
It helps to deliver oxygen throughout the body.
A typical Grade 6 student needs 0.008 g of iron each day.
How much iron does a Grade 6 student need in one week?

What happens if you use front-end estimation
to check your answer?

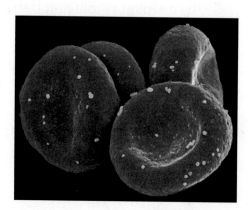

Explore

You will need a calculator.

Copy and complete the multiplication statements.
Use a calculator to find the products in the 2nd and 3rd columns.

1 × 1 =	0.1 × 1 =	0.01 × 1 =
1 × 2 =	0.1 × 2 =	0.01 × 2 =
1 × 3 =	0.1 × 3 =	0.01 × 3 =
1 × 4 =	0.1 × 4 =	0.01 × 4 =
1 × 5 =	0.1 × 5 =	0.01 × 5 =
1 × 6 =	0.1 × 6 =	0.01 × 6 =
1 × 7 =	0.1 × 7 =	0.01 × 7 =
1 × 8 =	0.1 × 8 =	0.01 × 8 =
1 × 9 =	0.1 × 9 =	0.01 × 9 =

➤ Describe the patterns you see.
➤ Insert a column to the right.
    Use your patterns to predict the entries in this new column.

Show and Share

Share your patterns with another pair of students.
How are the products in each row alike? How are they different?
What do you notice about the product when you multiply 0.1 by a 1-digit whole number?
0.01 by a 1-digit whole number? 0.001 by a 1-digit whole number?

When you multiply a decimal less than 1 by a whole number, the product is less than the whole number.
You can use place value and estimation to multiply a decimal less than 1 by a 1-digit whole number.

➤ To multiply 0.9 by 2:
Use Base Ten Blocks.
Model 2 groups of 0.9.
0.9 is nine tenths.
Nine tenths multiplied by 2 is 18 tenths.
Trade 10 tenths for 1 one.

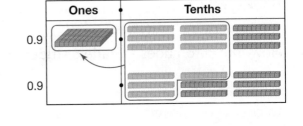

1 one + 8 tenths = 1.8
So, 0.9 × 2 = 1.8

➤ To multiply 0.15 by 4:
Use Base Ten Blocks.
Model 4 groups of 0.15.
0.15 is 15 hundredths, which is 1 tenth and 5 hundredths.

Ones	Tenths	Hundredths

Trade 10 hundredths
for 1 tenth.
Trade another 10 hundredths
for 1 tenth.

Ones	Tenths	Hundredths

0 ones + 6 tenths + 0 hundredths = 0.60
So, 0.15 × 4 = 0.60

0.60 is 60 hundredths, which is 6 tenths.

➤ To multiply 0.0138 by 9, multiply the whole numbers: 138 × 9

$$
\begin{array}{r}
138 \\
\times\ 9 \\
\hline
72 \\
270 \\
900 \\
\hline
1242
\end{array}
$$

Estimate to place the decimal point.

So, 0.0138 × 9 = 0.1242

To estimate, I use compatible numbers.
0.0138 is close to 0.01.
0.01 is 1 hundredth.
One hundredth multiplied by 9 is 9 hundredths.
Nine hundredths are close to 10 hundredths, or 1 tenth.
Place the decimal point so the product is close to 1 tenth; that is:
0.1242

Practice

1. Use Base Ten Blocks.
   Multiply.
   a) 0.6 × 4
   b) 0.12 × 3
   c) 0.21 × 2
   d) 0.34 × 5
   e) 0.215 × 3
   f) 0.408 × 2

2. Copy this place-value chart.
   Multiply. Record each product in the chart.

Ones	•	Tenths	Hundredths	Thousandths	Ten-Thousandths
	•				

   a) 0.005 × 7
   b) 0.42 × 9
   c) 0.029 × 5
   d) 0.0328 × 9
   e) 0.276 × 6
   f) 0.1036 × 8

3. Multiply. Describe your strategies.
   a) 0.9 × 3
      0.09 × 3
      0.009 × 3
   b) 0.25 × 6
      0.025 × 6
      0.0025 × 6
   c) 0.018 × 4
      0.0018 × 4
      0.000 18 × 4

   What patterns do you see?

4. Shona cut a ribbon into 8 equal lengths
to finish sewing her Fancy Shawl Regalia.
Each piece was 0.158 m long.

a) How long was the ribbon before Shona cut it?

b) How many cuts did she make?

Woman Dancing an Aboriginal
Fancy Dance

5.

Juice	Vitamin C per glass (g)
Pure Orange Juice	0.054
Pure Apple Juice	0.0009

a) Stefan drinks a glass of pure orange juice
each morning with his breakfast.
How much Vitamin C does Stefan get from orange juice each week?

b) Stefan went to Sasamat Outdoor Centre's overnight camp for one week.
He drank a glass of pure apple juice each morning with his breakfast.
How much Vitamin C did Stefan get from apple juice that week?

6. Without multiplying, choose the correct product
for each multiplication question.
Explain your choice each time. Multiply to check.

Question		Possible Products		
a)	0.063×9	5.67	0.567 ✓	0.0567
b)	0.349×7	2.443 ✓	0.2443	0.024 43
c)	0.0078×5	0.39	0.039 ✓	0.0039

7. Multiply as you would whole numbers. Estimate to place the decimal point.

a) 0.359×5 b) 0.0112×9 c) 0.083×4

d) 0.89×6 e) 0.0063×7 f) 0.097×8

8. A student said that since $11 \times 5 = 55$, then 0.0011×5 is 0.55.
Is the student's reasoning correct?
Give reasons for your answer.

Reflect

How can you use your knowledge of multiplication facts to help you
multiply a decimal less than 1 by a 1-digit whole number?

Dividing Decimals by a Whole Number

The Paralympic Games are an international sports competition for athletes with disabilities.
They are held in the same year and city as the Olympic Games. Vancouver was named host of the 2010 Paralympic Games.

For most paralympic sports, the athletes are grouped into classes according to their balance, coordination, range of motion, and skills required for the sport.

Chantal Petitclerc, French-Canadian Paralympian and 5-Time Gold Medalist, Beijing 2008

Explore

One event in the Paralympics is the men's 1-km time trial cycling.
Each competitor completes 4 laps of a 250-m track.
In 2004, the winner of the gold medal in the CP3/4 class was Darren Kenny of Great Britain. He completed the 4 laps in 74.472 s.

The Canadian competitor in this event was Jean Quevillon.
He finished in 10th place, with a time of 83.848 s.

About what time did each cyclist take to complete one lap?
Use any materials you think may help.
Estimate first. Then calculate the times.

Show and Share

Share your solutions with another pair of classmates.
Discuss the strategies you used to estimate and to solve the problems.
How can you verify your answers?
In a race, do you think the time to complete each lap would be the same? Explain.

LESSON FOCUS | Divide decimals to thousandths by a 1-digit number.

St-Pierre-Jolys is a small town in Manitoba. Every August, it is home to the *Frog Follies* frog-jumping contest. The longest jump on record is 5.18 m.

➤ Rochelle entered 3 frogs into the *Frog Follies*.
The total distance the frogs travelled was 4.92 m.
About how far did each frog travel?
Divide: 4.92 ÷ 3

Rochelle used Base Ten Blocks to model 4.92.

Rochelle recorded her work:

	o	t	h
	1		
3)	4	9	2
−	3		
	1		

Rochelle arranged the ones blocks into 3 equal rows.

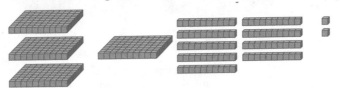

Each row has 1 one, with 1 one, 9 tenths, and 2 hundredths left over.
Rochelle traded 1 one for 10 tenths. Now there are 19 tenths.

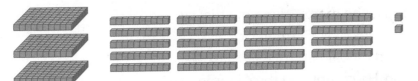

	o	t	h
	1	6	
3)	4	9	2
−	3	↓	
	1	9	
−	1	8	
		1	

Rochelle arranged the 19 tenths among 3 groups. Each group has 1 one and 6 tenths, with 1 tenth and 2 hundredths left over.

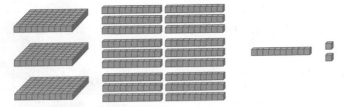

Rochelle traded 1 tenth for 10 hundredths.
Now there are 12 hundredths.
She shared the hundredths blocks equally among the 3 groups.
Each group has 4 hundredths.

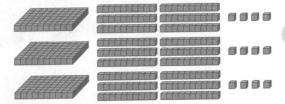

Each group has 1 one, 6 tenths, and 4 hundredths.

	o	t	h
	1	6	4
3)	4	9	2
−	3	↓	
	1	9	↓
−	1	8	↓
		1	2
−		1	2
			0

So, $4.92 \div 3 = 1.64$
Each frog travelled 1.64 m.

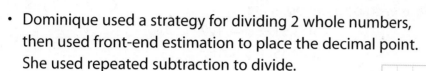

➤ Luc's frog travelled 16.64 m in 4 jumps.
About how far did the frog travel in 1 jump?

Divide: $16.64 \div 4$

• Dominique used a strategy for dividing 2 whole numbers,
then used front-end estimation to place the decimal point.
She used repeated subtraction to divide.

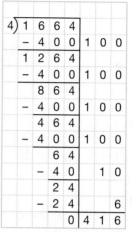

Write 16.64 as 16.
$16 \div 4 = 4$
Dominique placed the decimal
point in the answer so the whole
number part is a number close
to 4; that is: 4.16

So, $16.64 \div 4 = 4.16$

We can use multiplication
to check:
$4.16 \times 4 = 16.64$
So, the answer is correct.

• Marcel used a strategy for dividing 2 whole numbers,
then used estimation to place the decimal point.
To divide: $1664 \div 4$

Marcel broke 1664 into numbers that he could divide easily by 4.
$1664 = 1000 + 600 + 64$

$1000 \div 4 = 100 \text{ tens} \div 4$ $600 \div 4 = 60 \text{ tens} \div 4$ $64 \div 4 = 16$
        $= 25 \text{ tens}$ $= 15 \text{ tens}$
        $= 250$ $= 150$
So, $1664 \div 4 = 250 + 150 + 16$
            $= 416$

Marcel estimated to place the decimal point.
Since 16.64 is about 16, and $16 \div 4 = 4$, he placed the decimal point
between the 4 and the 1.
So, $16.64 \div 4 = 4.16$

Luc's frog travelled about 4.16 m in 1 jump.

1. Use Base Ten Blocks to divide.
   a) 6.25 ÷ 5   b) 4.24 ÷ 4   c) 1.68 ÷ 3   d) 3.9 ÷ 6

2. The decimal point is missing in each quotient.
   Use estimation to place each decimal point.
   a) 8.2 ÷ 2 = 41   b) 3.81 ÷ 3 = 127
   c) 1.992 ÷ 8 = 249   d) 9.45 ÷ 5 = 189
   e) 11.916 ÷ 9 = 1324   f) 62.8 ÷ 8 = 785

3. Estimate each quotient. Which strategies did you use?
   a) 26.34 ÷ 8   b) 15.27 ÷ 3   c) 2.304 ÷ 4
   d) 5.8 ÷ 8   e) 8.088 ÷ 6   f) 2.316 ÷ 2

4. Divide. Multiply to check your answers.
   a) 27.025 ÷ 5   b) 3.42 ÷ 6   c) 7.735 ÷ 7
   d) 16.072 ÷ 8   e) 30.9 ÷ 5   f) 3.438 ÷ 6

5. Estimate to choose the correct quotient for each division question.

	Question	Possible Quotients		
a)	8.124 ÷ 6	1.354	13.54	135.4
b)	37.92 ÷ 3	0.1264	1.264	12.64
c)	7.624 ÷ 8	0.953	9.53	95.3

6. Aqpik Peter is a young Inuit speed skater from Nunavut. He is one of 3 First Nations athletes being showcased for the 2010 Vancouver Olympics. At practice, Aqpik skated 2.75 km in 5 min. About how far did Aqpik skate in 1 min?

7. Eric cycled 2.25 km in 5 min.
   Josie cycled 2.72 km in 8 min.
   Who travelled farther in 1 min?
   Show your work.

8. Sharma paid $58.50 to board her cat at a kennel in Yellowknife for 5 days.
   Her friend Miles paid $12.50 each day to board his cat at a different kennel for 5 days.
   Who paid the lesser amount?
   Explain how you know.

9. The decimal point in some of these quotients is in the wrong place. Identify the mistakes, then write each quotient with the decimal point in the correct place.
   a) $44.8 \div 8 = 0.56$
   b) $14.805 \div 5 = 2.961$
   c) $3.15 \div 6 = 5.25$
   d) $8.127 \div 1 = 0.8127$

10. A student divided 1.374 by 4 and got 3.435.
    a) Without dividing, how do you know the answer is incorrect?
    b) What do you think the student did wrong?
    c) What is the correct answer? How can you check?

11. Write a story problem that can be solved by dividing 14.28 by 3.
    Trade problems with a classmate and solve your classmate's problem.

12. A square park has a perimeter of 14.984 km.
    How long is each side of the square?

13. In good weather, Hannah rides her bike to school and back each day.
    One week, Hannah rode her bike on 4 days.
    That week, Hannah rode 10.832 km in total.
    The following week, she rode her bike all 5 days.
    How far did Hannah ride the second week?

Reflect

Why is estimating important when dividing with decimals?
Use words, pictures, or numbers to explain.

Dividing Decimals

You and 2 friends have found $10.
You want to share the money.
How much will each person get?

Explore

A group of hikers on a 4-day trip travelled
96.575 km on the Trans Canada Trail.
About how far did the group travel each day?

To pay for the trip, each group of 3 hikers
had to raise at least $125.50.
How much did each hiker have to raise?

Use any materials you want.
Solve the problems. Show your work.

Show *and* Share

Share your work with another pair of classmates.
What strategies did you use?
Are your answers exact? How do you know?
What strategies can you use to check your answers?

Connect

➤ Four hikers want to share a 9.45-L jug of water equally.
How much water will each hiker get?

Divide: 9.45 ÷ 4

Use long division.
Divide as with whole numbers.

```
        2  3  6  2  5
    4 ) 9  4  5  0  0
      - 8
        1  4
      - 1  2
           2  5
         - 2  4
              1  0
            -    8
                 2  0
               - 2  0
                    0
```

Since there is a remainder, write a 0 in the dividend so we can continue to divide.

There is still a remainder. Write another 0 in the dividend.

Estimate to place the decimal point.
The closest whole-number benchmark to 9.45 is 9.

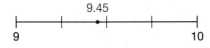

9 ÷ 4 is a little more than 2.
So, place the decimal point in the quotient so the whole number part is a number close to 2; that is: 2.3625

So, 9.45 ÷ 4 = 2.3625   This quotient is *exact*.

When a quotient is a measurement, we give the answer
in a form that makes sense.
Since the volume of water was given to a hundredth of a litre,
we write the quotient to the closest hundredth.
2.3625 is closer to 2.36 than to 2.37,
so write the quotient as 2.36.

Each hiker got about 2.36 L of water.

Check the answer by multiplying the quotient
by the divisor.
$2.36 \times 4 = 9.44$
9.44 is close to the dividend, 9.45.
So, the answer is reasonable.

➤ One morning, the hikers travelled 10.4 km in 3 h.
About how far did the hikers travel in 1 h?

Divide: $10.4 \div 3$
Divide as whole numbers. Use short division.
Write zeros in the dividend.

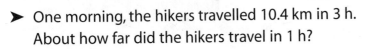

Sometimes you may never
stop dividing, no matter how
many zeros you write in the
dividend.

Estimate to place the decimal point.
The closest whole-number benchmark to 10.4 is 10.
$10 \div 3$ is a little more than 3.
So, place the decimal point between the 3 and the 4;
that is: 3.4666 …

So, $10.4 \div 3 = 3.4666 …$ This quotient is
                                  approximate.

The dots indicate that
the decimal places
go on forever.

Since the distance was given to a tenth of a kilometre,
we write the quotient to the closest tenth.
3.4666 … is closer to 3.5 than to 3.4,
so, write the quotient as 3.5.

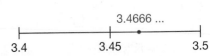

The hikers travelled about 3.5 km in 1 h.

Check the answer by multiplying the quotient by the divisor.
$3.5 \times 3 = 10.5$
10.5 is close to the dividend, 10.4.
So, the answer is reasonable.

1. Estimate to choose the correct quotient for each division question.

	Question	Possible Quotients		
a)	4.4 ÷ 5	0.88	8.8	88
b)	10.32 ÷ 6	0.172	1.72	17.2
c)	87.2 ÷ 4	0.218	2.18	21.8

2. Divide. Estimate to place the decimal point.
   a) 8.235 ÷ 6   b) 12.6 ÷ 5   c) 39.77 ÷ 2
   d) 88.2 ÷ 5   e) 2.367 ÷ 4   f) 4.573 ÷ 5

3. Divide. Write each quotient to the same number of decimal places as there are in the dividend.
   a) 3.05 ÷ 2   b) $49.67 ÷ 6   c) 6.1 ÷ 9
   d) 1.189 ÷ 3   e) 24.73 ÷ 9   f) $26.53 ÷ 6

4. In a snail-racing contest, Noba's snail crawled 1.677 m in 5 min. About how far did the snail travel each minute?

5. Check each division below. For each incorrect quotient, explain the error, then write the correct quotient.
   a) 1.44 ÷ 6 = 0.24   b) $15.97 ÷ 5 = $3.194
   c) 4.422 ÷ 3 = 14.74   d) 17.27 L ÷ 3 = 5.756 L

6. Richard divided a 1.954-L bottle of spicy tomato juice equally among 5 glasses. How much juice is in each glass?

7. Marina packed eight 2.54-L bottles of fruit juice for a 3-day camping trip to Beauvais Lake Provincial Park in Alberta. About how many litres of fruit juice does that allow for each day?

8. Three friends rent a movie for $6.49 and buy a package of popcorn for $1.82. They share the cost equally. How much should each person pay? Show your work.

Reflect

How do you know if a quotient is exact or approximate? Include examples in your explanation.

Dividing a Decimal Less than 1 by a Whole Number

How can you find 0.06 ÷ 3?
What happens if you use front-end estimation to check your answer?

Explore

You will need a calculator and a place-value chart.

➤ Use a calculator to find each quotient.

a)	b)	c)
1 ÷ 4	25 ÷ 5	168 ÷ 8
0.1 ÷ 4	2.5 ÷ 5	16.8 ÷ 8
0.01 ÷ 4	0.25 ÷ 5	1.68 ÷ 8
0.001 ÷ 4	0.025 ÷ 5	0.168 ÷ 8
	0.0025 ÷ 5	0.0168 ÷ 8
		0.001 68 ÷ 8

Record the quotients in a place-value chart.

Division	Tens	Ones	•Tenths	Hundredths	Thousandths	Ten- Thousandths	Hundred- Thousandths
1 ÷ 4			•				
0.1 ÷ 4			•				

➤ What patterns do you see in the expressions and their quotients?
Use these patterns to find the quotients below.

d) 2 ÷ 8	0.2 ÷ 8	0.02 ÷ 8	0.002 ÷ 8	0.0002 ÷ 8
e) 35 ÷ 7	3.5 ÷ 7	0.35 ÷ 7	0.035 ÷ 7	0.0035 ÷ 7
f) 198 ÷ 9	19.8 ÷ 9	1.98 ÷ 9	0.198 ÷ 9	0.0198 ÷ 9

Show *and* Share

Share the patterns you found with another pair of students.
What patterns do you see in the dividends? In the quotients?
How can you use the quotient of 12 ÷ 4 to help you find 0.12 ÷ 4?
To find 0.012 ÷ 4?

Connect

Here are two strategies to divide a decimal less than 1 by a whole number.

➤ Use Base Ten Blocks.

- To divide 0.8 by 2:
  0.8 is eight tenths.
  Eight tenths divided by 2 is 4 tenths.
  So, 0.8 ÷ 2 = 0.4

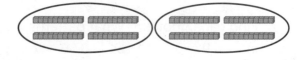

- To divide 0.15 by 3:
  0.15 is fifteen hundredths.
  Fifteen hundredths divided by 3 is 5 hundredths.
  So, 0.15 ÷ 3 = 0.05

➤ Use place value.
To divide 0.074 by 8:

Estimate first. 0.074 is close to 0.072.
0.072 is 72 thousandths.
Seventy-two thousandths divided by 8 is 9 thousandths.
So, 0.074 ÷ 8 is about 0.009.

> We know 72 ÷ 8 = 9.

	o	t	h	th	Tth	Hth
	0	0	0	9	2	5
8)	0	0	7	4	0	0
			−	7	2	↓
				2	0	
			−	1	6	↓
					4	0
				−	4	0
						0

> Write zeros in the dividend until there is no remainder.

So, 0.074 ÷ 8 = 0.009 25
Since 0.009 25 is close to the estimate, 0.009, the answer is reasonable.

1. Divide.
   a) 0.28 ÷ 4   **b)** 0.042 ÷ 7   **c)** 0.015 ÷ 3
   d) 0.024 ÷ 6   **e)** 0.16 ÷ 8   **f)** 0.0036 ÷ 9

2. Find each quotient. What patterns do you see?
   a)   0.9 ÷ 3   **b)**   0.56 ÷ 7   **c)**   0.108 ÷ 9
           0.09 ÷ 3   0.056 ÷ 7   0.0108 ÷ 9
           0.009 ÷ 3   0.0056 ÷ 7   0.001 08 ÷ 9

3. Quincy has 0.926 m of string.
   Suppose he cuts the string into 4 equal lengths.
   What is the length of each piece of string?

4. **a)** A typical hamster eats 0.084 kg of food a week.
       About how much food does a hamster
       eat in one day?
   b) Jiri's hamster was put on a special diet.
       Over 5 days, his hamster ate about 0.054 kg of food.
       About how much food did Jiri's hamster eat in one day?

5. Without dividing, choose the correct quotient for each division question.
   Explain your choice each time. Divide to check.

	Question	Possible Quotients		
a)	0.072 ÷ 9	0.8	0.08	0.008
b)	0.124 ÷ 8	0.155	0.0155	0.001 55
c)	0.0045 ÷ 2	0.225	0.0225	0.002 25

6. A student said that since 51 ÷ 3 = 17, then 0.051 ÷ 3 is 0.17.
   Is the student's reasoning correct? Give reasons for your answer.

7. Divide. Which strategies did you use to estimate?
   a) 0.66 ÷ 8   **b)** 0.058 ÷ 4   **c)** 0.375 ÷ 5
   d) 0.05 ÷ 8   **e)** 0.0061 ÷ 2   **f)** 0.039 ÷ 6

Reflect

How can you use division facts to help you divide a decimal less
than 1 by a whole number?

Make the Lesser Product

You will need a spinner with 10 congruent sectors, labelled 0 to 9,
an open paper clip as a pointer, and a sharp pencil to keep it in place.

Players create a product of a decimal and a whole number.
The object of the game is to make the lesser product.

Decide who will be Player A and Player B.

➤ Each player copies the grid and triangle below.

➤ Player A spins the pointer on the spinner.
   In a box on his grid, Player A writes the number the pointer lands on.
   If Player A decides that he does not want to use that number,
   he writes it in the triangle.
   Only one number can be written in the triangle.
➤ Player B has a turn.
➤ Players continue to take turns until all the boxes are full.
   Once a number is placed, it cannot be changed.
➤ Players find the product of their numbers.
   The player with the lesser product wins.
➤ Play the game again. This time, the greater product wins.

Strategies Toolkit

Explore

Suppose you are asked to solve this problem: Discuss what this question asks you to do. Solve the problem.

Show *and* Share

Share your work with another pair of classmates. Describe what you did to make sure you understood the problem. Compare your solutions.

> Use each of the digits 3, 4, 5, and 6 once.
> Replace each □ with a digit to make the greatest possible product.
>
> □ . □ □
> ×   □

Connect

Here are some strategies you can use to understand what the problem is about:

- Copy the problem.
- Underline the important words.
- Look at each part, one at a time. Think about what each part means.
- Highlight what you are asked to find.
- Decide what form your answer should take. Will your answer include:
  - a number?
  - a table?
  - a diagram?
  - a written explanation?
  - a graph?
- Think about how many parts your answer needs.

Strategies for Success

- **Check and reflect.**
- **Focus on the problem.**
- **Represent your thinking.**
- **Explain your thinking.**

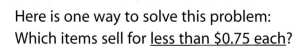

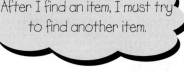

Here is one way to solve this problem:
Which items sell for <u>less than $0.75 each</u>?

Shower scrunchies   5 for $4.00
Lip gloss   6 for $3.90
Plush pens   9 for $6.57
Yoyos   3 for $2.43
Candy necklaces   4 for $2.76

> After I find an item, I must try to find another item.

Find as many items as you can.
<u>Write</u> the price of <u>each item you find</u> in <u>dollars</u>.

There are 3 items. They are:
lip gloss, $0.65; plush pen, $0.73; candy necklace, $0.69

Practice

The table shows the results of the men's
4 × 100 m relay final at the Melbourne 2006
Commonwealth Games.
Use the data in the table to answer the questions.
Describe what you did to understand each problem.

Country	Time (s)
Antigua and Barbuda	40.76
Canada	39.21
Jamaica	38.36
Mauritius	39.97
South Africa	38.98

1. a) Which country won the men's relay race?
        How do you know?
    b) Where did Canada place? How did you find out?

2. a) Each of the 4 relay team members runs a distance
        of 100 m. About how long did each country's
        team members take to run 100 m?
        Show your solution.
    b) Do you think each team member took the same
        amount of time? Explain.

Reflect

Describe what you can do to understand a problem.
Use examples to explain.

Show What You Know

1

1. Write each number in standard form.
    a) 2 and 12 ten-thousandths
    b) 7 millionths
    c) 16 and 46 hundred-thousandths
    d) 1 and 51 millionths

2. How are the values of the red digits in each number related?
    a) 0.626   b) 5.489 48   c) 0.000 355   d) 9.39

3. The Bigleaf Maple tree is native to the
    Queen Charlotte Islands. It produces winged seeds
    that can be carried long distances by the wind.
    A seed has a mass of about 0.126 582 g.
    Write this number as many ways as you can.

2

4. Estimate. Which strategies did you use?
    Tell if your estimate is an overestimate or an underestimate.
    a) 6.23×4 b) 21.872×3 c) 9.49×7
    d) $18.39 \div 3$ e) $125.431 \div 5$ f) $19.8 \div 4$

3

5. The decimal point is missing in each product.
    Use front-end estimation to place each decimal point.
    a) $6.9 \times 7 = 483$ b) $7.53 \times 3 = 2259$
    c) $11.288 \times 4 = 45152$ d) $2.307 \times 5 = 11535$
    e) $3.005 \times 4 = 1202$ f) $4.916 \times 5 = 2458$

6. The Giant Fan Palm produces the world's largest seed.
    A seed has a mass of about 9.075 kg.
    What is the combined mass of 6 of these seeds?

4

7. Multiply. Estimate to place the decimal point.
    a) 0.321×6 b) 0.0249×5 c) 0.0043×7

8. The recipe Sebastian wants to make requires
    1.5 L of evaporated milk.
    He has four 0.385-L cans.
    Does he have enough milk? Show your work.

5

9. Estimate each quotient. Which strategies did you use?
   a) 36.57 ÷ 6
   b) 22.41 ÷ 4
   c) 4.189 ÷ 2
   d) 42.3 ÷ 9
   e) 8.27 ÷ 4
   f) 7.1348 ÷ 8

10. Estimate to choose the correct quotient for each division question.

Question		Possible Quotients		
a)	9.348 ÷ 3	3.116	31.16	311.6
b)	52.925 ÷ 5	0.105 85	1.0585	10.585
c)	1.888 ÷ 8	0.236	2.36	23.6

11. James Steacy of Saskatoon won the silver medal in the men's discus throw at the 2006 Commonwealth Games in Melbourne, Australia. In the finals, James threw the discus 6 times for a total distance of 431.94 m. About how far did he throw each discus?

6

12. Divide.
    a) 24.15 ÷ 6
    b) $31.87 ÷ 8
    c) 9.3 ÷ 6
    d) 14.523 L ÷ 4
    e) 3.5 m ÷ 9
    f) $11.68 ÷ 9

13. The Coulter Pine produces the world's most massive pine cones. The combined mass of 8 of these cones is 25.259 kg. Find the mass of one Coulter Pine cone to the nearest hundredth of a kilogram.

UNIT

7

14. Divide. Which strategies did you use to estimate?
    a) 0.58 ÷ 8
    b) 0.066 ÷ 4
    c) 0.142 ÷ 8
    d) 0.0075 ÷ 6
    e) 0.081 ÷ 6
    f) 0.09 ÷ 5

15. Darcy takes one chewable multivitamin each morning. Each week, Darcy gets 0.0119 g of riboflavin from the vitamins. How much riboflavin is in one multivitamin? Show your work.

3 Learning Goals

☑ use place value to represent numbers less than one thousandth
☑ multiply decimals by a 1-digit number
☑ divide decimals by a 1-digit number

Unit Problem

Harnessing the Wind

Every day, thousands of people *ride the wind* in Calgary.
Calgary's C-Train is North America's first wind-powered
public transit system.
It runs on electricity generated by 12 wind turbines.

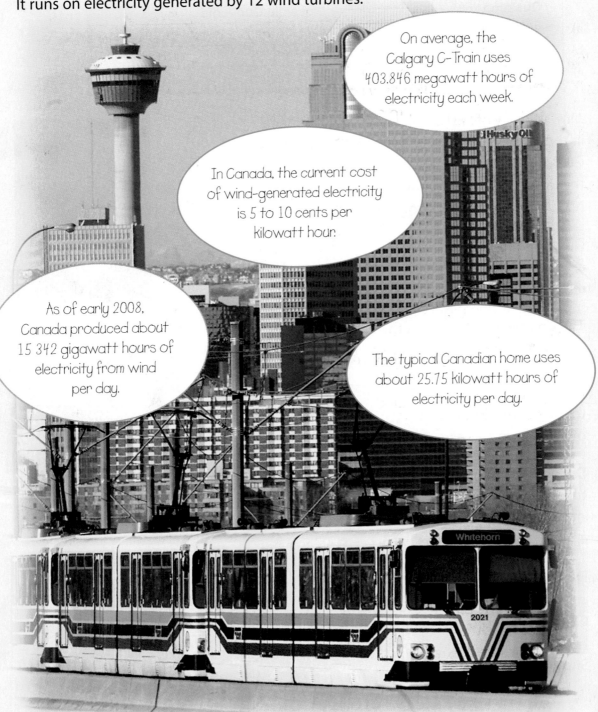

On average, the Calgary C-Train uses 403.846 megawatt hours of electricity each week.

In Canada, the current cost of wind-generated electricity is 5 to 10 cents per kilowatt hour.

As of early 2008, Canada produced about 15 342 gigawatt hours of electricity from wind per day.

The typical Canadian home uses about 25.75 kilowatt hours of electricity per day.

1. How many megawatt hours of electricity does the Calgary C-Train use in one day?

2. It takes about 2.34 kilowatt hours of electricity to do one load of laundry.
   A large family does one load of laundry each day.
   a) About how many kilowatt hours of electricity does the family use on laundry in one week?
   b) Suppose this electricity was wind generated. How much would it cost to generate the electricity for the weekly laundry? Explain your answer.

3. A wind farm in Saskatchewan has 9 identical turbines. Together they generate 18.9 gigawatt hours of electricity in 1 year. How much electricity does 1 turbine generate?

4. Use some of the data on pages 87 and 120. Write a problem about wind energy. Solve your problem. Show your work.

Reflect on Your Learning

What did you find easy about working with decimals?
What was difficult for you?
Give examples to illustrate your answers.

Unit

1

1. The pattern rule that relates the input to the output is:
   Add 2 to the input. Then divide by 5.
   Find the missing numbers in the table at the right.
   How can you check your answers?

Input	Output
3	1
?	3
18	?
43	?
?	14

2. The table, below right, shows the input and output for
   a machine with two operations.
   a) Identify the numbers and operations in the machine.
   b) Write a pattern rule that relates the input to the output.
   c) Graph the data in the table.
      Describe the relationship shown on the graph.
   d) Write an expression to represent the pattern.
   e) Find the output when the input is 14.
      Which strategy did you use?

Input	Output
5	11
6	14
7	17
8	20

3. a) Make an Input/Output table for this graph.
   b) How does the graph represent the pattern?

```
     24                    •
     20                •
Output 16           •
     12        •
      8     •
      4
      0  1 2 3 4 5
          Input
```

4. Which of the scales are balanced? How do you know?
   a) Left pan: 4 × 12   Right pan: 60 − 12
   b) Left pan: 27 + 8   Right pan: 8 × 4
   c) Left pan: 37 − 23   Right pan: 42 ÷ 3

2

5. In 2007, about 304 000 people visited the Telus
   World of Science in Calgary. About 54 500 of these
   visitors were students. In 2006, the total number of
   visitors was 263 000.
   a) By how much did the attendance increase
      from 2006 to 2007?
   b) How many of the visitors in 2007 were not students?
   c) What was the total attendance over the 2 years?

Unit

6. Find all the common multiples of 3 and 4 between 10 and 100.

7. Find all the factors of each number. Record the factors as a "rainbow."
Which factors are prime numbers?
   a) 49   **b)** 32   **c)** 66   **d)** 96

8. Evaluate each expression. Explain why the answers are different.
   a) $15 + 6 \div 3$ **b)** $(15 + 6) \div 3$

9. Use a number line. Order these integers from least to greatest.
$+5, -6, -8, 2, 0, -5, -1$

3

10. Write the number in each fact in as many different forms as you can.
   a) The Asian watermeal is the world's smallest flowering plant.
      It has a mass of about 0.000 15 g.
   b) The typical length of a human liver cell is about 0.000 05 m.

11. Jenny paid $19.25 for 7 admission tickets to the Assiniboine Park Zoo
in Manitoba. Estimate the cost of 1 admission ticket.
How did you find out?

12. Multiply.
   a) 3.7×9 **b)** 4.03×5
   c) 6.841×6 **d)** 0.004×9
   e) 0.0013×3 **f)** 0.093×7

13. In the 2006 Turin Olympics, Cindy Klassen
of Winnipeg, Manitoba won a silver medal
in the women's 1000-m speed skating event.
She skated 9 laps in 76.09 s. About how long
did it take Cindy to skate 1 lap?

14. Divide.
   a) $3.192 \div 7$ **b)** $11.59 \div 5$
   c) $36.752 \div 8$ **d)** $0.049 \div 7$
   e) $0.0096 \div 8$ **f)** $0.0567 \div 9$

U N I T

4

Angles and

Designing a Quilt Block

Learning Goals

- name, describe, and classify angles
- estimate and determine angle measures
- draw and label angles
- provide examples of angles in the environment
- investigate the sum of angles in triangles and quadrilaterals

Polygons

The Heritage Park Historical Village in Calgary, Alberta, hosts *A Festival of Quilts* each May. It is Western Canada's largest outdoor quilt show.

Key Words

angle

arm

right angle

straight angle

acute angle

obtuse angle

reflex angle

protractor

standard protractor

degree

interior angle

diagonal

Look at these quilts.

• What shapes do you see?

• Which shapes have sides that are perpendicular? How do you know?

Naming Angles

An **angle** is formed when 2 lines meet.

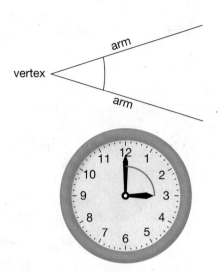

You can think of an angle as a turn about a vertex.
The angle shows how far one **arm** is turned to get
to the other arm.

The hour hand and the minute hand on a clock
form an angle at the centre of the clock.
What angle is formed by the hands on this clock?

Explore

You will need a drinking straw and grid paper.

To make an angle:
• Place the straw horizontally on the grid paper.
• Trace the bottom edge of the straw to make one arm.
• Use one end of the straw
  as the point of rotation.
  Rotate the straw.
• Trace the bottom edge of
  the rotated straw to make the other arm.

➤ Rotate the straw. Draw each angle:
  • a right angle
  • an angle less than a right angle
  • an angle greater than a right angle

➤ Trade drawings with another pair of students.
  Find a way to check their angles.

Show and Share

Compare the strategies you used to check the angles.
Which strategy worked best?
Did the length of the lines you drew affect the size of the angle?

Right angles and straight angles are all around us.

We name angles for the way they relate to a right angle or a straight angle.

An **acute angle** is less than a right angle.

An **obtuse angle** is greater than a right angle, but less than a straight angle.

A **reflex angle** is greater than a straight angle.

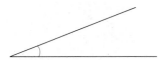

Practice

Use a piece of paper with a square corner when it helps.

1. Which angle is an acute angle? A right angle? An obtuse angle? A straight angle? A reflex angle?

a)

b)

c)

MANITOBA

d)

e)

2. Name each angle as a right angle, an acute angle, an obtuse angle, a straight angle, or a reflex angle. How did you find out?

a)
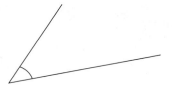

b)
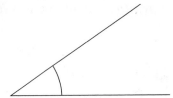

c)

d)
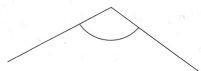

e)

f)

g)
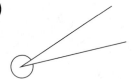

h)

i)

j)

3. Your teacher will give you a large copy of these flags.
   List the flags with:
   a) a right angle   **b)** an acute angle
   c) an obtuse angle   **d)** a reflex angle
   On each flag, label an example of each type of angle you find.

British Columbia

Saskatchewan

Nunavut

Canada

4. Draw a line segment on grid paper.
   Visualize rotating the line segment about one of its end points.
   Which type of angle is formed by each rotation?
   a) a $\frac{1}{2}$ turn
   b) a $\frac{1}{4}$ turn clockwise
   c) a $\frac{3}{4}$ turn counterclockwise
   Use tracing paper to check.

5. a) For each time below, which type of angle is formed
      by the hour hand and minute hand on a clock?
      How did you find out?

      i) 2:15
      ii) 3:35
      iii) 9:00
      iv) 12:30
      v) 1:45

   b) Would the size of each angle
      change if the minute hand was shorter?
      Justify your answer.

Steam Clock, Gastown, Vancouver

6. Find 5 angles in your classroom.
   Try to find one example of a right angle, an acute angle,
   an obtuse angle, a straight angle, and a reflex angle.
   Sketch each angle.
   Write where you found each angle, then label the
   angle with its name.
   How did you decide how to name each angle?
   Which angle was easiest to find?
   Why do you think so?

7. Use square dot paper.
   How many different angles can you draw on a 3-by-3 grid?
   Classify the angles.
   Show your work.

Reflect

When you see an angle, how can you tell which type of angle it is?
How many ways can you find out?
Use words and pictures to explain.

Exploring Angles

These angles are both acute.
Describe the angles.

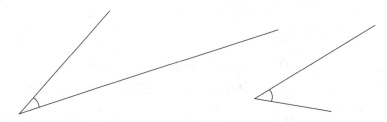

Explore

You will need Pattern Blocks, an index card, a ruler, and scissors.

➤ Use a ruler to draw an acute angle on the card.
   Cut out the angle.

➤ Use the cutout as a unit of angle measure.
   Choose the green triangle.
   Estimate how many times your angle unit will
   fit in each of its angles.
   Measure each angle of the green triangle with your
   angle unit.
   Record your measure in a table.
   Repeat with each of the other Pattern Blocks.

Pattern Block	Angle Measure (units)

Show *and* Share

Compare your angle measures with those of another pair of students.
Did you get the same measures for the same block? Explain.
What could you do so everyone does get the same measures for the same block?

Connect

We can use a square piece of tracing paper or wax paper to make an angle measurer.
The angle measurer is called a **protractor**.

➤ Carefully fold the paper in half and make a crease along the fold.
Fold the paper in half again so the folded edges meet. Make a crease.
Fold in this way one more time. Cut or tear as shown.

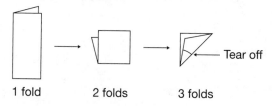

1 fold   2 folds   3 folds

Open up the paper.
It should look like this:

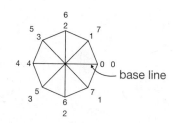

base line

> The protractor is divided into 8 equal slices. Each slice is 1 unit of angle measure. Label the slices from 0 to 7 clockwise and counterclockwise.

➤ To measure this angle, count how many units fit the angle:
- Place the protractor on the angle.
- Line up one arm of the angle with the base line of the protractor.
  The vertex of the angle is at the centre of the base line.
- Use the scale, starting at 0, to count the units that fit between the arms.

vertex

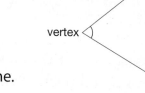

About 1.5 units

The angle is between 1 unit and 2 units.
The angle is about 1.5 units.

Practice

You will need an 8-unit protractor.

1. Use your protractor to measure the angles in:
   a) the yellow hexagon
   b) the blue rhombus
   c) the red trapezoid
   d) the orange square
   e) the green triangle
   f) the tan parallelogram
   Record your measures.

2. Use your protractor to measure each angle below.
   Record the measures.

   a)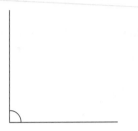

   b)

   c)

   d)

   e)

   f)

3. Use your protractor to measure the angles in each polygon below.
   Record the measures.

   a)

   b)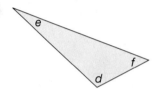

   c)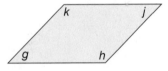

   d)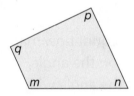

4. Use a ruler. Draw an angle.
   Use the protractor to measure the angle.
   Explain how you did it. Show your work.

5. How many units will fit in each angle below?
   a) a right angle
   b) a straight angle
   c) a reflex angle
   d) an angle one-half the size of a right angle
   For which angle were you able to find more than one answer? Explain.

Reflect

You have used two different angle measurers in this lesson.
What are the advantages and disadvantages of each angle measurer?
Which angle measurer do you prefer? Justify your choice.

Measuring Angles

In Lesson 2, you used an 8-unit protractor to measure angles.

To measure angles more accurately, we use a **standard protractor**.

The standard protractor divides a straight angle into 180 congruent slices.

Each slice is 1 **degree**. We write 1°.

The protractor shows angle measures from 0° to 180°.

From now on, we will refer to a standard protractor as a protractor.

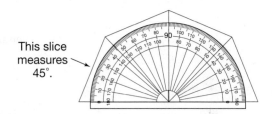

This slice measures 45°.

What is the measure of each angle?

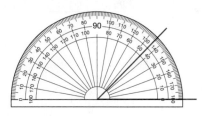

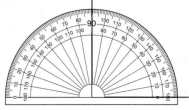

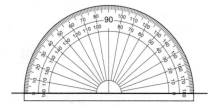

Explore

You will need a ruler.

➤ Use a ruler to draw an angle.
➤ Have your partner:
  • use the 45°, 90°, and 180° angles above as reference angles to estimate the size of the angle
  • record the estimate
➤ Trade roles. Continue until you have 6 different angles.
  Try to make angles that are acute, right, and obtuse.
➤ Order the estimates from least to greatest.

Show and Share

Share your work with another pair of students.
How did you estimate the size of each angle?
How did the estimate of one angle help you estimate the measure
of another angle?

Connect

● ●

A protractor has 2 scales so that we can measure
angles opening different ways.

➤ To measure this angle using a protractor:

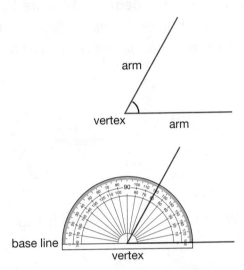

Step 1

Place the protractor on top
of the angle.
The vertex of the angle is at the
centre of the protractor.
One arm of the angle lines up with
the base line of the protractor.

Step 2

Find where the other arm of the
angle meets the protractor.
Since the arm along the base line
passes through 0° on the inner scale,
use the inner scale.
Follow the inner scale around.
The angle measures 60°.

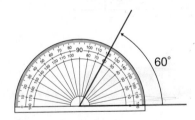

➤ This diagram shows when you would use
the outer scale to measure an angle.

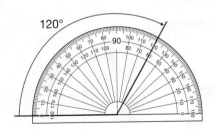

Since the arm along the
base line of this angle passes
through 0° on the outer scale,
use the outer scale. The angle
measures 120°.

➤ We can use a protractor to measure this reflex angle. A reflex angle is the outside angle of an acute, right, or obtuse angle.

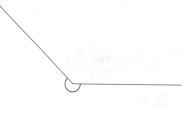

Step 1

Use the protractor to measure the inside angle.
The inside angle measures 135°.

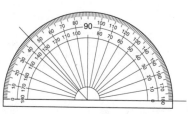

Step 2

A complete turn is 360°.

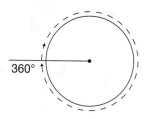

To find the measure of the reflex angle, we subtract:
360° − 135° = 225°

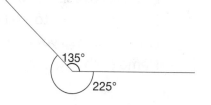

➤ We name angles according to their measures in degrees.

The measure of an **acute angle** is less than 90°.

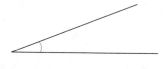

The measure of a **right angle** is 90°.

The measure of an **obtuse angle** is between 90° and 180°.

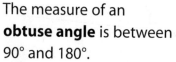

The measure of a **straight angle** is 180°.

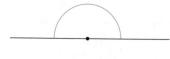

The measure of a **reflex angle** is between 180° and 360°.

The measure of one-half a right angle is 45°.

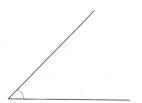

To estimate the measure of an angle, we can use 45°, 90°, and 180° as reference angles.

Practice

1. What is the measure of each angle? Explain how you know.

a)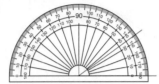
b)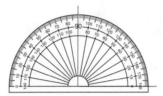
c)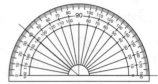

2. For each angle:
   - Choose an appropriate reference angle: 45°, 90°, 180°
     Estimate the size of the angle.
   - Use a protractor to find the angle measure.
     How close was your estimate to the actual measure? Explain.
   - Name each angle as acute, right, obtuse, or straight.

a)

b)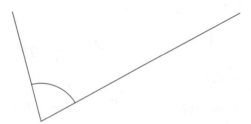

c)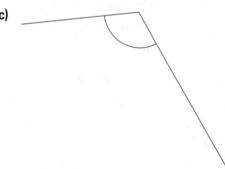

d)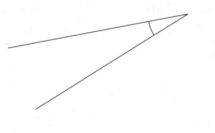

e)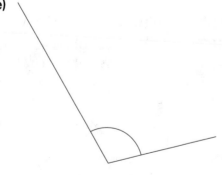

f)

3. Which of these angles do you think measures 45°?
   Check your estimates with a protractor. What did you find out?

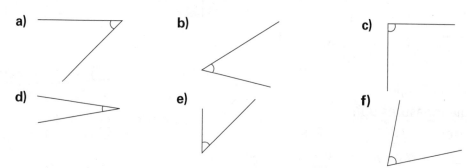

a)   b)   c)

d)   e)   f)

4. Measure each angle.
   Do the angles in each pair have the same measure?

   a)

   b)

   Do the lengths of the arms affect the measure of the angle? Explain.
   Does the position of the angle affect the measure? Explain.

5. How can you tell whether you used the correct scale on the
   protractor to measure an angle?
   Include an example in your explanation.

6. Use a protractor to find the measure of each reflex angle.
   How can you check that your measure is correct?

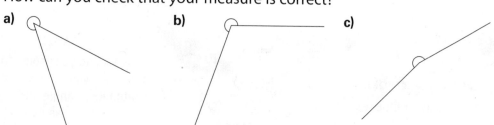

   a)   b)   c)

7. Use a protractor to solve each riddle.

a) I have 4 equal angles.
   Each angle measures 90°.
   Which letter am I?

b) I do not have any angles that
   measure 90°.
   I have 3 angles that measure 60°.
   I have 2 angles that measure 120°.
   Which letter am I?

c) I have 2 right angles.
   I have 1 acute angle.
   I have 1 obtuse angle.
   Which letter am I?

d) Make up your own letter riddle.
   Trade riddles with a classmate.
   Solve your classmate's riddle.

8. Name 4 objects in your classroom that have:
   a) an angle greater than 100°
   b) an angle less than 60°
   Use a protractor to check your answers.

9. A student measured this angle and said it measured 60°.
   Do you agree? Explain.

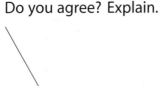

Reflect

How can you use a piece of paper
to help estimate the measure
of an angle?

Drawing Angles

Without using a protractor, how could you draw a 90° angle?
A 45° angle? A 135° angle?

You will need a ruler and a protractor.

Angle Aim!

The object of the game is to draw angles as close as possible to the given measures.
Decide who will be Player A and Player B.

➤ Player A writes an angle measure.
  Without using a protractor, Player B draws an angle
  as close as possible to Player A's measure.
  Players switch roles and repeat the activity.
➤ Players measure each other's angle.
  The player whose angle is closer to the stated measure gets 1 point.
➤ Players play 4 more rounds. The player with more points after 5 rounds wins.

Show and Share

Share the strategies you used to draw your angles with your partner.
How did you use estimation to help you draw the angles?
How could you draw the angles more accurately?

Connect

To draw an angle with a given measure, we use a ruler and a protractor.

➤ To draw an angle that measures 145°:

- Use a ruler. Draw a horizontal line.
  Use the line as one arm of the angle.

- Place the protractor on the arm.
  One end of the arm is at the centre
  of the protractor.
  The arm lines up with the base line
  of the protractor.
  Start at 0° on the arm along the base line.
  Count around the protractor until you reach 145°.
  Make a mark at 145°.

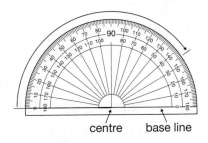

centre   base line

> You can measure from
> 0° to 180° clockwise or
> counterclockwise. Remember
> to start at 0° when you draw
> an angle.

- Remove the protractor.
  Draw a line to join the end of the
  arm at the centre of the protractor
  with the mark at 145°.
  Label the angle with its measure.

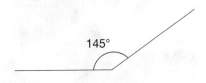

145°

➤ To draw an angle that measures 280°:

A 280° angle is a reflex angle.

So, draw the angle that makes up
a complete turn:
360° − 280° = 80°
Then, 280° is the outside angle.

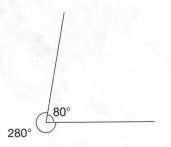

80°

280°

280° + 80° = 360°

140

Practice

1. Use a ruler and a protractor.
   Draw an acute angle with each measure.
   a) 20° **b)** 15° **c)** 75° **d)** 50°

2. Use a ruler and a protractor.
   Draw an obtuse angle with each measure.
   a) 120° **b)** 155° **c)** 95° **d)** 170°

3. Use a ruler and a protractor.
   Draw a horizontal line segment AB.
   Each angle you draw should have its vertex at A.
   a) Using AB as one arm, draw a 70° angle.
   b) Use the line you drew in part a as one arm
      of another angle. Draw a 55° angle.
   c) Use the line you drew in part b as one arm
      of another angle.
      Draw a 105° angle.
   d) Without using a protractor, find the measure
      of the angle formed by the horizontal line
      and the line you drew in part c.
      How did you find out? Measure to check.

4. Use only a ruler to draw an angle that you think measures:
   a) 90°
   b) a little less than 90°
   c) about 45°
   d) a little more than 90°
   e) a little less than 180°
   How can you check to see if you are correct?
   Show your work.

5. Copy these line segments. Use a ruler and a protractor.
   Using each line as one arm, draw a 50° angle.
   Label each angle with its measure.
   How did you decide which scale to use?
   a) **b)** **c)** **d)**

ASSESSMENT FOCUS | Question 5

Unit 4 Lesson 4   **141**

6. Use a ruler and a protractor.
   Draw an angle with each measure.
   a) 205°   **b)** 200°   **c)** 270°
   d) 320°   **e)** 350°   **f)** 300°

7. Draw an acute angle. Without using a
   protractor, draw an angle that is 90°
   greater than the angle you drew.
   Measure the angle with a protractor to check.
   Explain how you drew the angle.

8. **a)** Without using a protractor, draw a 90° angle.
       How can you use this angle to draw a 180° angle?
       How are the two angles related?
   b) Without using a protractor, draw a 180° angle.
       How can you use this angle to draw a 90° angle?
       A 45° angle?
       How are the three angles related?
   Show your work.

9. **a)** Draw an obtuse angle.
       Use a protractor to find its measure.
       Label the angle with its measure.
   b) Use tracing paper to copy the angle.
       Rotate the angle $\frac{1}{4}$ turn clockwise about its vertex.
       Measure the angle. What do you notice?
   c) Choose a different rotation.
       Predict what would happen to the size of the angle under this rotation.
       Rotate the angle to check. How can you explain this?

10. Is it possible to draw a reflex angle so the other angle formed
    by the arms is:
    a) acute?   **b)** obtuse?   **c)** straight?
    Use examples to explain.

Science

It takes about 365 days for the
Earth to make one complete
revolution around the Sun.
The number of degrees in a
complete turn is 360°. So, the
Earth travels about 1° around
the Sun each day.

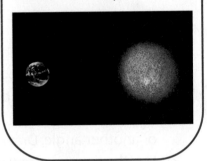

Reflect

Explain how to use a protractor to draw an angle of 315°.
Use words and pictures to explain.
How could you draw an angle of 315° without using a protractor?

Angle Hunt

Angles and shapes are everywhere.
In this game, you search for angles and shapes in your classroom.

You will need a protractor, a ruler, a pencil, paper, and game cards.
Work in a group of 4.

➤ Shuffle the game cards.
  Place the cards face down in the centre of the table.
  Decide who will go first.

➤ Player 1 draws a card.
  She looks for an object in the classroom that matches the description.
  If a sketch card is drawn, she sketches a shape with the attribute.
  Each shape may only be used once.
  The other players identify the object and check that Player 1 is correct.
  If the answer is correct, Player 1 keeps the card and it is the next
  player's turn.
  If the answer is incorrect, the card is passed to the next player to try.
  The card is passed until it is answered correctly.

➤ Players take turns until all the cards have been drawn.
  The player with the most cards is the winner.

Strategies Toolkit

Explore

Draw a pentagon with:
- no lines of symmetry
- exactly one obtuse angle
- exactly one pair of parallel sides

Is Paolo's solution correct? How do you know?
If Paolo's solution is not correct,
describe how he could change the shape
so his solution is correct.

Show and Share

Share your work with a classmate.
Is it possible to draw more than one shape to solve
this problem? Explain.

Connect

➤ Marg drew this shape to solve the problem below.

Draw a pentagon with:
- at least one reflex angle
- at least one right angle
- no parallel sides

Strategies for Success
- **Check and reflect.**
- **Focus on the problem.**
- **Represent your thinking.**
- **Explain your thinking.**

Marg checked that the shape
she drew meets all the criteria.

- The shape is a pentagon.   Yes
- The shape has at least one reflex angle.   Yes
- The shape has at least one right angle.   No
- The shape does not have any parallel sides.   Yes

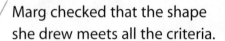

Marg's shape is a pentagon with at least one reflex angle,
no right angles, and no sides parallel.
She must change the shape
to include at least one right angle.

➤ When you solve problems, always check your solution.

✓ What was I asked to find? Did I answer the question?
✓ Did I include all the parts I needed?
✓ Is my answer reasonable?
✓ Are the calculations correct?
✓ How well did my strategy work?

Practice

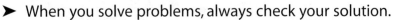

1. Find the mystery attribute.
   Show how you checked your answer.

All of these have it.	None of these has it.	Which of these has it?

2. Draw a quadrilateral with:
   • no lines of symmetry
   • exactly one pair of parallel sides
   • exactly two right angles
   • exactly one obtuse angle
   What shape have you drawn?

Reflect

Why is it important to always check your solution?

LESSON

Investigating Angles in a Triangle

Without using a protractor, what is the
measure of angle A?
How do you know?

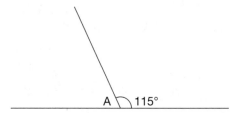

A ⟩ 115°

Explore 👥

You will need a ruler, scissors, and a protractor.

➤ Draw a triangle to match each description below:
  • a triangle with one right angle
  • a triangle with one obtuse angle
  • a triangle with all acute angles
  Use a protractor to measure the angles
  in each triangle.
  Record the measures in a table.
➤ Cut out one of the triangles. Cut off its angles.
  Place the vertices of the three angles together
  so adjacent sides touch. What do you notice?
➤ Repeat the activity with the other two triangles.
  What can you say about the sum of the angles in each triangle?
➤ Use the measures in your table.
  Find the sum of the angles in each triangle.
  Does this confirm your results from cutting off the angles?
  Explain.

Show and Share

Compare your results with those of another pair of classmates.
What can you say about the sum of angles in a triangle?
Do you think this would be true for all triangles?
Explain your thinking.

146   **LESSON FOCUS** | Investigate the sum of the angles in a triangle.

Connect

➤ We can show that the sum of the **interior angles** in a triangle is the same for any triangle.

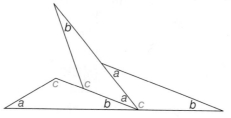

An interior angle is an angle inside a triangle or other polygon.

Arrange 3 congruent triangles as shown.

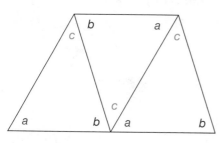

The arrangements show that angles *a, b,* and *c* make a straight angle.

So, $a + b + c = 180°$

The sum of the angles in a triangle is 180°.

➤ We can use the sum of the angles in a triangle to find the measure of the third angle in this triangle.

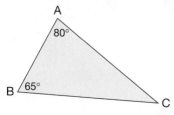

We often refer to an angle using the letter of its vertex. For example, the 80° angle in triangle ABC is ∠A.

The sum of the angles in a triangle is 180°.

So, $\angle A + \angle B + \angle C = 180°$

Since $\angle A = 80°$ and $\angle B = 65°$,

$80° + 65° + \angle C = 180°$ Add the angles.

$145° + \angle C = 180°$

Solve the equation by inspection.
Which number do we add to 145 to get 180?
The measure of ∠C is 35°.

I could count on to find out.

To check, we can find the sum of the 3 angles:

$\angle A + \angle B + \angle C = 80° + 65° + 35°$
$= 180°$

So, the answer is correct.

Practice

1. Draw 3 different triangles on dot paper. Measure and record each angle.
   Find the sum of the measures of the angles for each triangle.

2. Determine the measure of the third angle without measuring.

   a)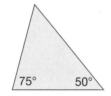
   75° 50°

   b)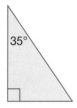
   35°

   c)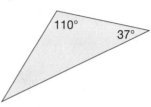
   110° 37°

3. The two unknown angles in each triangle below are equal.
   Determine the measure of each unknown angle without measuring.
   Explain the strategy you used.

   a)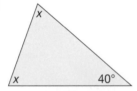
   x
   x 40°

   b)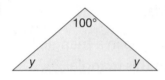
   100°
   y y

   c)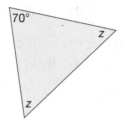
   70°
   z
   z

4. Two angles of a triangle are given.
   Find the measure of the third angle.
   a) 55°, 105°   b) 45°, 90°
   c) 30°, 60°   d) 25°, 125°

5. Vegreville, Alberta, is home to the world's largest
   known Ukrainian egg. It has 1108 triangular pieces
   with three angles of equal measure.
   Find the measure of each angle.
   Explain your strategy.

6. Is it possible for a triangle to have:
   a) more than 1 obtuse angle?
   b) 2 right angles?
   c) 3 acute angles?
   Explain your thinking.
   Use pictures and words.

7. Find the measure of the third angle in each triangle
   described below. Then, draw the triangle.
   Explain how you found each measure.
   a) A triangle with two angles measuring 65° and 55°
   b) A triangle with two equal angles; each measures 40°
   c) A right triangle with a 70° angle

8. Find the measures of the angles labelled *m* and *n*.
   Explain the strategy you used.

a)

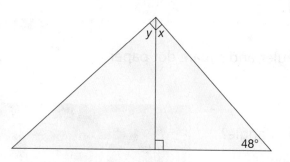

b)

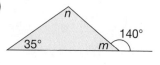

c)

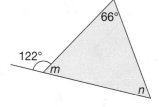

9. Find the measures of the angles labelled *x* and *y*.
   Show your work. Explain the strategy you used.

a)

b)

10. Use a geoboard and geobands or square dot paper.
    Construct △ABC.
    a) Find the unknown angle measures.
       Check your answers by measuring with a protractor.
    b) Extend AB 1 unit right to D.
       Extend AC 1 unit down to E. Join DE.
    c) Predict the measure of each angle in the new triangle.
       Use a protractor to check. Record your work.
    d) Repeat steps b and c two more times.
    e) What do you notice about all the triangles you created? Explain.

Reflect

Suppose your classmate missed today's lesson.
Explain how you know the sum of the angles in any triangle.

Investigating Angles in a Quadrilateral

How are these quadrilaterals alike?
How are they different?

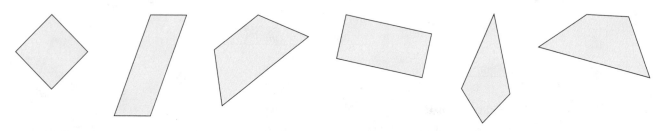

Explore

You will need a geoboard, geobands, a ruler, and square dot paper.
Draw each shape you make on dot paper.

➤ Make a square.
What do you know about each interior angle?
What is the sum of the angles in a square?

➤ Make a rectangle.
What do you know about each interior angle?
What is the sum of the angles in a rectangle?

➤ Make 2 different quadrilaterals.
None of the angles can be right angles.
Suppose you don't have a protractor.
How can you find the sum of the angles
in each quadrilateral?

➤ What can you say about the sum of the angles
in a quadrilateral? Explain.

Show *and* Share

Compare your results with those of another pair of students.
How can you use what you know about triangles to find the sum
of the angles in a quadrilateral?
Do you think this is true for all quadrilaterals? Why or why not?

Connect

➤ The sum of the interior angles in a quadrilateral
is the same for any quadrilateral.
A **diagonal** divides any quadrilateral into 2 triangles.

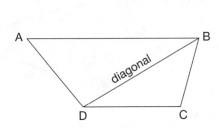

We can use 3 letters to name
an angle. The middle letter tells
the vertex of the angle.

The sum of the angles in each triangle formed is 180°.
In △ABD, ∠ABD + ∠BDA + ∠DAB = 180°
In △DBC, ∠DBC + ∠BCD + ∠CDB = 180°
So, the sum of the angles in quadrilateral ABCD is 2 × 180° = 360°.

➤ We can use the sum of the angles in a quadrilateral to find the
measure of ∠S in quadrilateral PQRS.

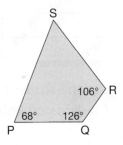

The sum of the angles in a quadrilateral is 360°.
So, ∠P + ∠Q + ∠R + ∠S = 360°
Since ∠P = 68°, ∠Q = 126°, and ∠R = 106°,
68° + 126° + 106° + ∠S = 360°   Add the angles.
        300° + ∠S = 360°

Solve the equation by inspection.
Which number do we add to 300 to get 360?
The measure of ∠S is 60°.

Practice

1. Draw 3 different quadrilaterals on dot paper.
   Measure and record each angle.
   Find the sum of the measures of the angles for each quadrilateral.

2. Find the unknown angle measure in each quadrilateral.

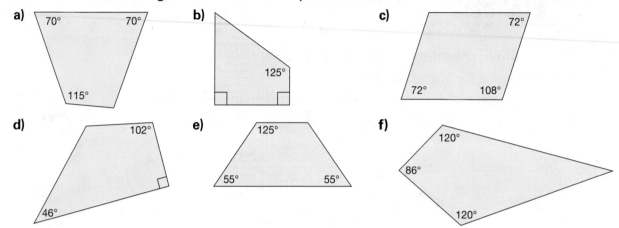

a) 70° 70° 115°

b) 125°

c) 72° 72° 108°

d) 102° 46°

e) 125° 55° 55°

f) 120° 86° 120°

3. A student drew 4 different quadrilaterals.
   She recorded the angle measures in a table.

Quadrilateral	∠A	∠B	∠C	∠D
a)	225°	36°	47°	42°
b)	81°	99°	81°	99°
c)	90°	45°	120°	105°
d)	123°	66°	108°	73°

Did the student measure the angles in each quadrilateral correctly?
How do you know?

4. Use a geoboard and geobands and/or dot paper.
   Try to make each quadrilateral below.
   If you can make the quadrilateral, record your work on dot paper.
   If you cannot make the quadrilateral, use what you know about
   the sum of the angles in a quadrilateral to explain why.
   a) a quadrilateral with 4 right angles
   b) a quadrilateral with 2 acute angles and 2 obtuse angles
   c) a quadrilateral with only one right angle
   d) a quadrilateral with 4 acute angles
   e) a quadrilateral with 4 obtuse angles

5. Look at this pentagon.
   a) Find the measure of ∠A.
   b) Find the measure of ∠DBC.
   Show your work. Explain your thinking.

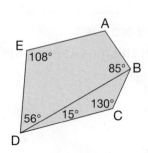

E 108°   A   85° B   130° C   15°   56°   D

6. Find the measure of the angles labelled *a*, *b*, and *c*.
Show your work.

a)

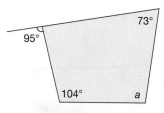

73°
95°
104°
a

b)

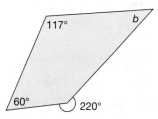

117°
b
60°
220°

c)

50°
c
c
50°

7. Find the measure of ∠ABC.
Show all the steps you took to find its measure.

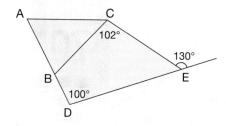

A   C
102°
130°
B
100°
D
E

8. Draw a rectangle. Draw its diagonals.
Measure one of the angles formed where the diagonals intersect.
Without using a protractor, find the measures of the other 3 angles.
Explain your strategy.
Repeat for 2 different quadrilaterals.
What do you notice?

9. Look at parallelogram ABCD.

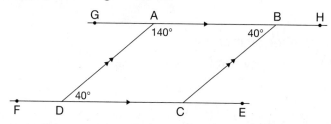

G   A   B   H
140°   40°
40°
F   D   C   E

a) Without using a protractor, find the measure of ∠BCD.
b) Find the measure of ∠BCE, ∠CBH, ∠ADF, and ∠DAG.
What strategy did you use?
c) List pairs of angles that have the same measure.
d) List pairs of angles that add to 180°.

Reflect

How did you use what you know about the sum of the angles
in a triangle in this lesson?

Unit 4 — Show What You Know

LESSON

1

1. Identify as many different angles as you can in the signs below.
   Name each angle as acute, obtuse, right, straight, or reflex.
   Tell how you know. Describe the location of each angle.

   a)
   Iqaluit, Nunavut

   b)
   Northwest Territories

   c)
   Jasper National Park, Alberta

2. Draw a line segment on grid paper.
   Visualize rotating the line segment about one of its end points.
   Which type of angle is formed by each rotation?
   a) $\frac{1}{4}$ turn clockwise
   b) between a $\frac{1}{2}$ turn and a full turn clockwise
   c) between a $\frac{1}{4}$ turn and a $\frac{1}{2}$ turn counterclockwise
   d) less than a $\frac{1}{4}$ turn counterclockwise

   Use tracing paper to check.

3

3. Owen says he can make an angle smaller by making the arms shorter. Do you agree? Why or why not?

4. For each angle:
   • Choose an appropriate reference angle: 45°, 90°, 180°
     Estimate the size of the angle.
   • Use a protractor to measure each angle.
   • Order the angles from least to greatest measure.
   • Name each angle as acute, right, obtuse, straight, or reflex.

   a) b) c)

   d) 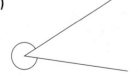 e)  f)

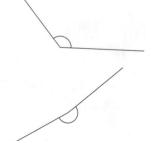

5. A student used a protractor to measure this angle.
   The student says the angle measures 65°.
   Is the student correct?
   If your answer is yes, explain how you know.
   If your answer is no, describe the student's mistake.

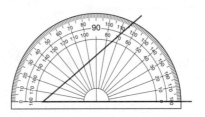

4

6. a) Use a protractor to draw a 40° angle.
   b) Do not use a protractor.
      Draw an angle that is 90° greater. Describe the strategy you used.
   c) Use a protractor to check the angle in part b.

7. Copy these line segments. Use a ruler and a protractor.
   Using each line as one arm, draw a 125° angle.

   a)   b)   c)

   Does the position of an angle on the page affect its measure?
   Explain how you know.

6

8. Use a ruler and a protractor.
   a) Draw, then label each angle below with its measure:
      • a right angle
      • an acute angle
      • an obtuse angle
   b) For each angle in part a:
      • Join the arms together to make a triangle.
      • Measure and label one of the other angles.
      • Without using a protractor, label the third
        angle with its measure.
   c) Explain the strategy you used to find the
      measure of the third angle each time.

9. Two angles of a triangle are given.
   Find the measure of the third angle.
   a) 70°, 25°   b) 62°, 71°   c) 58°, 74°   d) 115°, 43°

7

10. A quadrilateral has angles measuring 60°, 50°, and 120°.
    What is the measure of the 4th angle? How do you know?

UNIT
4 Learning Goals

☑ name, describe, and
   classify angles
☑ estimate and determine
   angle measures
☑ draw and label angles
☑ provide examples of angles
   in the environment
☑ investigate the sum of angles in
   triangles and quadrilaterals

Designing a Quilt Block

You will need:
- square grid paper
- large piece of paper (30 cm by 30 cm)
- scissors
- glue or tape
- construction paper
- rulers
- protractors

A quilt is usually made in square sections called blocks.
Here are some examples of quilt blocks.

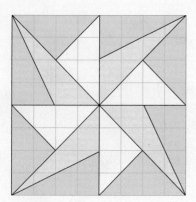

Part 1

Design your own quilt block.
Use a sheet of square grid paper.
Make a square pattern for your quilt block.
Your pattern should include triangles and quadrilaterals.

Part 2

To reproduce your pattern on a large piece of paper:
Use a ruler and a protractor to draw the shapes you used
on different colours of construction paper. Cut out the shapes.
Glue or tape the shapes onto the large sheet of paper.
Use pencil crayons or markers to add more colour to your block.

Part 3

Write about your block.
Describe at least one example of each type of angle:

- acute angle
- obtuse angle
- right angle
- reflex angle
- straight angle

Include the angle measure of each angle you chose.
Describe how you can use angles in your block to show
the sum of the angles in a triangle and in a rectangle.

Part 4

Combine your block with those of other groups to
make a bulletin board quilt.

Reflect on Your Learning

Write about what you have learned about angles, triangles,
and quadrilaterals. Use diagrams and words to explain.

Investigation

Ziggurats

Ziggurats were built by the ancient Assyrians and Babylonians.
A ziggurat is a tiered pyramid that was used as a temple.
Each tier of a ziggurat is smaller than the one below it.

> Tiers are layers arranged one on top of another.

You will need linking cubes, triangular dot paper, and grid paper.

Part 1

➤ Use linking cubes.
Build a ziggurat with each number of tiers:
1 tier   2 tiers   3 tiers
Each tier is centred on the tier below it.

Each block covers the block below it.

You can   You cannot
do this.   do this.

➤ Draw each ziggurat on triangular dot paper.

➤ Predict the number of cubes required to build a 4-tier ziggurat.
Build it to check your prediction.

Part 2

➤ Find the volume of each ziggurat in Part 1.
Record the numbers of tiers and
the volumes in a table.

Number of Tiers	Volume
1	
2	

Graph the table of values.
Explain how the graph represents the pattern.
Write a pattern rule for the volumes.

➤ Use the pattern rule.
What is the volume of a 6-tier ziggurat? Explain.

Display Your Work

Create a summary of your work. Describe all the patterns you used.
Use pictures, numbers, and words.

Take It Further

Suppose you built staircases like this one.
Predict a pattern rule for the volumes of staircases
with different numbers of tiers.
Build the staircases to check your prediction.
Draw each staircase on triangular dot paper.

Fractions, Ratios,

Designing a Floor Plan

This is a floor plan for a Youth Centre to be built in Vancouver, British Columbia. What is the total area of the floor plan?

Learning Goals

- relate improper fractions to mixed numbers
- compare mixed numbers and fractions
- use ratios for part-to-part and part-to-whole comparisons
- explore equivalent ratios
- explore percents
- relate percents to fractions and decimals

and Percents

Key Words
· · · · · · · · · · · · · · · · · · ·

improper fraction

mixed number

ratio

part-to-part ratio

part-to-whole ratio

terms of a ratio

equivalent ratios

percent

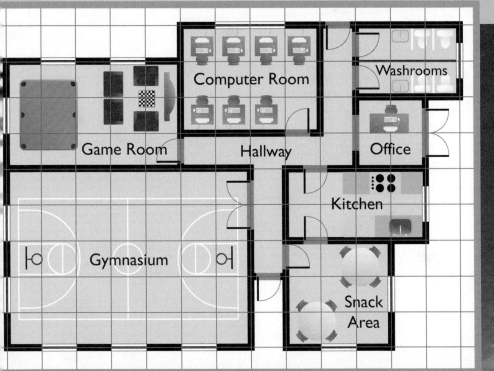

- Which room takes up the most space? The least space?
  What fraction of the entire floor plan does each room cover?
- Which room takes up $\frac{15}{100}$ of the floor plan?
  What is an equivalent fraction for $\frac{15}{100}$?
- Which 2 rooms together take up 0.5 of the floor plan?
  What fraction of the floor plan is 0.5?
- Which room is one-half the size of the kitchen?

Mixed Numbers

How would you describe the number of sandwiches on the tray?

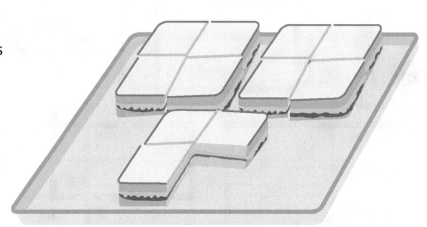

Explore •

You will need Pattern Blocks and triangular grid paper.
Use Pattern Blocks to show fractions
greater than 1 whole.
Use the yellow Pattern Block as 1 whole.

➤ Take a handful of red, blue, and
 green Pattern Blocks. Choose a colour.
 Arrange the blocks to show how many
 yellow hexagons you could cover.
 Name the amount covered in different ways.
 Record your work on grid paper.
➤ Repeat the activity with another colour
 of Pattern Blocks.

Show *and* Share

Share your work with another pair of students.
Did you draw the same pictures? Explain.
How did you decide what to name the amounts covered?
Which Pattern Blocks did you not use? Why not?

You can use whole numbers and fractions to describe amounts greater than 1.

Suppose the red trapezoid is 1 whole.

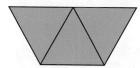 1 whole

Three green triangles cover the trapezoid.
So, each green triangle represents $\frac{1}{3}$.

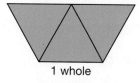 $\frac{3}{3} = 1$ whole

Then, eight green triangles represent $\frac{8}{3}$.

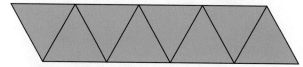 $\frac{8}{3}$

These triangles can be grouped to show that $\frac{8}{3}$ is equal to 2 and $\frac{2}{3}$.

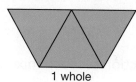
1 whole   1 whole $\frac{2}{3}$

We write 2 and $\frac{2}{3}$ as $2\frac{2}{3}$.

$\frac{8}{3}$ and $2\frac{2}{3}$ represent the same amount.
They are equivalent.
$\frac{8}{3} = 2\frac{2}{3}$

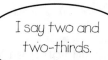
I say two and two-thirds.

The numerator, 8, of $\frac{8}{3}$ is greater than the denominator, 3.
So, we call $\frac{8}{3}$ an **improper fraction**.

$2\frac{2}{3}$ has a whole number part, 2, and a fraction part, $\frac{2}{3}$.
So, we call $2\frac{2}{3}$ a **mixed number**.

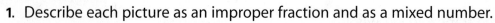

Practice

1. Describe each picture as an improper fraction and as a mixed number.

   a)

   b)

   c)

   d)

   e)
   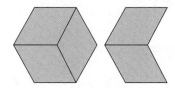

   f)
   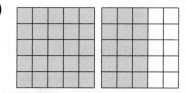

2. **a)** Match each improper fraction with a mixed number.
      Draw pictures to record your work.

   $\dfrac{5}{4}$ $\dfrac{9}{4}$ $\dfrac{7}{4}$ $2\dfrac{3}{4}$

   $1\dfrac{3}{4}$ $1\dfrac{1}{4}$ $2\dfrac{1}{4}$ $3\dfrac{1}{4}$

   b) Draw a picture to show an improper fraction for each mixed number
      that did not match.

3. Use Pattern Blocks. Are the numbers in each pair equivalent?
   Show your work.

   a) $3\dfrac{2}{3}$ and $\dfrac{11}{3}$ **b)** $\dfrac{8}{6}$ and $1\dfrac{1}{6}$ **c)** $2\dfrac{1}{2}$ and $\dfrac{5}{2}$

4. Which scoop would you use to measure each amount?
   How many of that scoop would you need?

   a) $1\dfrac{1}{6}$ cups   **b)** $2\dfrac{1}{2}$ cups   **c)** $1\dfrac{2}{3}$ cups   **d)** $1\dfrac{5}{6}$ cups

5. The Fernandez family drank $3\frac{1}{2}$ pitchers of water on a picnic. Draw pictures to show the amount, then write this mixed number as an improper fraction. Show your work.

6. Kendra mowed her lawn for $2\frac{1}{2}$ h.
   Mario mowed his lawn for $\frac{1}{4}$ h, then stopped. He did this 7 times.
   Who spent more time mowing the lawn?
   How do you know?

7. Carlo baked pies for a party. He cut some pies into 6 pieces and some into 8 pieces. After the party, more than $2\frac{1}{2}$ but less than 3 pies were left. How much pie might have been left? Show how you know.

8. Renée was making crepes by the dozen. Renée's family ate $2\frac{1}{3}$ dozen crepes. How many crepes did they eat? Show your work.

9. How can you find out if $2\frac{1}{2}$ and $\frac{10}{4}$ name the same amount? Use words, numbers, and pictures to explain.

Reflect

Can $\frac{5}{6}$ be written as a mixed number?
Use words and pictures to explain.

LESSON 2

Converting between Mixed Numbers and Improper Fractions

I have $\frac{5}{3}$ slices of French toast.

I have $1\frac{2}{3}$ slices of French toast.

How are $\frac{5}{3}$ and $1\frac{2}{3}$ related?

**Explore**

You will need Cuisenaire rods or strips of coloured paper.

Use the numbers given.

$1\frac{1}{4}$	$2\frac{1}{3}$	$\frac{9}{7}$
$\frac{11}{4}$	$3\frac{2}{5}$	$2\frac{1}{2}$
$1\frac{3}{10}$	$\frac{5}{3}$	$\frac{11}{8}$

When the dark green rod is one whole, the red rod is one-third.

➤ Choose a mixed number.
  Use Cuisenaire rods to model the mixed number.
  Write the mixed number as an improper fraction.
  Repeat for 2 different mixed numbers.
➤ Choose an improper fraction.
  Use Cuisenaire rods to model the improper fraction.
  Choose an appropriate rod to represent 1 whole.
  Write the improper fraction as a mixed number.
  Repeat for 2 different improper fractions.
➤ If you did not have Cuisenaire rods, how could you:
  • rewrite a mixed number as an improper fraction?
  • rewrite an improper fraction as a mixed number?
  Record each method.

Show *and* Share

Compare your methods with those of another pair of students.
Use Cuisenaire rods to show why your methods make sense.

Connect

➤ To write $2\frac{3}{4}$ as an improper fraction:
- Alison thinks about money.

$2:   3 quarters:

There are 11 quarters altogether.
So, $2\frac{3}{4} = \frac{11}{4}$

- Hiroshi draws a diagram to represent $2\frac{3}{4}$.

Hiroshi then divides each whole to
show quarters.

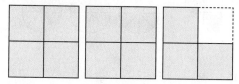

So, $2\frac{3}{4}$ is the same as $\frac{11}{4}$.

- Nadia uses mental math.

> Two wholes are the same as 8 quarters. Eight quarters and 3 quarters equals 11 quarters.

> I know there are 4 quarters in 1 whole. So, in 2 wholes there are $2 \times 4 = 8$ quarters. Eight quarters plus 3 more quarters equals 11 quarters. So, $2\frac{3}{4}$ is the same as $\frac{11}{4}$.

➤ To write $\frac{13}{5}$ as a mixed number:
- Edna draws a diagram to show 13 fifths.

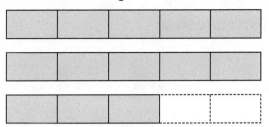

There are 5 fifths in 1 whole, and 10 fifths in 2 wholes. There are 2 wholes, with 3 fifths left over.

So, $\frac{13}{5}$ is the same as $2\frac{3}{5}$.
- Chioke gets the same result using division.

There are 5 fifths in 1 whole. To find how many wholes are in 13 fifths, I divide: $13 \div 5 = 2$ with remainder 3. There are 2 wholes with 3 fifths left over.

So, $\frac{13}{5} = 2\frac{3}{5}$

Practice

Use Cuisenaire rods or coloured strips when they help.

1. Write an improper fraction and a mixed number to describe each picture.

a)

b)

c)

2. Draw a picture to represent each number.

   a) $1\frac{5}{8}$ b) $1\frac{2}{3}$ c) $\frac{7}{4}$ d) $\frac{9}{2}$

3. Write each mixed number as an improper fraction.

   a) $1\frac{1}{6}$ b) $4\frac{3}{8}$ c) $1\frac{3}{4}$ d) $3\frac{3}{5}$ e) $8\frac{1}{2}$ f) $7\frac{1}{4}$

4. Write each improper fraction as a mixed number.

   a) $\frac{17}{5}$ b) $\frac{9}{4}$ c) $\frac{18}{4}$ d) $\frac{14}{3}$ e) $\frac{20}{3}$ f) $\frac{20}{6}$

5. Which of these improper fractions are between 4 and 5? How do you know?

   a) $\frac{13}{3}$ b) $\frac{13}{4}$ c) $\frac{13}{5}$ d) $\frac{13}{6}$

6. Mary baked 5 round bannock for a bake sale at
   the Chief Kahkewistahaw Community School in
   Saskatchewan. She cut each bannock into
   12 equal pieces. Mary sold 41 pieces of bannock.
   a) How many bannock did Mary sell?
      Give your answer 2 ways.
   b) How many bannock are left?
      Give your answer 2 ways.

7. Suppose you have 14 quarters.
   Do you have $4? Explain.

8. The pizza at Kwame's party is cut into eighths.
   Kwame eats 3 slices and the rest of the family eats 18 slices.
   There are 3 slices left over.
   How many pizzas had been ordered?

9. Maybelline has $3\frac{5}{6}$ loaves of bread in her diner in Regina.
   The whole loaves are cut into 6 equal slices.
   To how many customers can Maybelline serve a slice of bread?
   Draw a diagram to show your solution.

10. Hair scrunchies come in packages of 5.
    Suppose you have $2\frac{1}{5}$ of these packages to share among
    4 friends.

    a) Do you have enough scrunchies to give each friend
       three scrunchies? How do you know?
    b) Do you have enough scrunchies to give each friend two?
       How do you know?

11. Suppose you get 0 as the remainder when you divide
    the numerator of an improper fraction by the denominator.
    What does that tell you?
    Use drawings and words to explain.

Reflect

What is the difference between a mixed number and
an improper fraction?
Use pictures, words, and numbers to show how to rename an
improper fraction as a mixed number.

Fraction Match Up

Your teacher will give you a set of game cards.

The object of the game is to find the most pairs of game cards with equivalent numbers.

➤ Shuffle the game cards.
   Arrange cards, face down, in 4 rows of 5 cards.
➤ Player 1 turns over two cards.
   If the numbers are equivalent, Player 1 keeps the cards.
   If the numbers are not equivalent, turn both cards face down again.
➤ Player 2 has a turn.
➤ Continue to play until all the cards have gone.
   The player with more cards wins.

Comparing Mixed Numbers and Improper Fractions

Kenda watched a TV program for $1\frac{1}{2}$ h.
Garnet watched 5 half-hour programs.
Who watched TV for a longer time?

Explore

You will need Cuisenaire rods or strips of coloured paper.

Akna and Tootega shovelled snow to earn money to buy new snowshoes.
Akna shovelled snow for $1\frac{2}{3}$ h. Tootega shovelled snow for $\frac{3}{2}$ h.
Who spent more time shovelling snow?

Use Cuisenaire rods to find out.

Show *and* Share

Share your solution with another pair of students.

How did you decide which rods to use to represent one whole, one-third, and one-half?

How did you find out which number was greater?

How could you compare $1\frac{2}{3}$ and $\frac{3}{2}$ without using rods?

Connect ••

➤ Here are three strategies students used to place $2\frac{1}{4}$, $\frac{2}{3}$, and $\frac{11}{6}$ on a number line.

• Ella used benchmarks and estimation.

$\frac{2}{3}$ is between $\frac{1}{2}$ and 1, but closer to $\frac{1}{2}$.

$\frac{11}{6}$ is the same as $1\frac{5}{6}$. $1\frac{5}{6}$ is close to 2, but less than 2.

$2\frac{1}{4}$ is halfway between 2 and $2\frac{1}{2}$.

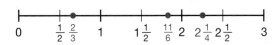

• Rahim drew three number lines of equal length, each labelled from 0 to 3.

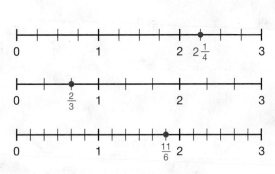

The denominators are 4, 3, and 6. So, I divided the first number line to show quarters. I divided the second line to show thirds. I divided the third line to show sixths.

- Maggie wrote each number as an equivalent fraction with the same denominator, then placed the fractions on a number line.

  Maggie wrote $2\frac{1}{4}$ as an improper fraction: $2\frac{1}{4} = \frac{4}{4} + \frac{4}{4} + \frac{1}{4} = \frac{9}{4}$

  Since 12 is a multiple of 3, 4, and 6,

  she wrote each fraction with denominator 12.

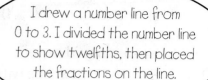

I drew a number line from 0 to 3. I divided the number line to show twelfths, then placed the fractions on the line.

$$\frac{9}{4} \xrightarrow{\times 3} \frac{27}{12} \qquad \frac{2}{3} \xrightarrow{\times 4} \frac{8}{12} \qquad \frac{11}{6} \xrightarrow{\times 2} \frac{22}{12}$$

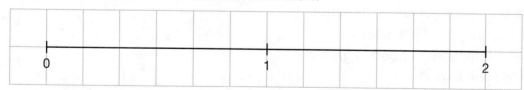

We can use the placement of the numbers on the line to order the numbers.

The numbers increase from left to right.

So, the order from least to greatest is:

$\frac{8}{12}, \frac{22}{12}, \frac{27}{12}$ or $\frac{2}{3}, \frac{11}{6}, \frac{9}{4}$ or $\frac{2}{3}, \frac{11}{6}, 2\frac{1}{4}$

Practice

Your teacher will give you copies of number lines for questions 3, 6, and 7.

1. Use 1-cm grid paper.

Draw a 12-cm number line like the one below.

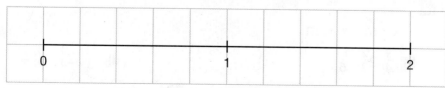

Place these numbers on the line: $\frac{5}{6}, 1\frac{1}{6}, \frac{9}{6}$

2. Use 1-cm grid paper.

Draw a 10-cm number line like the one below.

Place these numbers on the line: $1\frac{3}{5}, \frac{7}{5}, \frac{4}{5}$

3. Find equivalent fractions so the fractions in each pair have the same denominator.
   Place each pair of fractions on a number line.
   a) $\frac{8}{3}$ and $\frac{6}{4}$ b) $\frac{12}{5}$ and $\frac{8}{3}$
   c) $\frac{14}{6}$ and $\frac{17}{8}$ d) $\frac{11}{10}$ and $\frac{20}{15}$
   e) $\frac{9}{5}$ and $\frac{8}{6}$ f) $\frac{12}{9}$ and $\frac{11}{5}$

4. Use 1-cm grid paper.
   Draw a number line with the benchmarks 0, 1, 2, and 3 as shown below.

   Place these numbers on the number line:
   $\frac{1}{2}$, $\frac{23}{8}$, $1\frac{3}{4}$

5. Use 1-cm grid paper.
   Draw a number line with the benchmarks 0, 1, 2, 3, and 4 as shown below.

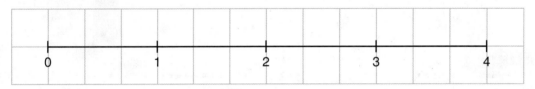

   Place these numbers on the number line:
   $\frac{5}{2}$, $\frac{2}{3}$, $1\frac{5}{6}$

6. For each pair of numbers below:
   • Place the two numbers on a number line.
     Which strategy did you use?
   • Which of the two numbers is greater?
     How do you know?
   a) $\frac{5}{8}$; $\frac{7}{16}$ b) $\frac{3}{4}$; $\frac{9}{12}$ c) $2\frac{1}{2}$; $\frac{9}{2}$
   d) $\frac{13}{10}$; $1\frac{1}{5}$ e) $\frac{29}{5}$; $6\frac{2}{10}$ f) $3\frac{5}{6}$; $3\frac{8}{12}$

7. Place the numbers in each set on a number line.
   Show how you did it.
   List the numbers from least to greatest.
   a) $\frac{5}{6}$, $\frac{15}{9}$, $1\frac{5}{12}$ b) $\frac{9}{4}$, $2\frac{2}{3}$, $\frac{11}{6}$ c) $\frac{9}{10}$, $\frac{7}{5}$, $\frac{11}{4}$ d) $\frac{10}{3}$, $2\frac{1}{4}$, $\frac{3}{2}$

8. Hisa says that $\frac{17}{3}$ is greater than $5\frac{3}{4}$. Is she correct?
   Use pictures, numbers, and words to explain.

9. Adriel watched a $1\frac{3}{4}$-h movie on TV.
   Nadir watched 3 half-hour sitcoms.
   Who watched more TV? How do you know?

10. Justine played a board game for $3\frac{1}{2}$ h.
    Marty played the same board game for $\frac{37}{12}$ h.
    Who played longer?
    Sketch a number line to show how you know you are correct.

11. Ratu, Addie, and Penny cooked pancakes
    for their school's maple syrup festival
    in McCreary, Manitoba.
    Ratu made $4\frac{1}{2}$ dozen pancakes,
    Addie made $\frac{28}{6}$ dozen pancakes,
    and Penny made $\frac{13}{3}$ dozen pancakes.
    Who made the most pancakes?
    Who made the least?
    Sketch a number line to show how you know.

McCreary is the maple syrup
capital of Manitoba.

12. Florence and her friends Rafael and Bruno race
    model cars.
    Florence's car completed $2\frac{1}{4}$ laps of a track in 1 min.
    Rafael's car completed $\frac{8}{3}$ laps of the track in 1 min.
    Bruno's car completed $\frac{11}{12}$ laps of the track in 1 min.
    Whose car was fastest? How do you know?

13. Use your ruler as a number line.
    Visualize placing these fractions on your ruler: $4\frac{3}{5}$, $\frac{11}{2}$, $\frac{83}{10}$
    Describe where you would place each fraction.
    Which fraction is the greatest? The least?

Reflect

How do you use a number line to compare fractions and mixed
numbers? Include an example.

Exploring Ratios

On her bird-watching expedition in Elk Island National Park, Alberta, Cassie spotted 6 sapsuckers and 3 Baltimore orioles sitting on a fence.

Here are some ways Cassie compared the birds she saw.
- The number of sapsuckers compared to the number of orioles:
  6 sapsuckers to 3 orioles
- The number of sapsuckers compared to the number of birds:
  6 sapsuckers to 9 birds

Cassie could also have compared the birds using fractions.
What fraction of the birds were sapsuckers? Orioles?

Explore

You will need twelve 2-colour counters and a paper cup.

➤ Put twelve 2-colour counters in the cup. Shake the cup and spill the counters onto the table.
➤ Compare the counters in as many ways as you can. Record each comparison.

The number of red counters compared to the total number of counters is 7 to 12.

Show and Share

Share your results with another pair of students. In which result did you compare one part of the set to another part of the set? In which result did you compare one part of the set to the whole set?

Mahit has 4 brown rabbits and 5 white rabbits.

A **ratio** is a comparison of 2 quantities with the same unit.

➤ You can use ratios to compare the numbers of white and brown rabbits.

The ratio of white rabbits to brown rabbits is 5 to 4.
The ratio 5 to 4 is written as 5 : 4.

white rabbits to brown rabbits:

5 to 4 or 5 : 4

The ratio of brown rabbits to white rabbits is 4 to 5, or 4 : 5.

These are **part-to-part ratios**.

The numbers 4 and 5 are the **terms of the ratio**.
Order is important in a ratio.
5 to 4 is not the same as 4 to 5.

➤ You can also use ratios to compare the parts to the whole.

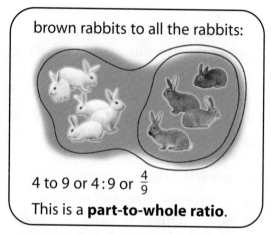

brown rabbits to all the rabbits:

4 to 9 or 4 : 9 or $\frac{4}{9}$
This is a **part-to-whole ratio**.

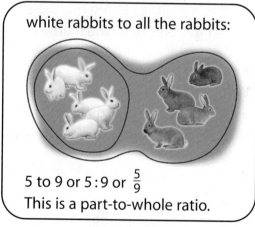

white rabbits to all the rabbits:

5 to 9 or 5 : 9 or $\frac{5}{9}$
This is a part-to-whole ratio.

A ratio that compares
a part of a set to the whole set is a fraction.
When we read a ratio like $\frac{4}{9}$,
we say "four to nine."

Practice· Unit 5 Lesson·

1. Write each ratio 2 ways.
   a) apples to pears

   b) caps to scarves

   c) roses to daisies

2. Write a ratio to show the numbers of:
   a) ladybugs to ants
   b) ants to ladybugs
   c) ladybugs to insects
   d) ants to insects

3. Write each ratio in as many ways as you can.
   a) red marbles to green marbles
   b) green marbles to all the marbles
   c) green marbles to red marbles
   d) red marbles to all the marbles

4. Ms. Zsabo has 13 girls and 11 boys in her class.
   Write each ratio.
   a) girls to boys   **b)** boys to girls
   c) boys to students   **d)** girls to students

5. What is being compared in each ratio?
   a) 3 : 4   **b)** $\frac{4}{7}$
   c) 3 to 7   **d)** 4 : 3

6. Use counters to model the ratio 3:5 in 2 different ways.
   Draw diagrams to record your work.
   Explain each diagram.

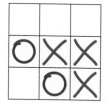

7. Write 4 different ratios for this picture.
   Explain what each ratio compares.

8. A penny can show heads or tails.
   Place 10 pennies in a cup. Shake and spill.
   Write as many ratios as you can for the pennies.

9. Write a ratio to show the numbers of:
   a) triangles to squares
   b) squares to rectangles
   c) triangles to all shapes
   d) red shapes to yellow shapes
   e) yellow triangles to yellow rectangles
   f) red triangles to yellow squares

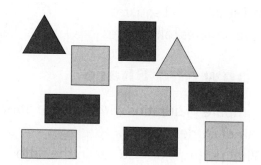

10. Write as many ratios as you can for the trail mix recipe.
    Explain what each ratio compares.

TRAIL MIX

1 scoop raisins

3 scoops nuts

2 scoops dried papaya

1 scoop sunflower seeds

11. Use 11 counters to show each ratio.
    Sketch counters to record your work.
    a) 5:6   b) 8 to 3   c) $\frac{2}{11}$ d) 6:11

Reflect

When you see a ratio, how can you tell
if it is a part-to-part or part-to-whole ratio?

LESSON 5

Equivalent Ratios

 **Explore** ⋯⋯⋯⋯⋯⋯⋯⋯⋯⋯⋯⋯⋯⋯⋯⋯

How many different ways can you write each ratio?
red squares : blue squares
red squares : all squares
blue squares : all squares

Show *and* Share

Compare your ratios with those of another
pair of students.
What patterns do you see in the ratios?
Try to write more ratios that extend each pattern.

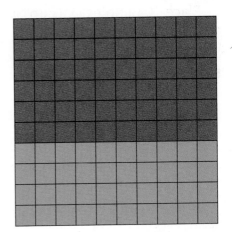

Connect ⋯⋯⋯⋯⋯⋯⋯⋯⋯⋯⋯⋯⋯⋯⋯⋯⋯⋯⋯⋯⋯

Kim is planting a border in her garden in Trail, BC.
She plants 5 yellow daisies for every 3 red petunias.
The ratio of daisies to petunias is 5 : 3.

How many petunias would Kim plant
for each number of daisies?

- 10 daisies
- 15 daisies
- 20 daisies

In each case, what is the ratio of daisies to petunias?

Here are 2 ways to solve the problem.

➤ You can use Colour Tiles to represent the plants.
  Use yellow tiles to represent daisies.
  Use red tiles to represent petunias.

  - Start with 10 yellow tiles.

  Think: For every 5 yellow tiles, you need 3 red tiles.
  Arrange your yellow tiles into groups of 5 tiles.
  You can make 2 groups.
  So, you need 2 groups of 3 red tiles.

 180 **LESSON FOCUS** | Solve problems involving equivalent ratios.

That makes a total of 6 red tiles.
These represent 6 petunias.
The ratio of daisies to petunias is 10 : 6.

- Add a group of 5 yellow tiles.
  You now have 15 yellow tiles.
  Add another group of 3 red tiles.
  You now have 9 red tiles.
  These represent 9 petunias.
  The ratio of daisies to petunias is 15 : 9.

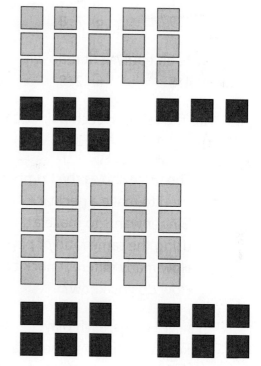

- Add a group of 5 yellow tiles.
  You now have 20 yellow tiles.
  Add another group of 3 red tiles.
  You now have 12 red tiles.
  These represent 12 petunias.
  The ratio of daisies to petunias is 20 : 12.

➤ You can use a table and patterns to find the ratios.

There are 5 daisies for every 3 petunias.
10 daisies are **2** groups of 5 daisies.
15 daisies are **3** groups of 5 daisies.
20 daisies are **4** groups of 5 daisies.

So, to keep the balance, you need the same numbers of groups of petunias.

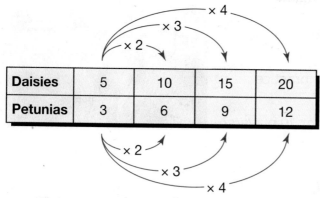

Daisies	5	10	15	20
Petunias	3	6	9	12

The numbers in the Daisies row are multiples of 5. The numbers in the Petunias row are multiples of 3.

The ratios of daisies to petunias are:
10 : 6, 15 : 9, and 20 : 12
Each ratio can be written as 5 : 3.
So, we say that 5 : 3, 10 : 6, 15 : 9, and 20 : 12
are **equivalent ratios**.

1. Write 2 equivalent ratios for each ratio.
   a) 3:1   **b)** 4:2   **c)** 1:2   **d)** 5:6   **e)** 3:5
   f) 4:9   **g)** 7:8   **h)** 8:3   **i)** 1:1   **j)** 2:5

2. Write an equivalent ratio with 20 as one of the terms.
   a) 4:5   **b)** 2:8   **c)** 7:4   **d)** 10:3

3. Are the ratios in each pair equivalent? Explain how you know.
   a) 7 to 14 and 1 to 2   **b)** 6:9 and 3:2   **c)** 1 to 10 and 4 to 40

4. The table shows the number of beads
   used to make a necklace.
   Ginger wants to make a smaller necklace
   using the same ratio of pink to white beads.
   How many different necklaces could Ginger make?
   How do you know?

Colour	Number
Pink	30
White	35

5. In a card game, each player is dealt 5 cards.
   Make a table to show the total number of cards
   dealt for each number of players from 3 to 6.
   Write each ratio of players to cards dealt.

Number of Players	Total Number of Cards Dealt

6. Ms. Olivieri's class plays a game in teams.
   Each team has the same number of students.
   The ratio of teams to players is 8:32.
   a) How many students are in Ms. Olivieri's class?
   b) How many students are on each team?

7. Atiba plays for the Linden Woods Vipers in the
   Winnipeg Youth Soccer League.
   The ratio of players to soccer balls at practice
   sessions is 5:2.
   How many soccer balls are needed for 20 players?

8. The word "fun" has a vowel-to-consonant ratio of 1:2.
   a) Find 3 words with a vowel-to-consonant ratio of 2:3.
   b) Choose a vowel-to-consonant ratio and find 3 words for it.

9. Su Mei's recipe for bean salad calls for 3 cans of lima beans, 2 cans of pinto beans, and 1 can of kidney beans. Su Mei is making bean salad for her family reunion. Suppose she uses 9 cans of lima beans.
    a) How many cans of pinto beans will she use?
    b) How many cans of kidney beans will she use?

10. Katherine has diabetes. At each meal, she must estimate the mass in grams of carbohydrates she plans to eat, then inject the appropriate amount of insulin. Katherine needs 1 unit of insulin for 15 g of carbohydrates. Katherine's lunch has 60 g of carbohydrates. How many units of insulin should Katherine inject?

11. To make a jug of plant fertilizer, Malaika uses 6 cups of water and 3 scoops of fertilizer. Bart uses 8 cups of water and 5 scoops of fertilizer. Will Malaika's and Bart's plant fertilizer have the same strength? Explain.

12. Use counters to find all the ratios that are equivalent to 2 : 3 and have a second term that is less than 40. List the ratios.

Math Link

Your World

A contrast ratio is associated with televisions and computer monitors. It is a measure of the difference between the brightest and darkest colours displayed on a screen. A high contrast ratio, such as 800 : 1, delivers a better image than a low contrast ratio, such as 150 : 1.

Reflect

Write two ratios that are equivalent.
Explain how you know they are equivalent.
Write two ratios that are not equivalent.
Explain how you know they are not equivalent.

Strategies Toolkit

Explore

A frog climbed up a tree 20 m tall.
Each day, the frog climbed up 4 m.
Each night, it slid back 2 m.
How many days did it take the frog to climb to the top of the tree?

Solve the problem.
Represent your thinking as many different ways as you can.

Show *and* Share

Share your work with another pair of students.
Compare the ways you represented your thinking.
Which way do you like best? Why?

Connect

Here are some ways to represent your thinking.

Strategies for Success

- Check and reflect.
- Focus on the problem.
- Represent your thinking.
- Explain your thinking.

With words

A written explanation can give lots of information.
You can use math language to describe the steps you
followed, the patterns you noticed, and your ideas.

With a diagram

You can draw a diagram to show important details.
Your diagram can show how you visualized the
problem, what parts changed, or how they changed.

With numbers

You can use numbers to show your thinking in a formal way.
The numbers may be in a table, in calculations, or in equations.

More than one way

Sometimes, the best way to represent your thinking
is with words, diagrams, and numbers.

When you have completed your answer, ask yourself:

Would someone else be able to understand
my thinking by looking at my answer?
What could I add to make my answer more clear?

Practice

Solve each problem. Each time, show
your thinking at least 2 different ways.

Name	Mass	Equipment	Food
Shawn	60 kg	38 kg	25 kg
Martha	56 kg	42 kg	33 kg
Bubba	75 kg	63 kg	35 kg

1. Three hikers want to cross a river
   to get to a campsite on the other shore.
   The boat holds a maximum of 300 kg.
   Describe how the hikers can cross the river
   making the fewest trips.
   Can they do this more than one way? Explain.

2. Suppose a yellow Pattern Block is worth $3.00,
   a red Pattern Block is worth $1.50,
   a blue Pattern Block is worth $1.00,
   and a green Pattern Block is worth $0.50.
   Create 5 different designs that are each worth $10.00.

Reflect

Describe some ways you can represent your thinking.
Give an example of when you might use each way.

Exploring Percents

Suppose a Base Ten flat represents 1 whole.
What fraction does this picture represent?
Which decimal names this amount?

 **Explore** •

You will need Base Ten Blocks.

A group of students was planning to go
hiking in Dinosaur Provincial Park in Alberta.

The students were surveyed to find out
which hike they would most like to take.

Hike	Number of Students
Camel's End Coulee Hike	21
Centrosaurus Bone Bed Hike	24
Great Badlands Hike	33
Fossil Safari Hike	22

➤ How many students are in the group?
   How do you know?
➤ What fraction of the students chose each hike?
➤ How else can you name each amount?
   Use Base Ten Blocks to model each amount.
➤ What fraction of the students did not choose
   the Great Badlands Hike? How did you find out?

Show *and* Share

Compare strategies for renaming each amount with another pair of students.
If you used the same strategy, work together to find a different way.

The hundredths grid represents 1 whole.

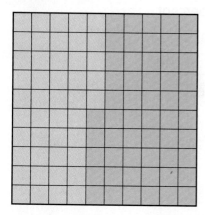

Here are 4 ways to describe the green part of the grid.

➤ Compare the number of green squares to the total number of squares:
45 out of 100 squares are green

➤ Write a fraction.
$\frac{45}{100}$ of the grid is green.

➤ Write a decimal.
0.45 of the grid is green.

➤ Write a **percent**.
45% of the grid is green.
Percent is another name for *hundredths*.

> % is the percent symbol.

A percent is a special ratio that compares a number to 100.
45% means "45 out of 100" or "45 per hundred."

We can describe the blue part of the grid in the same 4 ways.

➤ 55 out of 100 squares are blue.

➤ $\frac{55}{100}$ of the grid is blue.

➤ 0.55 of the grid is blue.

➤ 55% of the grid is blue.

> You read 55% as 55 percent. Percent means "per hundred" or "out of 100."

1. Write:
   - a fraction with hundredths
   - a decimal
   - a percent

   to name the shaded part of each grid.

   a)

   b)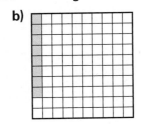

   c)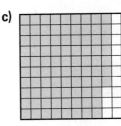

2. Write:
   - a fraction with hundredths
   - a decimal
   - a percent

   to name the unshaded part of each grid in question 1.

3. For each grid in question 1, add the percents you used to name the shaded and unshaded parts.
   What do you notice? Why do you think this happens?

4. Estimate the percent of each grid that is shaded.
   Then count the squares to check.

   a)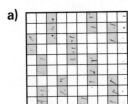

   b)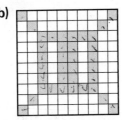

   c)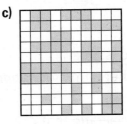

5. Use Base Ten Blocks to show each percent.
   Then write each percent as a decimal.
   a) 84%   b) 17%   c) 25%   d) 100%

6. a) Use a hundredths grid. Colour 20% red, 13% blue, 32% green, and 23% yellow.
   b) Write a fraction to describe the part of the grid that is each colour.
   c) Write a decimal and a percent to describe the part of the grid that is not coloured.

7. a) Use a hundredths grid. Choose a different colour for each hike in *Explore*.
      Colour a section of the grid to show the fraction of students who chose that hike.
   b) Write a percent to describe each section of the grid in part a.

8. Write as a percent. Then write as a decimal.

   a) 64 out of 100
   b) $\frac{50}{100}$
   c) 1 out of 100
   d) $\frac{17}{100}$

9. Write each percent as a fraction with hundredths. Then write as a decimal.

   a) 13%
   b) 5%
   c) 79%
   d) 64%

10. Ninety-seven percent of Earth's water is salt water.
    What percent is fresh water?
    How do you know?

11. The graph shows the water contents of some foods.

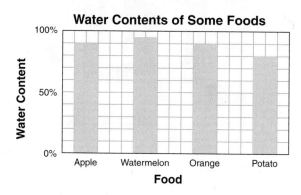

Water Contents of Some Foods

   a) About what percent of each food is water?
   b) About what percent of each food is not water?
   c) Write each percent in the graph as a fraction.

12. Janette bought a portable CD player on sale.
    The regular price was $100. She was charged $89.
    a) What percent of the regular price did Janette pay?
    b) What percent of the regular price did she receive
       as a discount?

13. Salvo said that of the 100 singers in a children's choir
    in Whitehorse, 62% are girls and 48% are boys.
    Is this possible?
    Use words and pictures to explain.

At Home

Reflect

What does percent mean?
Use words and pictures
to explain.

LESSON

Relating Fractions, Decimals, and Percents

How can you describe each part of this design?

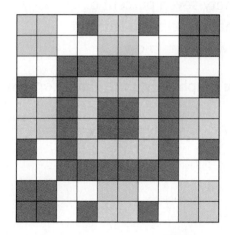

Explore

You will need a 10-cm by 10-cm grid.

➤ Make a design on the grid.
Your design must follow these guidelines:
  • The design must use only 4 colours:
    – orange
    – blue
    – green
    – red
  • At least $\frac{7}{10}$ of the squares must be coloured.
  • At least 4% of the squares must be coloured blue.
  • No more than 8% of the squares can be coloured orange.
  • At least 0.5 of the squares must be coloured green or red.
➤ Describe each colour of your design as a fraction, a decimal, and a percent.

Because of place value, I know I can write a fraction like $\frac{15}{100}$ as 15 hundredths, or 0.15.

Show and Share

Share your design with another pair of students.
How are your designs alike? How are they different?
What is the greatest percent of blank squares
you could have in your design? Explain.

➤ Fractions, decimals, and percents are 3 ways to describe parts of one whole.

A fraction can be written as a decimal or a percent.
A decimal can be written as a fraction or a percent.
A percent can be written as a fraction or a decimal.

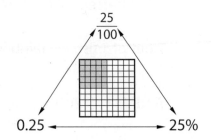

$\frac{25}{100}$

0.25 ◄──────► 25%

You can use a percent to describe any part of one whole.
1 whole = 100%

➤ What percent of this shape is shaded?

$\frac{3}{4}$ of the shape is shaded.

Think: Percent means "out of 100," so we need to write an equivalent fraction with hundredths.

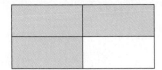

$$\frac{3}{4} = \frac{75}{100} = 75\%$$

$\frac{75}{100}$ is the same as 0.75. So, 0.75 of the shape is shaded.

75% of the shape is shaded.

➤ What percent of this set of counters are yellow?

$\frac{6}{12}$ of the counters are yellow.
$\frac{6}{12} = \frac{1}{2}$
And, $\frac{1}{2} = 0.50 = 50\%$
50% of the counters are yellow.

➤ A fish tank contains rainbow fish and goldfish.
The ratio of rainbow fish to goldfish in the tank is 1 : 4.
What percent of the fish are rainbow fish?

1 out of 5 fish are rainbow fish.

$\frac{1}{5} = 0.20$

And, $0.20 = 20\%$

20% of the fish are rainbow fish.

 Practice

1. Draw Base Ten Blocks or shade a hundredths grid to represent each fraction.
   Write each fraction as a percent and as a decimal.

   a) $\frac{6}{100}$ **b)** $\frac{81}{100}$ **c)** $\frac{17}{50}$ **d)** $\frac{3}{10}$

   e) $\frac{1}{50}$ **f)** $\frac{1}{5}$ **g)** $\frac{7}{20}$ **h)** $\frac{3}{4}$

2. Draw Base Ten Blocks or shade a hundredths grid to represent each decimal.
   Write each decimal as a fraction and as a percent.

   a) 0.97   **b)** 0.03   **c)** 0.16   **d)** 0.5

   e) 0.65   **f)** 0.24   **g)** 0.09   **h)** 0.7

3. Draw Base Ten Blocks or shade a hundredths grid to represent each percent.
   Write each percent as a fraction and as a decimal.

   a) 14%   **b)** 99%   **c)** 25%   **d)** 40%

   e) 35%   **f)** 6%   **g)** 90%   **h)** 15%

4. What percent of each whole is shaded?
   Show how you found your answers.

   a)   **b)**   **c)**

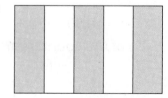

5. What percent of each set is shaded?
Show how you found your answers.

a)

b)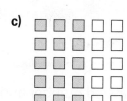

c)

6. Is each fraction greater than or less than 50%?
Explain how you know.

a) $\frac{7}{10}$ b) $\frac{3}{4}$ c) $\frac{11}{25}$ d) $\frac{6}{6}$

7. Luis used a calculator to find a decimal and a percent equal to $\frac{1}{4}$.
How might Luis have done this?

8. Use the data in the table. Is each statement true or false?
Explain how you know.

  a) More than 50% of the audience were adults or seniors.
  b) Of the audience, $\frac{58}{100}$ were children or teens.
  c) More than $\frac{1}{4}$ of the audience were adults.
  d) Less than 0.5 of the audience were teens or adults.

Members of the Audience

Age Group	Percent
Children	13%
Teens	45%
Adults	34%
Seniors	8%

9. Which is least? Which is greatest?
How do you know?

10% $\frac{1}{10}$ 0.01

10. Ravi got 18 out of 20 on a math quiz.
Karli got 85% on the quiz.
Whose mark was greater? How do you know?

11. Write a percent that represents:
  a) a very little of something
  b) almost all of something
  c) a little more than $\frac{3}{4}$ of something
  d) between 0.25 and 0.50 of something
How did you choose each percent?

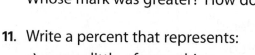

How are fractions, decimals, and percents alike?
How are they different?
Use examples in your explanations.

LESSON

1

1. Use a mixed number and an improper fraction to describe each picture.

   a)

   b)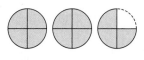

   c)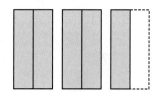

2. Jolene is making a traditional ham dish for Le Banquet de la Cabane à Sucre. She has a $\frac{1}{2}$-cup measuring cup. How many times will Jolene have to fill it to measure $3\frac{1}{2}$ cups of maple syrup? Draw a picture to show your solution.

2

3. Write each mixed number as an improper fraction.

   a) $3\frac{1}{4}$ b) $7\frac{2}{3}$ c) $4\frac{1}{2}$ d) $2\frac{7}{8}$

4. Write each improper fraction as a mixed number.

   a) $\frac{14}{5}$ b) $\frac{17}{8}$ c) $\frac{11}{3}$ d) $\frac{15}{6}$

1
2

5. A class ordered 12-slice pizzas for lunch. The students ate 40 slices.

   a) What is the least number of pizzas the class could have ordered?

   b) Write an improper fraction and a mixed number for the number of pizzas the students ate.

   c) Suppose the least number of pizzas were ordered. Write a fraction for how many pizzas were left over.

2
3

6. You will need triangular dot paper. Use the yellow hexagon Pattern Block to represent one whole.

   a) Draw a picture to show each improper fraction.

   $\frac{7}{3}$ $\frac{11}{6}$ $\frac{9}{2}$ $\frac{10}{3}$

   b) Draw a picture to show each mixed number.

   $2\frac{1}{6}$ $3\frac{2}{3}$ $5\frac{1}{2}$ $4\frac{5}{6}$

   c) Order the improper fractions in part a from least to greatest.

   d) Order the mixed numbers in part b from greatest to least.

1 whole

7. Place each pair of numbers on a number line.
   Which strategy did you use?

   a) $\frac{3}{2}$; $1\frac{1}{2}$ b) $\frac{8}{5}$; $1\frac{7}{10}$ c) $\frac{25}{8}$; $2\frac{3}{4}$

8. Place the numbers in each set on a number line.
   Show your work. List the numbers from least to greatest.

   a) $\frac{9}{2}$, $2\frac{1}{6}$, $\frac{2}{3}$ b) $\frac{7}{2}$, $3\frac{1}{4}$, $\frac{3}{4}$ c) $\frac{7}{20}$, $1\frac{1}{4}$, $\frac{15}{10}$

9. In a punch, 2 cups of orange juice are mixed
   with 3 cups of ginger ale.

   a) Use grid paper.
      Draw a diagram to show this ratio.

   b) How much ginger ale is needed for
      10 cups of orange juice?

   c) How much orange juice is needed for
      21 cups of ginger ale?

10. a) Write as many ratios as you can for the buttons.
       Explain what each ratio means.

    b) Suppose you doubled the number
       of each colour of buttons.
       What would the ratio 40 : 16 describe?

11. What percent of the buttons in question 10 are red?

12. Use a hundredths grid.
    a) Colour the grid so 14% is green, 45% is yellow,
       17% is blue, and the rest is red.
    b) Write a fraction with hundredths and a decimal
       to describe each colour of the grid.
    c) What percent of the grid is red?

13. Conner got 23 out of 25 on a spelling test.
    Rose got 88% on the test.
    Whose mark was greater? How do you know?

UNIT

5 Learning Goals

- ✓ relate improper fractions to mixed numbers
- ✓ compare mixed numbers and fractions
- ✓ use ratios for part-to-part and part-to-whole comparisons
- ✓ explore equivalent ratios
- ✓ explore percents
- ✓ relate percents to fractions and decimals

Dr. Cowper plans to open a new animal clinic in Winnipeg, Manitoba.
You have been hired to design the floor plan for the clinic.

You will need a ruler, 1-cm grid paper, and coloured pencils or markers.

The floor plan must follow these guidelines:

➤ The floor can be of any shape, but it must have an area of 100 square units.
➤ The plan must include:
  – a waiting room and reception area
  – an x-ray room
  – two exam rooms
  – an operating room
  – a kennel room
  – a washroom
  – a grooming room
➤ The operating room should be $1\frac{1}{2}$ times the size of the x-ray room.
➤ The kennel room and grooming room together should occupy 40% of the floor plan.
➤ The exam rooms should occupy $\frac{1}{5}$ of the floor plan.
➤ The ratio of the area of the washroom to the area of the grooming room should be 2:5.

Draw the floor plan on grid paper.
Colour and label each room or section of the floor plan.
Use a table to show the floor space of each room or section as a fraction, decimal, and percent of the entire floor.

Room or Section	Fraction	Decimal	Percent

Include calculations to show how your plan meets the design guidelines.

Reflect on Your Learning

Look back at the Learning Goals.
Which learning goal was easiest for you?
Which was most difficult?
Justify your choices.

UNIT 6

Geometry and

Puzzle Mania!

Learning Goals

- construct and compare triangles
- describe and compare regular and irregular polygons
- develop formulas for the perimeters of polygons, the area of a rectangle, and the volume of a rectangular prism

These pictures are ancient Egyptian characters called *hieroglyphs*.

Measurement

Over 2000 years ago, the Egyptians carved the same message in stone in different languages, including hieroglyphics and Greek.

By comparing the texts, scholars were able to solve the puzzle of Egyptian hieroglyphics.

Key Words

- equilateral triangle
- isosceles triangle
- scalene triangle
- acute triangle
- right triangle
- obtuse triangle
- non-polygon
- regular polygon
- irregular polygon
- convex polygon
- concave polygon
- congruent
- formula

- Which hieroglyphs resemble polygons?
- Which polygons do they resemble? What do you know about each polygon you identify?
- Which hieroglyphs are not polygons? How do you know?

Exploring Triangles

Which sorting rules can you use to sort these shapes?

Explore

You will need 9 toothpicks, a ruler, a protractor, and scissors.

➤ Use at most 9 toothpicks. Make a triangle on paper.

➤ Mark a dot at each vertex of the triangle.

➤ Remove the toothpicks.
Use a ruler to draw the triangle.

➤ Are there any equal sides? Equal angles?
Record your findings.

➤ Repeat the activity to draw at least
5 different triangles. Cut out the triangles.

➤ Choose a sorting rule. Sort the triangles.

Show and Share

Trade your sorted triangles with another group of students.
Identify the rule for your classmates' sorting.
Did you use the same rule to sort? Explain.
What else do you notice about the triangles?

Connect

➤ We can:
  • Use a ruler to measure the side lengths of a triangle.
  • Use a protractor to measure the angles in a triangle.
  • Fold a triangle, or use a Mira to find the lines of symmetry in a triangle.

So, we can use these attributes to sort triangles.

➤ We can name triangles according to how their side lengths compare.

An equilateral triangle has 3 equal sides.

An isosceles triangle has 2 equal sides.

A scalene triangle has no equal sides.

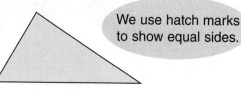
We use hatch marks to show equal sides.

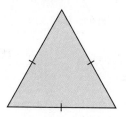

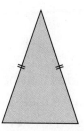

➤ Here are some other attributes of triangles.

• An equilateral triangle has 3 equal angles and 3 lines of symmetry.
   Since the sum of the angles in a triangle is 180°, each angle measure is: 180° ÷ 3 = 60°
   All equilateral triangles have angle measures of 60°.

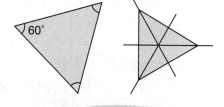

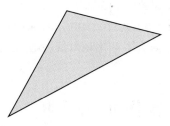
We use matching arcs to show equal angles.

• An isosceles triangle has 2 equal angles and 1 line of symmetry.

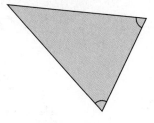

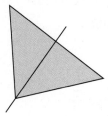

• A scalene triangle has no equal angles and no lines of symmetry.

Practice

1. Name each triangle as isosceles, equilateral, or scalene.
   How did you decide which name to use?

a)

b)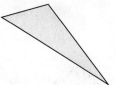

c)

d)

2. **a)** Which triangles are isosceles? How do you know?

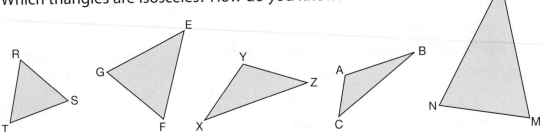

  b) For each isosceles triangle, name the sides that have the same length, and the angles that have the same measure.
  c) Which triangle is equilateral? How do you know?
  d) Which triangle is not isosceles and not equilateral? Which type of triangle is it?

3. Use a geoboard, geobands, and square dot paper.
  a) Make 3 different scalene triangles.
    Record each triangle on dot paper.
    How do you know each triangle is scalene?
  b) Make 3 different isosceles triangles.
    Record each triangle on dot paper.
    How do you know each triangle is isosceles?
  c) Try to make an equilateral triangle.
    What do you notice?

4. Work with a partner.
  a) Look around you. Find 2 examples of:
    • a scalene triangle   • an isosceles triangle   • an equilateral triangle
    Sketch each triangle. Describe where you found it.
  b) Which type of triangle was easiest to find? Why might this be?

5. Here is the truss of the Burrard Street Bridge in Vancouver, BC.
  Which types of triangles do you see in the truss? How could you check?

6. Your teacher will give you a large copy of these triangles.

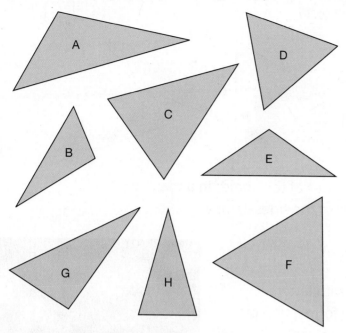

a) List the attributes of each triangle.
b) Sort the triangles by the number of equal sides.
c) Sort the triangles by the number of equal angles.
d) What do you notice about your sortings?

7. Identify each triangle as equilateral, isosceles, or scalene.
Which strategy did you use?

a) 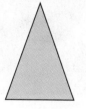 b)   c)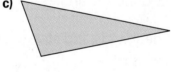

8. You will need drinking straws, a ruler, scissors, and pipe cleaners.
Cut the straws into 8 pieces as shown. Use pieces of pipe cleaner as joiners.

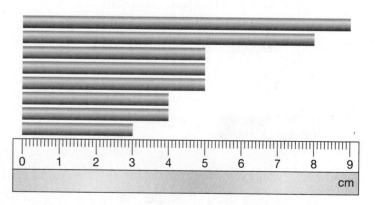

a) Make each triangle.
Trace and label your results.
• an equilateral triangle
• an isosceles triangle with the least perimeter
• a scalene triangle with the greatest perimeter

b) Which straws could not be used together to make a triangle? Explain.

Perimeter is the distance around a shape.

9. a) Name each triangle as scalene, isosceles, or equilateral.
Explain your choice each time.

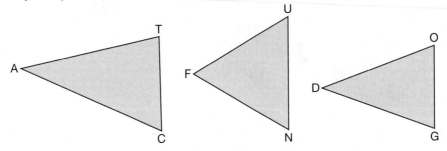

b) How can you use the measures of the angles in a triangle to predict how the lengths of the sides compare?

10. Your teacher will give you a copy of this picture of the Orion constellation.
The brightest stars are labelled with letters.

a) Connect points C, D, and F to form a triangle.
Which type of triangle did you form?
How do you know?

b) Connect points F, H, and J to form a triangle.
Which type of triangle did you form?
How do you know?

c) Which points would you connect to form an equilateral triangle?
Check by measuring the angles.

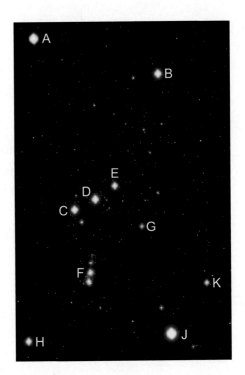

11. Use a geoboard, geobands, and square dot paper.

a) Make an isosceles triangle.
Draw the triangle on dot paper.

b) Use the triangle from part a.
Change the triangle so it is scalene.
Describe the changes you made.

Reflect

Explain how you remember how many equal sides each of these triangles has.
• an equilateral triangle
• an isosceles triangle
• a scalene triangle

LESSON

2

Naming and Sorting Triangles by Angles

Name each angle in △XYZ as acute, right, or obtuse.
What strategy did you use to find out?
What is the sum of the angles in the triangle?

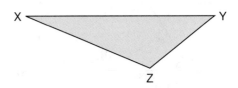

 **Explore**

You will need a protractor and scissors.
Your teacher will give you a large copy of these triangles.

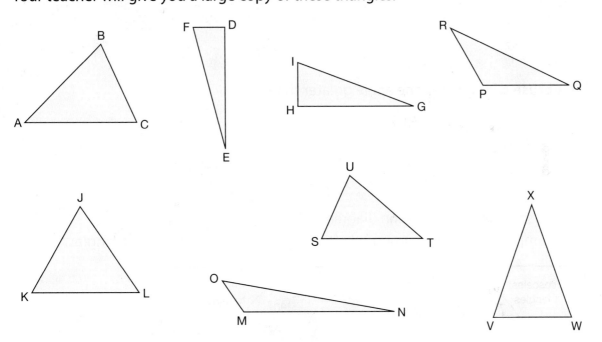

➤ Measure the angles in each triangle.
   Record the angle measures.
➤ Cut out the triangles. Choose a sorting rule, then sort the triangles.
   How are the triangles in each group the same? How are they different?

Show and Share

Trade your sorted triangles with another group of students.
Identify the rule for your classmates' sorting.
Did you sort the triangles the same way? Explain.

LESSON FOCUS | Name and sort triangles by types of angles.

205

➤ We can name triangles by the types of interior angles.
An **acute triangle** has all angles less than 90°.

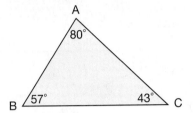

A **right triangle** has one 90° angle.

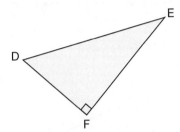

An **obtuse triangle** has one angle greater than 90°.

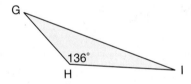

➤ We can sort triangles in a Venn diagram.
For example, choose the sorting rule "Isosceles triangles" and "Acute triangles."

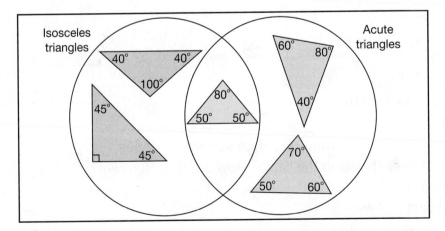

The triangles in the left loop have 2 equal angles.
The triangles in the right loop have all angles less than 90°.
The triangle in the overlap has 2 equal angles and all angles less than 90°.

1. Use a geoboard, geobands, and square dot paper.

   a) Make 3 different acute triangles.
      Draw each triangle on dot paper.
      How do you know each triangle is acute?

   b) Make 3 different obtuse triangles.
      Draw each triangle on dot paper.
      How do you know each triangle is obtuse?

   c) Make 3 different right triangles.
      Draw each triangle on dot paper.
      How do you know each triangle is right?

2. a) Predict whether each triangle is an acute,
      an obtuse, or a right triangle.
      How did you make your prediction?

   b) Use a protractor. Measure the angles in each triangle.
      Name each triangle as an acute, an obtuse, or a right triangle.

   c) Were your predictions correct? Explain.

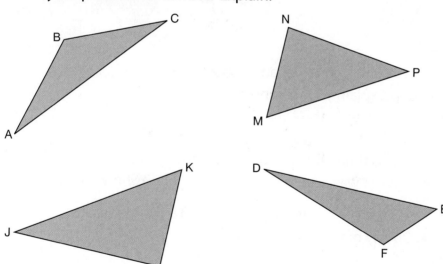

3. Akna drew these triangles. He noticed
   there were at least two acute angles
   in each triangle he drew.
   Akna made this conclusion: "All triangles
   must have at least two acute angles."
   Do you agree?
   Why or why not?

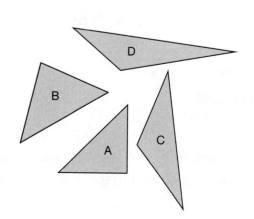

4. Is each statement true or false?
   Use pictures, words, or numbers to explain your thinking.
   a) A triangle can have more than one obtuse angle.
   b) A triangle can have only one 90° angle.
   c) A triangle can have 3 acute angles.

5. You will need scissors and a large copy of these triangles.

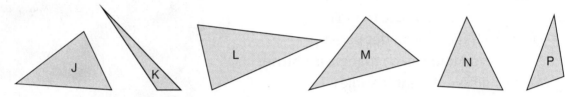

Cut out the triangles.
Sort the triangles as acute, obtuse, or right triangles.
How did you decide where to place each triangle?

6. You will need scissors and a large copy of these triangles.
   Cut out the triangles.

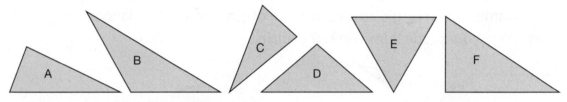

   a) Sort the triangles in a Venn diagram with 2 loops.
   Label each loop. Explain your sorting rule.
   Are there any triangles in the overlap?
   If there are, what attributes do these triangles have?
   b) Repeat part a. This time, choose a different sorting rule.
   How many different ways can you sort the triangles? Show your work.

7. Sort the triangles in question 6 using a Venn diagram with 3 loops.
   Record your work. Do any of the loops overlap?
   Why or why not?

8. **a)** Can an obtuse triangle be an equilateral triangle? Explain.
   b) Can a right triangle be an isosceles triangle? Explain.

Reflect

How many different ways can you describe a triangle?
Draw a triangle and describe it as many ways as you can.

Drawing Triangles

We can use a protractor to draw an angle.
What steps would you take to draw a 45° angle?

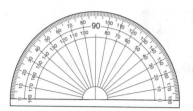

Explore

You will need rulers and protractors.

➤ Each group member chooses 2 triangles from the list:
  • acute
  • obtuse
  • right
  • scalene
  • isosceles
  • equilateral

➤ Draw each triangle you chose.

➤ Trade triangles with another group member.
  Identify each triangle.

LESSON FOCUS | Construct a specified triangle.

209

Show *and* Share

Compare your strategies for drawing with those of the others in your group.
How did you create each triangle?
How did you identify your group members' triangles?

Connect ·

We can use a ruler and a protractor to construct a triangle.

Construct scalene △MNP.
The length of MN is 4.5 cm.
The measure of ∠M is 40°.
The length of MP is 3.7 cm.

Step 1 Sketch the triangle first. Label each side and angle. This sketch is *not* accurate.	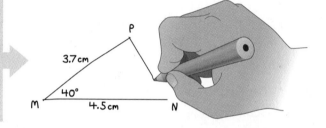
Step 2 Use a ruler to draw side MN 4.5 cm long.	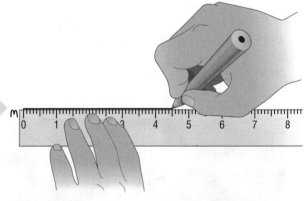
Step 3 Place the baseline of the protractor on MN, with its centre at M. From 0° on the inner circle, measure an angle of 40° at M.	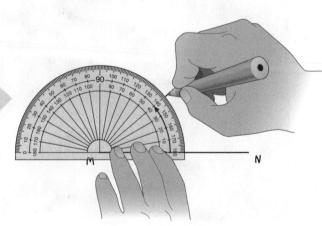

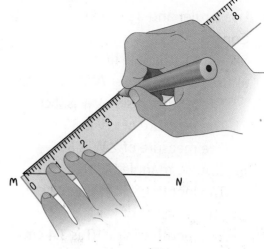

Step 4
Remove the protractor.
Join M to the mark at 40°.
Measure 3.7 cm from M.
Mark the point P.

Step 5
Use a ruler to join P to N
to form side NP.
Label the triangle with its measures.

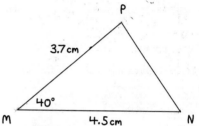

1. Use either or both of these tools: ruler and protractor
   • Construct each triangle listed below.
   • Explain how you know you have drawn that triangle.
   a) an acute triangle
   b) an equilateral triangle
   c) an isosceles triangle
   d) an obtuse triangle
   e) a right triangle
   f) a scalene triangle

2. Use a ruler and a protractor.
   Construct a triangle with angles 40°, 60°, and 80°.
   Compare your triangle with that of a classmate.
   Do your triangles match?
   How could you find out?

3. Use a ruler and a protractor.
    Construct each triangle.
    Sketch the triangle first.

    a) Isosceles triangle VWX
       The length of side VW is 7 cm.
       The measure of ∠V is 80°.
       The measure of ∠W is 50°.
    b) Obtuse triangle RST
       The length of side TS is 5.2 cm.
       The measure of ∠T is 30°.
       The length of side RT is 3.4 cm.
    Label each triangle with the measures of all the sides and angles.

4. You will need drinking straws, a ruler, scissors, and pipe cleaners.
    Cut the straws into 9 pieces as shown.

    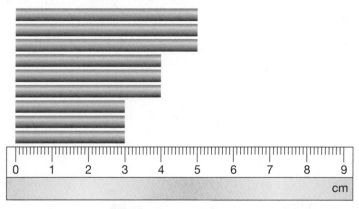

    Use pieces of pipe cleaner as joiners.
    Use combinations of 3 or more straws to make each triangle.
    Trace each triangle.
    Label each triangle with the measures of all the sides and angles.
    a) an isosceles triangle that is also an acute triangle
    b) an isosceles triangle that is also an obtuse triangle
    c) two different equilateral triangles
    d) two different right triangles

5. Use a geoboard and geobands.
    Construct a triangle with two 45° angles.
    Record your work on square dot paper.
    Do this 3 times to construct 3 different triangles.
    a) How are the triangles the same?
       How are the triangles different?
    b) What kind of triangle did you make?
       Give a different name to describe the triangle.

6. Construct a triangle that has one angle that measures 55°
   and one angle that measures 35°.
   What kind of triangle did you make?
   Give a different name to describe the triangle.

7. Construct a triangle that has one angle that measures 60° and
   one angle that measures 45°.
   a) What is the measure of the third angle?
   b) What kind of triangle did you make?
      How do you know?
   c) How else can you name the triangle?

8. A student said he had drawn △ABC with these measures:
   • AB = 4.2 cm
   • ∠A = 90°
   • ∠B = 95°
   Was the student correct?
   How do you know?

9. Construct isosceles △GHK.
   The measure of ∠H is 120°.
   Choose side lengths for HG and HK
   so that △GHK is isosceles.
   a) What are the measures of ∠G and ∠K?
      How long is side GK?
   b) Suppose side HG is longer.
      The length of side HK does not change.
      What happens to the measure of ∠K?
      What happens to the length of side GK?
   Show your work.

At Home

Reflect

Name the 6 types of triangles you know.
Which of them do you find
easiest to draw?
Explain why.

Look for triangles in your home.
They could be pictures of
triangles or objects with
triangular faces.
Name each triangle 2 ways.
Choose 1 triangle. Draw it.

Investigating Polygons

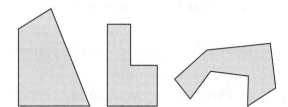

What do we call a polygon with 4 sides?
With 6 sides? With 8 sides?

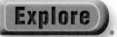

You will need a ruler and a protractor.
Your teacher will give you a large copy of these shapes.

Mystery Sort!
Set 1: All of these shapes have the same attribute.

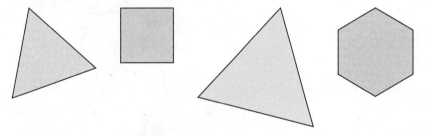

Set 2: None of these shapes has that attribute.

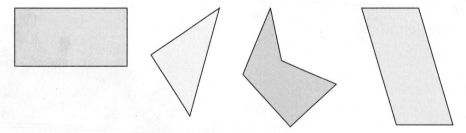

Set 3: Which of these shapes have that attribute?

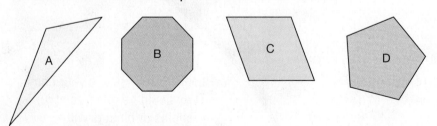

Which attribute do the shapes in Set 1 share?

Show *and* Share

Share your results with another pair of students.
Did you find the same attribute?
If not, check that both attributes are correct.
How did you decide which shapes in Set 3 have the attribute?
Which other shapes could you place in Set 1? Explain.

Connect

A polygon is a closed shape with sides that are straight line segments.
Exactly 2 sides meet at a vertex. The sides intersect only at the vertices.

This shape is a polygon.   These shapes are **non-polygons**.

               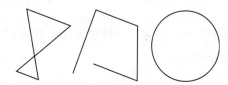

A **regular polygon** has all sides equal and all angles equal.
These polygons are regular.

A regular polygon has line symmetry.
A regular hexagon has 6 lines of symmetry.

Math Link

Your World

A *parfleche* is a container used by the Plains people
to carry dried meat, clothing, tools, and other goods.
It is usually made from buffalo hide, then painted with
a design. The design represents a particular band,
and is passed down from generation to generation.
Which polygons do you see in the design on this
parfleche of the Crow Nation?

An **irregular polygon** does not have all sides equal and all angles equal.
These polygons are irregular.

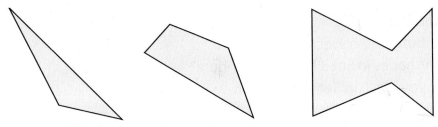

A **convex polygon** has all angles less than 180°.
These polygons are convex.

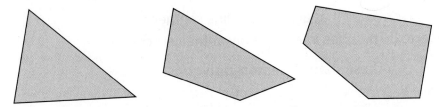

A **concave polygon** has at least one angle greater than 180°.
These polygons are concave.

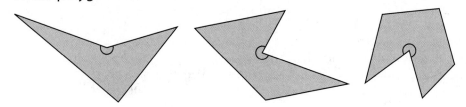

 Practice •

1. Explain why each shape is not a polygon.

   a)   b)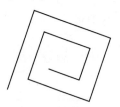

2. Is each polygon regular? How do you know?

   a) 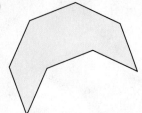   b) 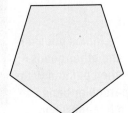   c)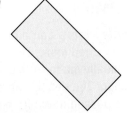

3. A cell in a honeycomb approximates a regular hexagon.
   a) Suppose ∠A = 120°. What are the measures of angles B, C, D, E, and F?
   b) Suppose side AB has length 9 cm.
      What are the lengths of sides BC, CD, DE, EF, and FA?

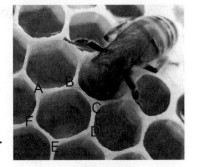

4. Your teacher will give you a large copy of these shapes.
   a) Sort these shapes into sets of polygons and non-polygons. Explain how you decided where to place each shape.

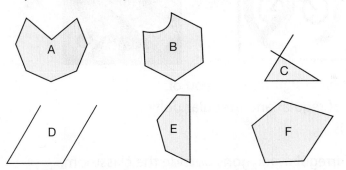

   b) Draw a different shape that belongs in each set.
      Explain how you know that it belongs.

5. Your teacher will give you a large copy of these polygons.

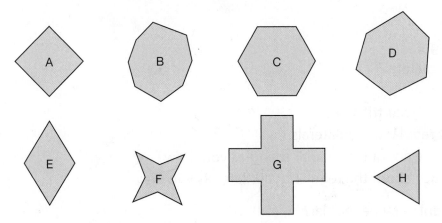

   a) Which polygons appear to be regular?
   b) How can you check that the polygons you identified in part a are regular? Use your strategy to check.
   c) Sort the polygons into sets of regular and irregular polygons.
   d) For each set in part c, draw a different polygon that belongs in that set.
   e) Sort the polygons into sets of convex and concave polygons.
   f) For each set in part e, draw a different polygon that belongs in that set.

6. Your teacher will give you a large copy of these road signs.

   a) Name the polygon that each sign reminds you of.
   b) Sort the signs into sets of regular and irregular polygons.
      Explain how you did this.

7. a) Find at least 3 different irregular polygons outside the classroom.
      Describe each polygon you find.
   b) Find at least 3 different regular polygons outside the classroom.
      Describe each polygon you find.
      Name each polygon.

8. a) What do we call:
      • a regular triangle?
      • a regular quadrilateral?
   b) Use dot paper.
      Draw 3 different regular triangles.
      Draw 3 different regular quadrilaterals.
   c) What do you notice about the regular triangles you drew?
      What do you notice about the regular quadrilaterals you drew?

9. Can a concave quadrilateral be regular?
   Explain.

Reflect

List the attributes of a regular polygon.
Which strategy do you prefer to use to check whether a polygon
is regular or irregular?
Explain your choice.

Congruence in Regular Polygons

Do these shapes match?
How could you find out?

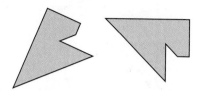

Explore ·

You will need tracing paper, a protractor, and a millimetre ruler.
Your teacher will give you a large copy of these polygons.

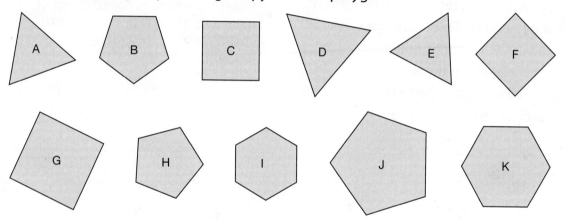

➤ Identify pairs of polygons that match.
How do you know that they match?

➤ Choose a pair of matching polygons.
Measure and record their side lengths.
Measure and record their angles.
Repeat these measures for other pairs of matching polygons.

➤ What do you notice about the side lengths and angle measures
of matching polygons? Explain.

Show *and* Share

Share your work with another pair of students.
Check that you found the same pairs of matching polygons.
What other strategy could you use to tell if two polygons match?

When polygons match exactly, the polygons are **congruent**.
Here are two ways to show that these pentagons are congruent.

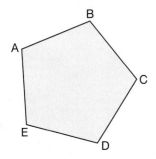

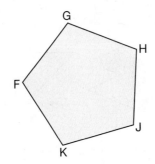

➤ Place one pentagon on top of the other.
If they match exactly, they are congruent.
You may need to flip or turn the shapes
to show they are congruent.
If you cannot move the pentagons:
Trace one pentagon, then place the tracing
on top of the other pentagon.

> When one shape is placed on top of
> another and the two shapes match
> exactly, we say they *coincide*. One
> shape is *superimposed* on the other.

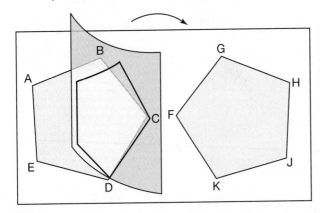

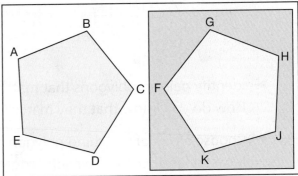

➤ Measure and record the lengths of all the sides.
Measure and record all the angle measures.

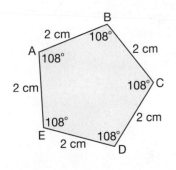

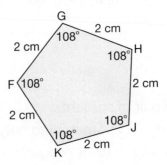

Compare the measures.

All sides have the same length.

AB = BC = CD = DE = EA = FG = GH = HJ = JK = KF

All angles have the same measure.

$\angle A = \angle B = \angle C = \angle D = \angle E = \angle F = \angle G = \angle H = \angle J = \angle K$

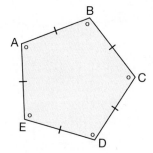
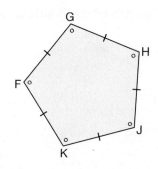

In pentagons ABCDE and FGHJK, all sides are equal and all angles are equal.
So, the pentagons are congruent.

We say: "Pentagon ABCDE is congruent to pentagon FGHJK."
We write: ABCDE ≅ FGHJK

Here is a regular octagon.
We can use a tracing of the octagon to show that all sides are equal and all angles are equal.

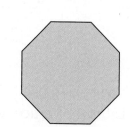

➤ Trace the octagon.
  Place the tracing to coincide with the octagon.
  Each angle in the tracing fits exactly over an angle in the original octagon.
  Each side in the tracing fits exactly over a side in the original octagon.

  Rotate the tracing until the octagons coincide again.
  Keep rotating until you have checked every side and every angle.
  Then you know that all the angles are congruent, and all the sides are congruent.

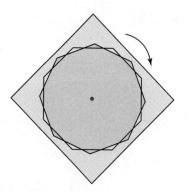

1. Quadrilaterals DEFG and JKMN are congruent.
   a) Without using a protractor, write the measure of each angle in JKMN.
   b) Without using a ruler, write the length of each side in JKMN.

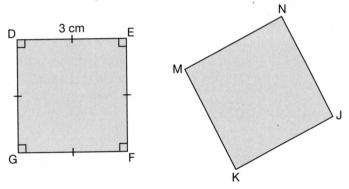

2. Which of these polygons are congruent?
   How can you tell?

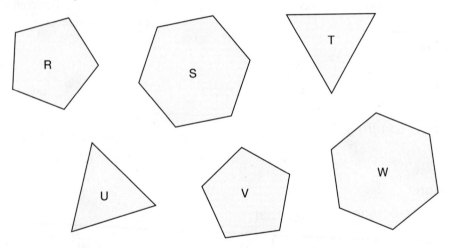

3. a) Use tracing paper. Trace hexagon HJKLMN on paper.
   Label the vertices of the traced hexagon UVWXYZ.

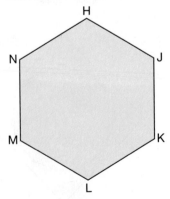

   b) Find the side lengths and angle measures of both hexagons.
   What do you notice?

4. Your teacher will give you a large copy of these polygons. Use whatever materials you need.

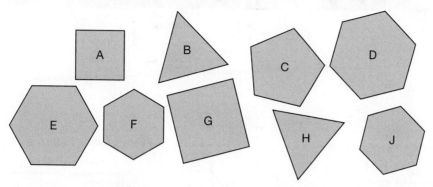

   a) Which pairs of polygons have corresponding angles congruent? Which strategy did you use to find out?
   b) Which pairs of polygons have corresponding sides congruent? Which strategy did you use to find out?
   c) Which pairs of polygons in parts a and b are congruent? How did you decide?
   Show your work.

5. Work with a partner. You will need tracing paper and a ruler. Each of you draws a triangle. Use tracing paper to draw 2 exact copies of the triangle in different orientations. Trade triangles with your partner. Check that your partner's triangles are congruent. Which strategy did you use to check?

6. Draw a regular hexagon on triangular dot paper. Use measuring and superimposing to show that all angles are congruent and all sides are congruent. Show your work.

7. A student drew a rectangle on grid paper. The student said, "Since all the angles measure 90°, the angles are congruent. So, the rectangle is a regular quadrilateral." Do you agree? Why or why not?

Reflect

What does it mean when we say two regular polygons are congruent? Include diagrams in your explanation.

Strategies Toolkit

Explore

You will need square dot paper.
Cerise and René have a square.
They draw diagonals to divide the square into triangles.
How many triangles will they make?
Are any of the triangles congruent? Explain.
Which types of triangles are made?

Show *and* Share

Describe the strategy you used to solve the problem.

Connect

➤ Josette has a convex octagon.
She draws all of its diagonals.
How many diagonals
did Josette draw?

What do you know?

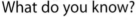

- An octagon has 8 sides.
- A diagonal is a line segment that joins
2 vertices of a polygon, but is not a side
of the polygon.

Think of a strategy to help you solve the
problem.

- You can **solve a simpler problem**,
then **extend a table**.

➤ Draw a convex quadrilateral.
Draw its diagonals.
Two diagonals are drawn.

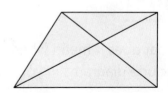

Strategies

- **Make a table.**

- **Solve a simpler problem.**
- **Guess and test.**
- **Make an organized list.**
- **Use a pattern.**

➤ Draw a convex pentagon.
  Draw its diagonals.
  Five diagonals are drawn.

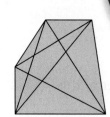

➤ Draw a convex hexagon.
  Draw its diagonals.
  Nine diagonals are drawn.

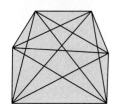

➤ Record your work in a table.

Shape	Number of Sides	Number of Diagonals
Quadrilateral	4	2
Pentagon	5	5
Hexagon	6	9

How many diagonals are in an octagon?
Extend the pattern in the number of diagonals column.
To check your answer, sketch the octagon.
Then draw the diagonals.

Practice

Choose one of the

Strategies

1. Draw three different polygons.
   Each polygon should have 5 diagonals.
   Which strategy did you use?

2. Draw a polygon with 2 diagonals
   so that the triangles formed are:
   • 4 congruent right triangles
   • 2 pairs of congruent isosceles triangles
   What shape have you drawn?

Reflect

Choose one of the *Practice* questions above.
Describe how you solved it.

Perimeters of Polygons

What is the perimeter of this quadrilateral?

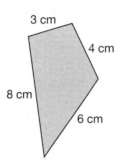

3 cm

4 cm

8 cm

6 cm

Explore

You will need geoboards, geobands, dot paper, and rulers.
Share the work.

Make 15 different polygons.
Make sure there are at least two of
each of these types of polygons:
- square
- rectangle
- parallelogram
- rhombus
- triangle

Record each polygon on dot paper.
Find the perimeter of each polygon.
For which types of polygons
can you write a rule to calculate
the perimeter? Write these rules.

Show and Share

Share your rules with another group of students.
Compare your rules. Discuss any differences.
For which types of polygons is it possible to write
more than one rule? Explain.

Perimeter is the distance around a polygon.
You discovered that we can use rules to find the perimeter of polygons.
For this hexagon:

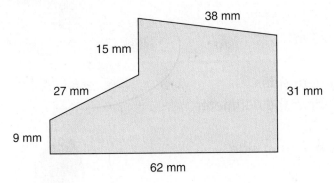

Perimeter = 38 + 31 + 62 + 9 + 27 + 15
          = 182

The perimeter of this hexagon is 182 mm.

Our rule is, for any polygon, we can find the perimeter by adding the side lengths.

We can also develop rules that apply to specific polygons.
➤ Here is Katy's way to find the perimeter of this square.

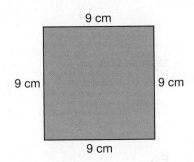

My rule was the same but I used a letter for the side length. I wrote $P = 4\ell$.

Perimeter = 9 + 9 + 9 + 9
          = 4 × 9
          = 36

The perimeter of this square is 36 cm.

A square has 4 equal sides.
Katy says this suggests a rule for finding the perimeter of any square:
Multiply the side length by 4.

➤ Here is Graeme's way to find the perimeter of this parallelogram.

Perimeter = 6 + 4 + 6 + 4
$\qquad$ = (6 + 4) + (6 + 4)
$\qquad$ = 2 × (6 + 4)
$\qquad$ = 2 × 10
$\qquad$ = 20

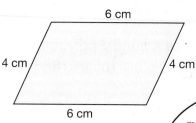

The perimeter of this parallelogram is 20 m.

A parallelogram has two pairs of congruent sides. Graeme says this suggests a rule for finding the perimeter of any parallelogram:
Add the measures of a longer side and a shorter side, then multiply by 2.

A rule for finding the perimeter of any parallelogram is:
Perimeter = 2 × (ℓ + s)

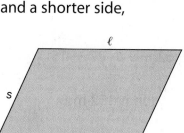

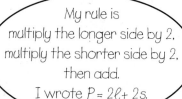

My rule is multiply the longer side by 2, multiply the shorter side by 2, then add.
I wrote P = 2ℓ + 2s.

➤ We can use these **formulas** to find the perimeter of the parallelogram below.

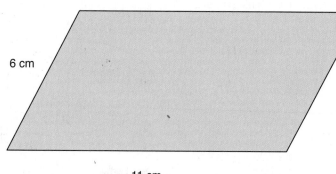

A *formula* is a short way to state a rule.

$P = 2 \times (\ell + s)$ $\qquad\qquad$ $P = 2\ell + 2s$

We replace each variable ℓ and s with the given side lengths.

When we replace a variable with a number, we *substitute*.

$P = 2 \times (11 + 6)$ $\qquad\qquad$ $P = 2(11) + 2(6)$
$\quad = 2 \times 17$ $\qquad\qquad\qquad\quad = 22 + 12$
$\quad = 34$ $\qquad\qquad\qquad\qquad\quad = 34$

The perimeter of this parallelogram is 34 cm.

We can check by adding the lengths of the 4 sides:
11 cm + 6 cm + 11 cm + 6 cm = 34 cm
This is the same as the answers we got using the formulas.

1. Find the perimeter of each polygon.

   a)
   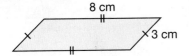
   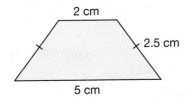

   b)
   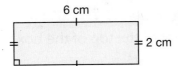
   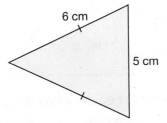

   c)
   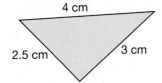

   d)
   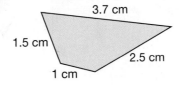

2. Describe the strategy you used to find the perimeter of each polygon in question 1.

3. Find the perimeter of each polygon.

   a)

   b)

   Can you write a rule to find the perimeter of each of these polygons? Why or why not?

4. Use Pattern Blocks like those below.

   Write a rule to find the perimeter of each Pattern Block.

5. Aldo wants to install a skylight in the roof of his house. The base of the skylight is a regular hexagon with side length 40 cm. What is the perimeter of the base of the skylight? Give your answer in metres.
   Which strategy did you use to find out?

6. Winnie is building a hexagonal storage box.
   Here is a drawing of the top of the box.
   a) Write a rule to find the perimeter of the top
      of the box.
   b) Write the rule as a formula.
   c) What is the perimeter of the top of the box?

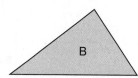

7. a) Find the perimeter of each polygon.

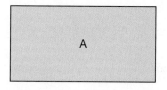

   b) Suppose the side lengths of each polygon are doubled.
      What would happen to each perimeter? Explain.

8. Your teacher will give you a large copy of these regular polygons.

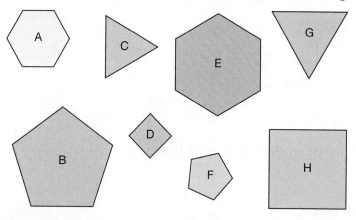

   a) Find and record the perimeter of each polygon.
   b) How is the perimeter of a regular polygon related
      to the number of its sides?
      Write a formula to find the perimeter of a regular polygon.

9. Saki has a remote control car. She enters her car in a race.
   The track is close to rectangular.
   a) Use a formula to find the perimeter of the track.
   b) Suppose the car completes 8 laps.
      How far did the car travel?

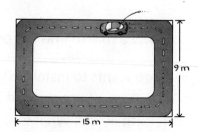

Reflect

How are the side lengths of a polygon and its perimeter related?
Use examples to explain.

LESSON

8

Area of a Rectangle

What is the area of this rectangle?
How did you find out?

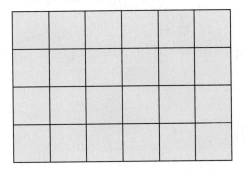

Explore

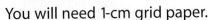

You will need 1-cm grid paper.
➤ Draw a 2-cm by 3-cm rectangle.
  Find the area of the rectangle.
➤ Suppose the length of the rectangle doubles.
  Predict the area of the new rectangle.
  Check your prediction.
➤ Suppose the width of the original rectangle
  doubles. Predict the area of the new rectangle.
  Check your prediction.
➤ Suppose both the length and the width double.
  Predict the area of the new rectangle.
  Check your prediction.
➤ How does the area of each new rectangle
  compare to the area of the original rectangle?
➤ Write a rule to calculate the area of a rectangle.
  Write the rule as a formula.
  Use the formula to check the area of the rectangles you drew.

Show *and* Share

Share your work with another pair of students.
Compare your formulas.
What do you think happens to the area of a rectangle when the
length triples? The width triples? Both the length and the width triple?
How could you use your formula to find out?

LESSON FOCUS | Develop and apply a formula to determine the area of a rectangle.

231

We can find a shortcut for calculating the area of a rectangle.

Measure the length of the rectangle.

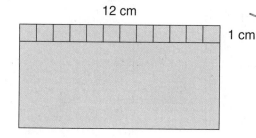

The length tells how many 1-cm squares fit along it. The length is 12 cm. So, twelve 1-cm squares fit along the length.

Measure the width of the rectangle.

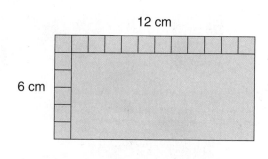

The width tells how many rows of 1-cm squares fit in the rectangle. The width is 6 cm, so there are 6 rows.

Multiply the length by the width.
$12 \times 6 = 72$
So, the area of the rectangle is 72 cm².

To find how many 1-cm squares fit in the rectangle, we multiply the length of a row by the number of rows.

We can write this rule:
To find the area of a rectangle, multiply the length by the width.

 This rule can be expressed as a formula.

Area = length × width
$A = \ell \times w$

We use: *A* to represent area, ℓ to represent length, and *w* to represent width.

Edmond built a dog crate for his dog.
The floor of the crate is a rectangle.
The dimensions of the floor are 80 cm by 120 cm.

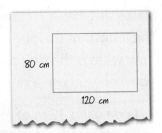

➤ You can use the formula for the area of a rectangle
to find the floor area of the crate.

$A = \ell \times w$
$\quad = 120 \times 80$
$\quad = 9600$

The floor area of the crate is 9600 cm².

Practice

1. Find the area of each rectangle.

   a)
   3 cm

   5 cm

   b)
   18 mm

   10 mm

   c)
   15 m

   7 m

2. Which rectangle below do you think has the greatest area?
   Estimate first. Use a formula to check.
   Order the areas from least to greatest.
   How does the order compare with your prediction?

   a)
   0.8 km

   1 km

   b)
   2 km

   0.5 km

   c)
   0.7 km

   1 km

3. Copy and complete this chart.

Rectangle	Length (cm)	Width (cm)	Area (cm²)
A	7	5	?
B	?	6	12.6
C	3	?	13.5
D	5.3	7	?

   Which strategy did you use to find the missing number each time?

4. Matt's dog has a rectangular dog run.
   The length of the dog run is 8 m. The total area enclosed is 56 m².
   How wide is the dog run? Draw a diagram.
   How can you use a number sentence to show your thinking?

5. Lena used 36 m of fencing to enclose a rectangular vegetable
   garden on her farm in Battleford, Saskatchewan.
   a) Sketch some possible rectangles and label their side lengths.
      What is the area of the enclosed section in each case?
   b) How many different answers can you find?

6. A banner for the Vancouver 2010 Olympics has length 226 cm
   and width 72 cm. What is the area of the banner?

7. Hailey bought a can of stain. The stain will cover
   50 m² of fencing. The fence has height 2 m.
   What length of fencing can Hailey stain before she
   runs out of stain? How did you find out?

8. A square has side length *s*.

   s

   Write a formula for the area of a square.

9. The Festival du Voyageur is a winter festival that
   takes place in St. Boniface, Manitoba, each February.
   The festival's logo contains a red rectangle.
   Suppose the logo is enlarged so the rectangle
   has width 4 cm and area 28.8 cm².
   What is the length of the rectangle?
   How did you find out?

10. Rectangle A has area 40 cm² and length 8 cm.
    The area of Rectangle B is one-half the area of Rectangle A.
    The rectangles have the same length.
    What is the width of Rectangle B?

Reflect

When might you use the formula for the area of a rectangle outside
the classroom?

Volume of a Rectangular Prism

A centimetre cube has a length, width, and height of 1 cm.
What is its volume?

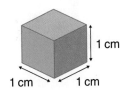

1 cm

1 cm   1 cm

Explore ·

You will need 2 empty boxes and centimetre cubes.

➤ Choose one box.
Estimate how many centimetre cubes
the box can hold.

➤ Fill the bottom of the box with
one layer of cubes.
How many cubes are in that layer?
How many layers can fit in the box?
How do you know?

➤ How many cubes can the box
hold altogether?
Describe how you found your answer.
Record your answer on the box.

➤ Without filling it completely, find how
many cubes the second box can hold.
Describe the strategy you used.
Use cubes to check your answer.

Show *and* Share

Share the boxes you used with the class.
How can you find the volume of a box without filling it completely?
Will your answer be exact? Explain.
How can you find the volume of a box without using cubes?

A rectangular prism is 10 cm long, 5 cm wide, and 6 cm high.

The length is 10 cm.
It is 1 row of 10 cubes.
Volume of 1 row = 10 cm³

The width is 5 cm.
Five rows of 10 cubes
make 1 layer of 50 cubes.
Volume of 1 layer = 5 × 10 cm³
= 50 cm³

The height is 6 cm.
Six layers of 50 cubes make
a volume of 300 cubes.
Volume of 6 layers = 6 × 50 cm³
= 300 cm³

We can use the descriptions above to develop a formula for the volume of a rectangular prism.

Volume in cubic centimetres
= number of 1-cm cubes in each layer × number of layers

The number of cubes in each layer is the area of the base of the prism. It is the length times the width.

The number of layers is the height of the prism.

So, Volume = base area × height

Another way to write the formula is:

Volume = length × width × height

$V = \ell \times w \times h$

> We use: V to represent volume, ℓ to represent length, w to represent width, and h to represent height.

➤ We can use the formula to find the volume of a rectangular prism 11 cm long, 4 cm wide, and 5 cm high.

Volume = $\ell \times w \times h$
= 11 cm × 4 cm × 5 cm
= 44 cm² × 5 cm
= 220 cm³

The volume of the prism is 220 cm³.

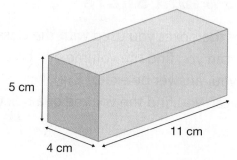

5 cm

4 cm

11 cm

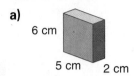

1. Find the volume of each rectangular prism.

a)
6 cm
5 cm   2 cm

b)
2 cm
7 cm   3 cm

c)
3 cm
15 cm   4 cm

2. Estimate, then calculate, the volume of a rectangular prism with these dimensions.

	Length (cm)	Width (cm)	Height (cm)
a)	6	2	2
b)	9	4	7
c)	18	9	12
d)	30	15	6

3. A dog box is built to fit in the back of a pick-up truck. It is used to transport sled dogs and supplies to a race. A dog box that holds 3 dogs is 117 cm long, 97 cm wide, and 61 cm tall. Each dog compartment is 38 cm long, 97 cm wide, and 46 cm tall.

   a) What is the volume of each dog compartment?
   b) What is the volume of the dog box that is not used to hold dogs? How did you find out?

4. During the buffalo hunt, the Métis used a Red River cart to carry buffalo meat and fur. The cart was made of wood and was usually pulled by oxen. The top of this cart has the shape of a rectangular prism with volume 1 350 000 cm³. The area of its base is about 13 500 cm². About how high is the top of the cart? Which strategy did you use to find out?

5. A rectangular prism has volume 90 cm³.
   The prism has length 9 cm and width 5 cm.
   What is its height? How do you know?

6. A rectangular prism has volume 192 cm³.
   a) The prism is 16 cm high. What is the area of its base?
      How do you know?
   b) What other possible measurements of height and
      base area could the rectangular prism have?
      What strategy did you use to find out?

7. Canada's Food Guide recommends that we eat
   2 to 4 servings of dairy products every day.
   a) This piece of cheese is 1 serving of dairy products.
      What is its volume?

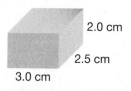

2.0 cm
2.5 cm
3.0 cm

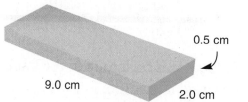

0.5 cm
9.0 cm
2.0 cm

   b) Is the block of cheese at the right more
      or less than 1 serving? How do you know?

8. Each block in a child's set of building blocks is
   15 cm long, 10 cm wide, and 5 cm high.
   Suppose you put the blocks in a box
   that is 50 cm long, 35 cm wide, and 30 cm high.

   a) What is the volume of each block? Of the box?
   b) Suppose you only consider the volume.
      How many blocks would you expect to fit in the box?
   c) Suppose you arrange the blocks neatly in layers.
      How many different ways can you layer the blocks?
      How many blocks fit in the box each way?
   d) Compare your answers to parts b and c.
      Explain any differences.
   e) Which is the best way to pack the blocks? Why?

Reflect

Explain why the volume of a rectangular prism is the product of its
length, width, and height. Include a diagram in your explanation.

Beat the Clock!

Your teacher will give you copies of 12 *Draw* cards,
12 *Explain* cards, and 12 *Size It Up* cards.
You will need scissors and a timer.
The goal of this game is to complete the most tasks and
to get the most cards.
Form 2 teams. Decide who will be Players A and B on each team.
For regular play, use 2-min timers.
For advanced play, use 1-min timers.

➤ Cut out the cards.
   Shuffle the cards and place them face down in a pile.

➤ Teams take turns. Player A draws a card.
   • If the card is a *Draw* card, Player A draws the shape.
     Player B guesses the shape.
   • If the card is an *Explain* card, Player A describes the attributes
     of the shape. Player B guesses the shape.
   • If the card is a *Size It Up* card, Players A and B work together
     to find the perimeter, area, or volume.
   When the team is ready to begin, the other team starts the timer.

➤ A team keeps a card if the task was completed correctly.
   If a team is not correct, the other team can steal the card by
   giving the correct answer. If neither team is correct,
   the card is returned to the pile.
   A team completes as many cards as it can in the allotted time.

➤ Teams continue to take turns.
   The team with more cards after an agreed time wins.

LESSON

1
2

1. **a)** Name each triangle as scalene, isosceles, or equilateral.
Explain how you decided on each name.

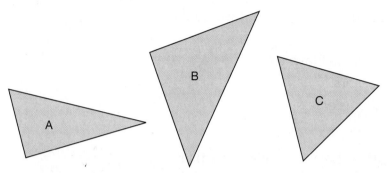

b) Rename each triangle as acute, obtuse, or right.
Tell how you know.

3
5

2. **a)** Use a ruler and a protractor.
Construct triangle RST: side RS is 5.6 cm, ∠R is 30°, and ∠S is 90°.
Sketch the triangle first.
b) What kind of triangle did you draw?
How else can you name the triangle?
c) Trace △RST.
Use the tracing to draw the triangle in a different orientation.
Explain how you know the two triangles are congruent.

4

3. **a)** Sort these shapes into sets of polygons and non-polygons.
Explain how you decided where to place each shape.

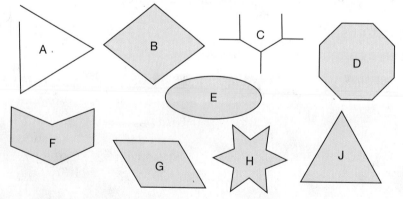

b) Sort the polygons in part a into sets of regular and irregular polygons.
Explain how you did this.

5

4. Draw a regular quadrilateral on square dot paper.
   a) What shape did you draw?
   b) Use measuring and superimposing to show that all angles are congruent and all sides are congruent.
      Show your work.

7

5. a) This sushi-platter pendant has the shape of a regular hexagon.
      The pendant has side length 1.9 cm.
      Calculate the perimeter of the pendant.
      Which strategy did you use?
   b) Write a formula to find the perimeter of any regular hexagon.
      Explain why the formula works.

8

6. The flag of the Métis Nation in Saskatchewan is rectangular.
   Suppose it has length 3 m and width 1.5 m.
   What is the area of the flag?
   How did you find out?

7
8

7. The top of Toby's desk has length 68 cm and width 50 cm.
   a) What is the area of the top of Toby's desk?
   b) Toby is working on a poster.
      The area of the poster is 2500 cm².
      Find 3 pairs of possible dimensions for the poster.
      How did you do this?
      Which dimensions are most likely?
   c) Can you tell if the poster fits on Toby's desk?
      Explain.

9

8. Estimate, then calculate, the volume of a rectangular prism with each set of dimensions.
   a) length 21 cm, width 19 cm, height 8 cm
   b) length 5 m, width 1.2 m, height 2 m

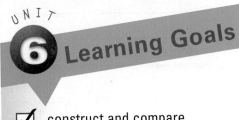

UNIT

6 Learning Goals

☑ construct and compare triangles
☑ describe and compare regular and irregular polygons
☑ develop formulas for the perimeters of polygons, the area of a rectangle, and the volume of a rectangular prism

You will solve 2 puzzles, then design your own puzzle for others to solve.

Part 1

Triangle Detection

Matina was organizing the math lab.
She sorted triangles, then placed them in
3 sealed envelopes labelled A, B, and C.
Each envelope contains one type of triangle:
equilateral, isosceles, or scalene.
Use the clues to solve the puzzle.

Clues

- Envelope B does *not* contain any regular polygons.
- Envelope A has some right triangles.
- All of the triangles in envelopes A and C have line symmetry.
- The triangles in envelope B do not have line symmetry.

Use the table to help.

Type of Triangle	Envelope A	Envelope B	Envelope C
Equilateral			
Scalene			
Isosceles			

Mark an X to eliminate a triangle from an envelope, and a ✓ to show a match.
Which type of triangle is in each envelope? Explain how you know.

Books by Size

You will need a calculator.
Li used the dimensions of his 4 favourite books to create a puzzle.
He wrote each dimension to the closest centimetre.

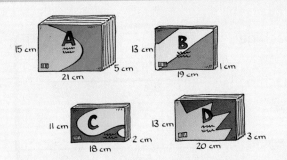

Use the clues and the table to match the books with their sizes. Show all calculations. Explain how you solved the puzzle.

Clues

- The front cover of *Stig of the Dump* has the least area.
- The volume of *The Little Prince* is less than that of *Stig of the Dump*, but the area of its front cover is greater.
- The front cover of *The Faraway Tree Collection* has the greatest perimeter.

Book	The Little Prince	Stig of the Dump	Swallows and Amazons	The Faraway Tree Collection
A				
B				
C				
D				

Part 2

Create your own geometry puzzle about regular and irregular polygons. Include at least 3 shapes and 3 clues. Make a table to record your reasoning. Explain how you created your puzzle. Solve your puzzle. Then trade problems with another pair of classmates and solve your classmates' puzzle.

Reflect on Your Learning

What have you learned about triangles and other polygons? Write about the different formulas you developed in this unit. Provide a real-world application for each formula.

Unit

1

1. The table shows the input and output for a machine with two operations.
   Identify the numbers and operations in the machine.

Input	Output
1	1
2	6
3	11
4	16
5	21

2

2. Use an integer to represent each situation.
   Then use yellow or red tiles to model each integer.
   Draw the tiles.
   a) 13°C above zero
   b) 8 m below sea level
   c) a withdrawal of $10
   d) an apartment 7 floors above ground level

3

3. Estimate each product or quotient. Which strategy did you use?
   Tell if your estimate is an overestimate or an underestimate.
   a) 6.89 × 3   b) 621.45 ÷ 4   c) 14.93 × 5   d) 41.625 ÷ 7

4

4. Measure each angle. Name each angle as acute, right, obtuse, straight, or reflex.

a)    b)    c)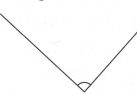

d) 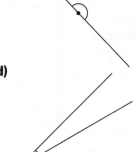   e) 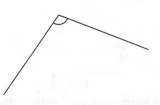   f)

5. Use a ruler and a protractor. Draw an angle with each measure.
   a) 35°   b) 160°   c) 310°   d) 95°

6. A backgammon board contains 24 congruent triangles.
   Here is one of the triangles.
   a) Find the measures of the unknown angles without measuring.
      Explain your strategy.
   b) Check your answers by measuring with a protractor.

12°

5

7. Place the numbers in each set on a number line.
Show how you did it. List the numbers from greatest to least.

a) $2\frac{1}{8}, \frac{5}{2}, \frac{9}{4}$ **b)** $\frac{3}{2}, \frac{5}{3}, 1\frac{5}{12}$

8. Chef Blanc uses 4 parts of oil for every 3 parts of vinegar to make a salad dressing for his restaurant in Hay River, NWT. Suppose he uses 12 parts of oil. How many parts of vinegar will he use?

9. Draw Base Ten Blocks or shade a hundredths grid to represent each amount.

a) $\frac{7}{50}$ **b)** 0.51   **c)** 29%   **d)** 0.02   **e)** $\frac{3}{20}$ **f)** 9%

6

10. Use a ruler and a protractor.
Measure the sides and angles of each triangle.

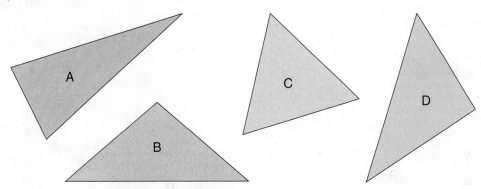

a) Name each triangle by the number of equal sides.
Use the words: scalene, equilateral, isosceles
b) Name each triangle by the angle measures.
Use the words: acute, right, obtuse

11. Use dot paper. Draw two congruent regular polygons.
Trade shapes with a classmate.
Explain how you know your classmate's shapes are congruent.

12. a) This dinner plate is shaped like a regular octagon.
The side length of the octagon is 9.5 cm.
Calculate the perimeter of the dinner plate.
Which strategy did you use?
b) Write a formula that you could use to find the perimeter of any regular octagon. Explain why the formula works.

Data Analysis and

Alien Encounters!

Learning Goals

- choose and justify an appropriate method to collect data
- construct and interpret line graphs to draw conclusions
- graph collected data to solve problems
- find theoretical and experimental probabilities
- compare theoretical and experimental probabilities

Probability

Aliens! Do living creatures really exist on other planets? To find out, scientists use space probes to collect data. In 2005, the Mars Express probe sent back images of the surface of Mars. The river-like patterns suggest that Mars may once have had liquid water. In 2008, the Phoenix Mars Lander collected soil samples from Mars. Studies of these samples may prove there was once water on Mars.

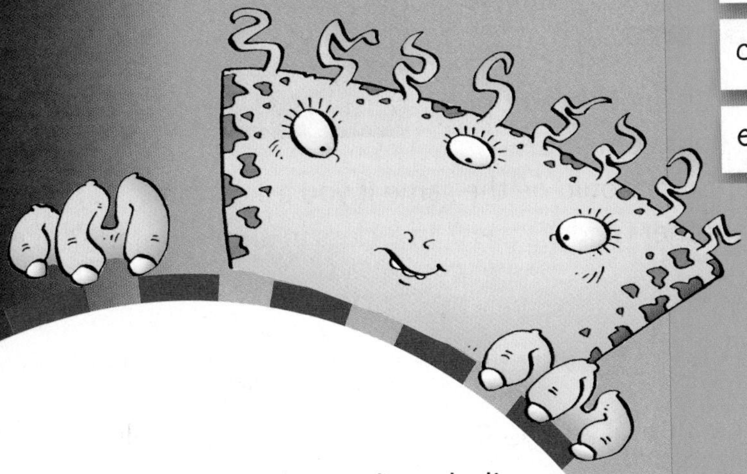

Key Words

fair question

biased question

database

electronic media

discrete data

line graph

continuous data

probability

theoretical probability

at random

experimental probability

- According to a survey, 62% of Canadians believe there is life on other planets. Do most of your classmates agree? How could you find out?

- Would the presence of water make Martian life more likely or less likely? Why?

- Does life exist on Mars today?
  Did life exist on Mars in the past?
  Use the words *certain*, *likely*, *unlikely*, or *impossible* in your answers.

LESSON

1

Using a Questionnaire to Gather Data

Electronic games are popular among Grade 6 students.
Store owners want to know which games to stock.
Which electronic games do students in your class like to play?

 **Explore** ·

Conduct a survey to find out
which electronic game is most popular
in your class.

Plan a survey. Write a question to ask.
Collect data from your classmates.
Record your results in a table.
Which electronic game is most popular?
How do you know?

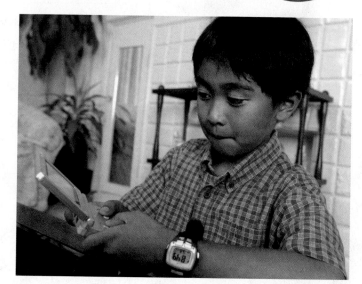

Show and Share

Share your results with another group.
How did your questions compare?
Do you think your results would be the same if you asked the
same question in another Grade 6 class? In a class in another grade? Explain.

Connect ·

Here are some guidelines for writing questions for a questionnaire.

➤ The question should be understood in the same way by all people.

Suppose you want to find out how much TV people watch.
You think of asking:

Do you watch a lot of TV?   ☐ *Yes* ☐ *No*

People may interpret "a lot" differently.
A better question would be:

How many hours of TV do you watch in a typical week? ___

➤ Each person should find an answer she would choose.

Suppose you want to find out people's favourite sports to watch on TV.
You think of asking:
What is your favourite sport to watch on TV?
☐ *Hockey* ☐ *Baseball*

Some people may prefer a different sport.
Others may not watch any sports on TV.
So, add more choices.
A better question would be:
What is your favourite sport to watch on TV?

☐ *Hockey*   ☐ *Baseball*   ☐ *Soccer*
☐ *Other (please specify)* _____ ☐ *None*

➤ The question should be **fair**.
It should not influence a person's answer.
If it does, it is a **biased question**.

Suppose you want to find out people's opinions
on how often students should have phys-ed classes.
You think of asking:
*Studies have shown that daily physical activity for children
is important. How often should elementary students
have phys-ed classes?* _____

The question provides extra information that might lead
a person to answer one way. A better question would be:
*How many times a week should elementary students
have phys-ed classes?*
☐ *never*   ☐ *once*   ☐ *twice*   ☐ *three times*   ☐ *four times*   ☐ *daily*

Mia wanted to find out which Canadian singer her classmates like best.
She handed out a questionnaire. She asked this question:

Who is your favourite Canadian singer:
Avril Lavigne _____, Susan Aglukark _____,
Nelly Furtado _____, Paul Brandt _____,
Brian Melo _____, or Other _____?

Mia recorded the results in a tally chart.
Mia concluded that Avril Lavigne was the
most popular singer of those named.
Mia's question was a fair question.
She did not give clues about her own
preference, nor did she try to influence a
person's answer.

Singer	Number of Students
Avril Lavigne	卌 ||||
Susan Aglukark	卌 ||
Nelly Furtado	卌
Paul Brandt	|||
Brian Melo	||
Other	||||

Practice

1. Design a questionnaire for collecting data to answer each question.
   Give at least 4 possible answers for your question each time.
   a) What is the favourite food of Grade 6 students?
   b) What is the favourite pet of students in your school?
   c) Who is the favourite athlete of people in your province or territory?

2. This graph shows the results of a questionnaire.
   a) Write what the question might have been.
   b) Can you tell how many students were
      given the questionnaire? Explain.
   c) Write 2 things you know from this questionnaire.

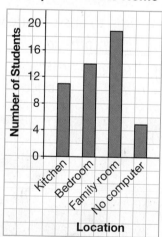

Computers in the Home

3. Think of a questionnaire you could hand out
   in your school.
   a) Write a question you could ask.
   b) How do you know if your question is a fair question?

4. Each question (written in italics) can be improved.
   Write a better question for each. Explain why you think it is better.
   a) To discover how much time each person spends doing homework each day:
      Do you spend a lot of time each day doing homework?
   b) To find out how students get to school:
      Do you usually walk to school or ride your bike?
   c) To find out the favourite type of TV programs:
      Do you prefer to watch mindless comedies or exciting dramas?

250

5. Ariel wanted to find out what the Grade 6 students in her school wanted to be when they left school. She wrote this question.

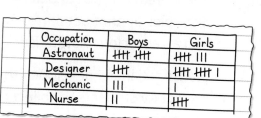

> What do you want to be when you leave school? Check one.
> Astronaut ☐   Designer ☐   Mechanic ☐   Nurse ☐

Ariel gave this question to the 76 students in Grade 6. Forty-five people answered the question. Here are the results.
Ariel concluded that most students will become astronauts or designers when they leave school.

a) Is Ariel's conclusion valid? Explain.

b) What might Ariel have done to improve her question?

Occupation	Boys	Girls
Astronaut	⫿⫿⫿⫿⫿ ⫿⫿⫿⫿⫿	⫿⫿⫿⫿⫿ ⫿⫿⫿
Designer	⫿⫿⫿⫿⫿	⫿⫿⫿⫿⫿ ⫿⫿⫿⫿⫿ ⫿
Mechanic	⫿⫿⫿	⫿
Nurse	⫿⫿	⫿⫿⫿⫿⫿

6. Two people want to open a shoe store at the local mall. They want to know what types of shoes they should stock.

a) How could a questionnaire be helpful?

b) Design a questionnaire the people could use to help them make the best decision.

7. What is your classmates' favourite way of keeping in touch with their friends?

a) Make a prediction.

b) Design a questionnaire you could use to find out.

c) Ask the question. Tally the results.

d) How did the results compare with your prediction?

8. What is the favourite type of music of students in your class?

a) Design a questionnaire you could use to find out.

b) Predict the results of your questionnaire.

c) Ask the question. Record the results.

d) How did the results compare with your prediction?

e) What else did you find out from your questionnaire?

At Home

Reflect

Why is it important to word a question carefully when you use a questionnaire? Include an example in your explanation.

Search the Internet.
Find a questionnaire.
Copy 3 questions in your notebook.
Is each question fair or biased?
How did you decide?

ASSESSMENT FOCUS | Question 7

Unit 7 Lesson 1 **251**

Using Databases and Electronic Media to Gather Data

A **database** is an organized collection of data.
There are two types of databases: print and electronic
Examples of print databases include a telephone book, a dictionary,
and an encyclopedia. Statistics Canada stores data in electronic databases.

Statistics Canada developed the *Census at School-Canada* Web site as a survey
project for students to collect data about themselves.

Here are some questions you can investigate.
- How many people usually live in your home?
- How long does it usually take you to travel to school?
- What is your favourite subject?
- In what sport or activity do you most enjoy participating?
- Whom do you look up to?

Your teacher can register your class so you can
complete the survey and access the data.
The Web site has data from other Canadian
students who have completed the survey.
To use *Census at School's* Canadian database,
follow these steps:

1. Open the Web site.

2. Under **Home Page**, click: **Data and results**

3. Under **Canadian summary results**, click
   on the most recent year and choose any
   topic that interests you.

4. Suppose you select:
   What is your favourite subject?
   A table similar to this appears.
   What conclusions can you make from
   these data?

| Statistics Canada | Statistique Canada | | | | Canadā |

Statistics Canada
www.statcan.gc.ca

| Français | Home | Contact Us | Help | Search | canada.gc.ca |

Home > Census at School > Data and Results > Canadian summary results for 2007/2008

Census at School

What's new
Teachers
Need help?
Students
Parents
Survey questions
Data and results
Learning activities
StatCan Learning Resources
Census of Canada
Privacy
International project

What is your favourite subject?

Subject	Elementary			Secondary		
	Girls	Boys	All students	Girls	Boys	All students
	%					
Physical education	23.8	44.6	34.0	16.9	37.4	26.8
Art	25.8	8.6	17.4	15.3	4.4	10.0
Math	11.7	14.6	13.1	11.9	12.1	12.0
Science	6.1	6.6	6.4	9.9	7.2	8.6
Computers	4.7	7.8	6.2	2.5	6.5	4.4
Music	7.7	4.4	6.1	5.0	4.5	4.7
English	6.7	2.2	4.5	12.8	4.6	8.8
History	2.5	3.4	2.9	4.5	5.0	4.8
French	3.8	1.6	2.7	3.1	0.8	2.0
Social studies	1.2	1.0	1.1	4.9	2.1	3.5
Geography	1.0	1.0	1.0	1.9	1.8	1.9
Other	5.1	4.1	4.6	11.3	13.6	12.4

Note: Favourite subjects appear in order of importance for all students.
Source: Statistics Canada, Census at School, 2007/2008.

Date Modified: 2008-08-13   ▲ Top of Page   Important Notices

Source: Statistics Canada

To find data from students in other countries, follow these steps:

5. Return to *Step 3*.
   Under **International results and random data selector**, click: random data selector. Follow the link to the *CensusAtSchool* International database.

6. Click Choose data, then click on a country to select it.

7. From the pull-down menu, select the most recent phase. Then click: Next >

8. Fill in all required information, then click: Get data

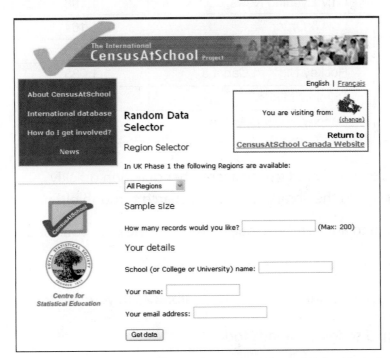

Source: International CensusAtSchool Project

Use data from *Census at School* to answer each question.
Print your data.

1. What percent of elementary students in Canada take more than 1 h to get to school?

2. What is the difference in percents of elementary students in Canada with blue eyes and with brown eyes?

3. a) In which month are most students in the United Kingdom born?
   b) Is this month the same for boys and girls? Explain.

We can also use electronic media to collect data.
Electronic media include radio, television, and the Internet.

Aria wanted to find the 10 most-watched television shows in
Canada for the week ending December 30, 2007.
She went to the Web site of the *National Post*, then searched *Top TV Programs*.
She looked through the results to find a link to a table like this.

Ranking	Program	Number of Viewers (millions)
1	The Amazing Race	1.618
2	CTV Evening News	1.196
3	Law & Order	1.164
4	CTV Evening News Weekend	1.110
5	Hockey Night in Canada	1.083
6	Criminal Minds	1.031
7	Sunday Evening Movie	0.948

By using this Web site, Aria found the answer to her question quickly.
She did not have to go to the library to find and search through old newspapers.

Use electronic media to answer these questions. Print the data you used.

4. Who are the leading point scorers in the NHL today?

5. What are the telephone numbers of 4 public libraries in your area?

6. What are the top 5 songs in Canada today?

7. Search electronic media to find a Web site of interest to you.
   Write a question that can be answered using data on the Web site.
   Use the data to answer the question.

Reflect

When do you think it is appropriate to use a database to collect data?
When are electronic media more appropriate?
Which electronic media and databases do you use regularly?

Conducting Experiments to Gather Data

Suppose you wanted to answer this question:
Which letter of the alphabet occurs most often in the English language?
How could you find out? Could you hand out a questionnaire?
Could you use a database or electronic media? Explain.

Explore

You will need a paper cup or Styrofoam cup.
Which way is the cup most likely to land when it falls?
To find out:

➤ Slowly slide an upright cup off the edge
of the desk. Record its position after it lands.
➤ Copy and complete this table for 50 results.

Position	Tally	Total

➤ Do you think the results would be different
if you rolled the cup off the desk?
How could you find out?

Show and Share

Compare your results with those of another pair of students.
What other ways could you have conducted this experiment?
Which way is a cup least likely to land when it falls? Explain.

Jasbir and Summer wanted to answer this question:
  Does doubling the height of the ramp double the
  distance a toy car travels?

To find out, they let a toy car roll down a ramp
of height 10 cm, then measured the distance
the car travelled from the end of the ramp.
Then, the students doubled the height of the ramp
to 20 cm, and then to 40 cm.
They did 3 trials for each height of the ramp,
and recorded the results.

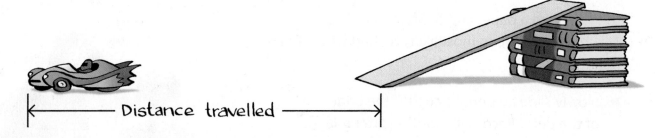

Distance travelled

Here are the data the students collected.

Ramp Height	Distance Travelled		
	Trial 1	Trial 2	Trial 3
10 cm	60 cm	58 cm	61 cm
20 cm	118 cm	120 cm	121 cm
40 cm	235 cm	241 cm	238 cm

The car travelled about 60 cm when the height of the ramp was 10 cm.
When the height of the ramp was doubled to 20 cm,
the distance travelled also doubled: 60 cm × 2 = 120 cm

When the height of the ramp was doubled to 40 cm,
the distance travelled also doubled: 120 cm × 2 = 240 cm

From the data, Jasbir and Summer concluded that doubling the height of the ramp
doubles the distance a toy car travels.

1. Work with a partner to answer this question:
   Which sum occurs most often when you roll 2 dice labelled 1 to 6?
   You will need two dice labelled 1 to 6.
   Take turns to roll the dice.
   Find the sum of the numbers on the dice.
   Each student rolls the dice 25 times.

Sum	Tally	Total
2		
3		
4		

   a) Record the results.
   b) Which sum occurred most often?
   c) How do your results compare with those of another pair of students?
   d) What other questions could you answer using these data? Explain.

2. Work with a partner to answer this question:
   Which way is a spoon more likely to land:
   rightside up or upside down?
   You will need a bag and 10 plastic spoons.
   Place the spoons in a bag, shake them up,
   then drop them on the floor.
   Count how many spoons land rightside up and
   how many land upside down. Record your results.
   Repeat the experiment 9 more times. Make sure you drop the spoons
   from the same height each time. Add the results.
   Which way is a spoon more likely to land? Why do you think so?

   rightside up

   upside down

3. Which letter of the alphabet occurs
   most often in the English language?
   a) Predict the answer to the question above.
      Explain your prediction.
   b) Design an experiment you can use
      to check your prediction.
   c) Conduct the experiment.
      Record the results.
   d) Use the data you collected to answer
      the question above.
      What other conclusions can you make
      from your data?

4. Morgan experimented with 3 different paper airplanes to answer this question: Which airplane travels the greatest distance? Morgan flew each plane 4 times and measured the length of each flight. Here are the data Morgan collected.

Airplane Design	Trial 1	Trial 2	Trial 3	Trial 4
The Dart	6.3 m	18.4 m	12.2 m	4.1 m
Flying Squirrel	11.3 m	10.5 m	9.8 m	11.2 m
Speed-o-matic	3.1 m	2.5 m	2.1 m	3.6 m

What answer would you give to the question above? Explain your choice.

5. A Grade 6 class experimented with radish seeds and bean seeds. The students wanted to answer this question:
Will the seeds sprout best in tap water, salt water, or sugar water?
Here are the data the students collected. Use these data.
What conclusion can you make?
Why do you think this might be?

Type of Seed	Percent of Seeds That Sprouted After One Week		
	Tap water	Sugar water	Salt water
Radish	60%	30%	10%
Bean	50%	18%	7%

6. How long does it take a Grade 6 student to write the alphabet backward: 30–44 s, 45–60 s, or more than 60 s?
   a) Predict the answer to the question above. Explain your prediction.
   b) Design an experiment you can use to check your prediction.
   c) Conduct the experiment. Record the results.
   d) Use the data you collected to answer the question above. What other conclusions can you make from your data?

7. Which method would you use to collect data to answer this question: How many times can you blink in 5 s? Explain your choice of method.
Collect the data. Answer the question. Show your work.

Reflect

What strategies did you use to keep track of your data during your experiments?

Interpreting Graphs

Meteorologists are scientists
who study weather.
They record weather data over days,
months, and years.
It is important that they display
these data for others to understand.

Explore

Look at this graph.

What does the graph show?
How do the highest temperatures
in May and November compare?
Which months have the same
highest temperature?
Write 4 other questions you can answer
from the graph.

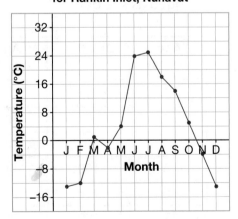

**Monthly High Temperature
for Rankin Inlet, Nunavut**

Show *and* Share

Trade questions with another pair of classmates.
Answer your classmates' questions.
How is this graph the same as a bar graph?
A pictograph? How is it different?

➤ Hard-Headed Helmet Company wanted to find out how many of its bicycle helmets had been sold in the last 6 months.
The company surveyed 10 bike stores in Manitoba.

Month	Number of Helmets Sold
April	12
May	21
June	56
July	63
August	37
September	18

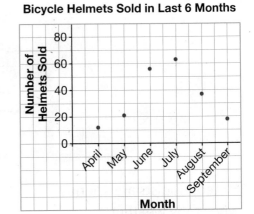

Bicycle Helmets Sold in Last 6 Months

Only whole numbers of helmets can be sold.
For example, a store cannot sell $12\frac{3}{8}$ helmets.
So, the graph is a series of points that are not joined.
These data are **discrete**. There are gaps between values.
Usually, discrete data represent things that can be counted.

From the table, we can see that the greatest number of helmets was sold in July.
This corresponds to the highest point on the graph.

➤ This table and graph show how Leah's height changed as she got older.

Age (years)	Height (cm)	Age (years)	Height (cm)
2	83	11	142
3	95	12	151
4	101	13	158
5	109	14	160
6	116	15	161
7	120	16	162
8	128	17	162
9	135	18	162
10	139	19	162

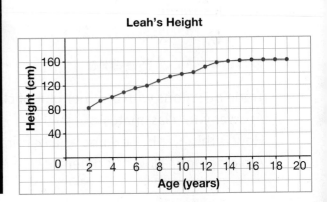

Leah's Height

Consecutive points on the graph are joined by line segments.
Points on the line between the plotted points have meaning.
For example, it is possible for Leah's height to have been 117.5 cm
when she was 6 years 3 months old.

From the graph, we see that from 2 to 16 years of age, the line segments go up
to the right. This shows that Leah's height increases.
From 16 years on, the line segments are horizontal.
This shows that Leah's height has stopped increasing.
She has stopped growing taller.

This type of graph is called a **line graph**. It shows **continuous data**.
Continuous data can include any value between data points.
Time, money, temperature, and measurements, such as length or
mass, are continuous.

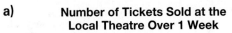

Practice

1. For each graph below:
   - What is the title of the graph?
   - What does each axis show?
   - Why are the points not joined or joined?
     Are the data discrete or continuous?
   - What conclusions can you make from the graph?

   a)
   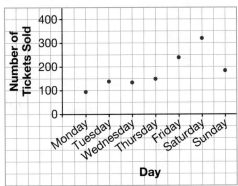

   b)
   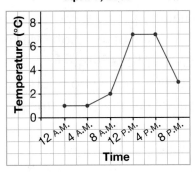

2. Would you use a line graph or a series of points to display each set of data?
   Explain your choices.
   a) the temperature of a cup of boiling water as it cools
   b) the number of goals scored by Jarome Iginla over the last 10 weeks
      of the 2007–2008 season
   c) the mass of a puppy in its first year
   d) the distance travelled by a cross-country skier as she completes the course

3. **a)** What does this line graph show?

   b) About how tall was Nathan at each age?
   - 8 years
   - 12 years
   - 15 years

   c) During which year did Nathan grow the most? The least? How does the graph show this?

   > We use a jagged line to indicate we are not showing all the numbers.

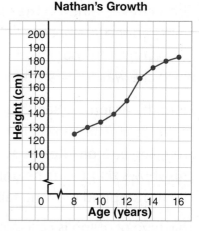

Nathan's Growth

4. Look at the three graphs below.

   i) My Baby Sister's First Year

   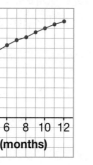

   ii) Population of Nunavut, 2001–2006

   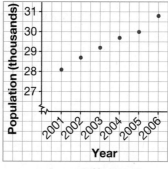

   iii) How My Hot Chocolate Cooled

   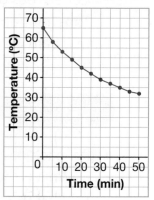

   a) How are the graphs alike? How are they different?

   b) What conclusions can you make from each graph?

5. Marina measured the life left in her cell phone battery every two hours for 24 h. She used a line graph to display the data.

   a) What happened in the first 4 h?

   b) What happened between hours 4 and 6?

   c) How many times might Marina have used her cell phone? Explain.

   d) Between which two hours did Marina use her cell phone the most? How do you know?

   e) What percent of the battery life remained after 24 h?

   f) What other conclusions can you make from the graph?

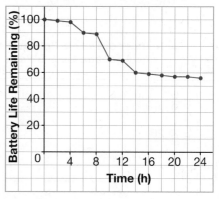

My Cell Phone Battery

Reflect

You can display data using a line graph or a series of points.
What do such graphs have in common?
Describe a situation where you might use each type of graph.

Drawing Graphs

Many science experiments involve
measuring time and distance
or temperature.
The data can be plotted on line graphs.
What experiments have you done in
science class?
How did you display the results?

Explore

You will need a paper cup, 100 mL of water at room temperature,
a large ice cube, a thermometer, a watch or clock, and grid paper.

➤ Place 100 mL of water in the cup.
Record the temperature of the water.

➤ Place a large ice cube in the water.
Record the temperature of the water
every minute for 10 min.

➤ Draw a graph to display the data you collected.
Did you join the points? Explain.

➤ What can you tell from looking at the graph?

Show and Share

Share your graph with another pair of classmates.
How are your graphs the same?
How are they different?
How did you decide whether to join the points?

On December 26, 2004, a massive underwater earthquake rocked the coast of Indonesia's Sumatra Island.
It caused a *tsunami*, or huge ocean waves.

➤ This table shows the height of the waves at different distances from land.

Distance from Land (km)	Height of Waves (m)
5	32
10	20
15	10
20	5
25	1
30	1

To display these data:

• Draw two axes.
The horizontal axis shows *Distance from Land* in kilometres.
The vertical axis shows *Height of Waves* in metres.

• Choose an appropriate scale.
Count by 5s for the scale on the horizontal axis.
The horizontal scale is 1 square represents 5 km.

Count by 5s for the scale on the vertical axis.
The vertical scale is 1 square represents 5 m.

• To mark a point for 5 km at 32:
32 is $\frac{2}{5}$ of the way between 30 and 35.
So, on the vertical line through 5,
mark a point $\frac{2}{5}$ of the way between 30 and 35.

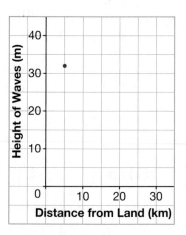

- Then mark points for the rest of the data in the same way.

- Both distance and height are continuous. So, use a ruler to join consecutive pairs of points, from left to right.

- Give the graph a title.

Since the line segments go down to the right, we know that the farther the tsunami is from land, the smaller the waves.

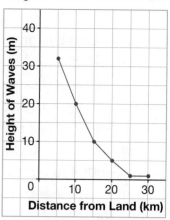

Height of Waves in a Tsunami

Practice

You will need grid paper.

1. Miners drill a hole in the earth's surface. They measure the temperature of the earth at intervals of 1 km. This table shows the data they collected.
   a) Draw a graph to display these data.
   b) Did you join the points? Explain.
   c) Write 2 things you know from the graph.

Distance (km)	Temperature (°C)
0	20
1	29
2	41
3	48
4	59
5	67

2. The population of killer whales along the British Columbia coast is counted each year. The table shows the data for 2002 to 2006.
   a) Draw a graph to display these data.
   b) Explain how you chose the vertical scale.
   c) Did you join the points? Explain.
   d) What conclusions can you make from the graph?

Year	Number of Killer Whales
2002	81
2003	82
2004	86
2005	85
2006	87

3. This table shows how far Rene's family travelled on a car trip to Regina.
   a) Draw a line graph to display these data.
   b) How did you choose the scale on the vertical axis?
   c) What was the distance travelled each hour from hours 2 to 4? From hours 6 to 8?
   d) What do you think was happening from hour 4 to hour 5 on the trip? Explain.
   e) What other conclusions can you make from the graph?

Time Passed (h)	Distance Travelled (km)
1	80
2	180
3	280
4	380
5	380
6	480
7	530
8	580

4. Rajiv measures the length of his cucumber vine at 9:00 A.M. each day.

Day	1	2	3	4	5	6	7	8	9	10
Length of Vine (mm)	0	1	7	15	27	35	41	48	53	57

   a) Draw a graph to display these data.
   b) Did you join the points? Explain.
   c) Write 2 things you know from the graph.

5. A ball is dropped from the top of a cliff. This table shows the distance travelled by the ball in the first 6 s.
   a) Draw a graph to display these data.
   b) Did you join the points? Explain.
   c) Write 2 things you know from the graph.

Time (s)	Distance (m)
0	0
1	5
2	20
3	45
4	80
5	125
6	180

6. This table shows the Aboriginal population in Canada from 1971 to 2001.

Year	1971	1981	1991	2001
Population (in thousands)	313	491	1003	1320

   a) Draw a graph to display these data.
   b) Explain how you chose the scale on each axis.
   c) Did you join the points? Explain.
   d) What do you know from looking at the graph?

Reflect

Do you find it easier to see how data change by looking at a table or a graph? Explain your choice.

5

Choosing an Appropriate Graph

Which types of graphs
do you know how to draw?

Your teacher will draw this table on the board.

Make a tally mark next to your shoe size.
Copy the completed table.
Draw a graph to display the data.
What conclusions can you make from the graph?

Shoe Size	Number of Students	
	Boys	Girls
$5\frac{1}{2}$		
6		
$6\frac{1}{2}$		
7		

Show and Share

Share your graph with another pair of students.
Did you draw the same type of graph?
If your answer is yes, how did you decide which type of graph to use?
If your answer is no, which type of graph better represents the data?

Connect

➤ Tao counted the number of red chocolates in
5 different boxes of candy-coated chocolates.
This table shows the data collected.
Tao displayed the data in a bar graph.
She chose a vertical bar graph so the heights of the bars
could be used to compare the numbers of chocolates.

Box	Number of Red Chocolates
1	8
2	12
3	13
4	9
5	12

From the bar graph, Tao knows that:

- The bar representing Box 3 is the tallest.
  So, Box 3 has the greatest number of red chocolates.
- Box 1 has the least number of red chocolates.

➤ Manuel recorded the contents of his family's recycling bin.
  This table shows what his family recycled each week for
  2 weeks.

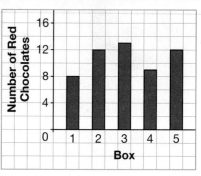

Number of Red Chocolates in a Box

Item	Week 1	Week 2
Plastic Items	21	23
Glass Items	11	9
Cans	7	9
Boxes	10	14

- Manuel wanted to compare the data for
  Week 1 and Week 2. So, he drew a double-bar
  graph to display the two sets of data.

  From the double-bar graph, Manuel
  knows that:
  - More plastic items, cans, and boxes
    were recycled in Week 2.
  - Fewer glass items were recycled in Week 2.

- Manuel then displayed the data to show
  the total amount recycled over the 2 weeks.
  The data are discrete and there are sets
  of items. So, Manuel drew a pictograph.

  Since each number is divisible by 4, he chose
  🥡 to represent 4 items.

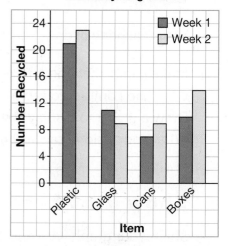

Our Recycling Bin

Item	Number
Plastic Items	44
Glass Items	20
Cans	16
Boxes	24

From the pictograph, Manuel knows that:
- In the 2 weeks, more plastic items were
  recycled than any other type of item.
- In the 2 weeks, cans were recycled the least

1. Jon surveyed the Grade 6 students in his
   school to answer this question:
   In which room of your home do you usually do
   your homework?
   This table shows the data he collected.
   a) Draw a graph to display these data.
      Explain your choice of graph.
   b) Where do most students do their homework?
      How does the graph show this?

Location	Number of Students
Kitchen	9
Bedroom	21
Living Room	14
Other	6

2. Zena surveyed the Grade 6 students in her class to answer this question:
   What is your favourite flavour of fruit juice?
   This table shows the data she collected.

Girls		Boys	
Flavour	Number of Students	Flavour	Number of Students
Apple	3	Apple	6
Orange	4	Orange	3
Cranberry	7	Cranberry	2
Grape	1	Grape	3
Other	0	Other	2

   a) Draw a graph to display these data.
      Explain your choice of graph.
   b) Which flavour of juice is most popular? Explain.

3. a) Choose an appropriate method to collect data
      to answer this question:
      What do the students in your class like most
      about summer?
      Explain your choice.
   b) Collect the data. Record the results.
   c) Draw a graph to display these data.
      Explain your choice of graph.
   d) Use the graph to answer the question in part a.
      Explain your answer.

4. Jeremy conducted an experiment to answer this question:
   How fast does the centre of a potato cool down after
   it is removed from boiling water?
   The table shows the data he collected.
   a) Draw a graph to display these data.
      Explain your choice of graph.
   b) What conclusions can you make from the graph?

Time (min)	Temperature (°C)
0	91
5	80
10	67
15	58
20	50
25	45
30	41
35	37
40	34

5. For each question below:
   • Choose an appropriate method to collect data to
     answer the question. Explain your choice.
   • Collect the data. Record the results.
   • Draw a graph to display the data.
     Explain your choice of graph.
   • Answer the question.
     What other conclusions can you make from your graph?
     a) What was the greatest temperature outside your classroom
        during a school day?
     b) When you toss 2 pennies, which outcome shows most often:
        2 heads, 2 tails, or a head and a tail?

6. Demetra used *The Globe and Mail* Web site to collect data to
   answer this question: In the first week of January 2008,
   when would I have had the most American money
   for a Canadian dollar?
   This table shows the data collected.
   a) Draw a graph to display these data.
      Explain your choice of graph.
   b) Answer the question above.
   c) What has happened to the value of the
      Canadian dollar since January 2008?
      How could you find out?

Day	Value of $1 Can in US cents
Jan. 1	100.9¢
Jan. 2	100.7¢
Jan. 3	100.9¢
Jan. 4	99.9¢
Jan. 5	99.4¢
Jan. 6	99.6¢
Jan. 7	99.0¢

Reflect

When you see a set of data, how do you decide the best way
to display the data?
Use examples from this lesson in your answer.

6 Theoretical Probability

Which of these numbers are prime
and which are composite?
How do you know?   7, 20, 23, 36, 47, 64

Explore ·  Game

In a game, students roll 2 dice. Each die is labelled 1 to 6.
If the sum of the numbers rolled is a prime number,
Player A scores a point.
If the sum of the numbers rolled is a composite number,
Player B scores a point.
The first player to score 20 points wins.

• Who do you predict is more likely to win? Why?
• Play the game with a partner.
   Decide who will be Player A and Player B.
   Record your results in a tally chart.

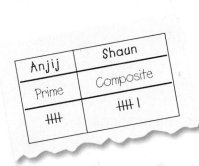

• Who won? How does this compare with your prediction?

Show and Share

Compare your results with those of another pair of students.
Explain any differences.
Work together to list the outcomes of the game.
Which sum is more likely: a prime number or a composite number?
How do you know?

Connect

Jamie and Alexis are playing *Predicting Products*.
They take turns to roll 2 dice, each labelled 1 to 6.
If the product of the 2 numbers rolled is odd,
Jamie gets a point.
If the product is even, Alexis gets a point.
The first person to get 20 points wins.
Who is more likely to win?

Jamie	Alexis
Odd Product	Even Product

Here is one way to help predict the winner:

Organize the possible outcomes in a table.
Each number on a die has an equal
chance of being rolled.

X	1	2	3	4	5	6
1	1	2	3	4	5	6
2	2	4	6	8	10	12
3	3	6	9	12	15	18
4	4	8	12	16	20	24
5	5	10	15	20	25	30
6	6	12	18	24	30	36

From the table:
- There are 36 possible outcomes.
- 27 outcomes are even products.
- 9 outcomes are odd products.

We say: The **probability** of getting an even product is 27 out of 36.
We write the probability of an even product as a fraction: $\frac{27}{36}$

We say: The probability of getting an odd product is 9 out of 36.
We write the probability of an odd product as: $\frac{9}{36}$

Each of these probabilities is a **theoretical probability**.
A theoretical probability is the likelihood that an outcome will happen.

$$\text{Theoretical probability} = \frac{\text{Number of favourable outcomes}}{\text{Number of possible outcomes}}$$

The probability that Alexis wins is $\frac{27}{36}$.
The probability that Jamie wins is $\frac{9}{36}$.
Since $\frac{27}{36} > \frac{9}{36}$, Alexis is more likely to win.

➤ A jar contains 5 blue marbles, 6 red marbles, 7 green marbles, and 7 white marbles.
Without looking, a student picks a marble from the jar.

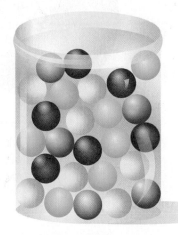

When we pick a marble without looking, we say the marble is picked **at random**.

- What are the possible outcomes?
  The outcomes are: a blue marble, a red marble, a green marble, and a white marble.

- What is the theoretical probability of picking a green marble?
  Each marble has an equal chance of being picked.
  There are 7 green marbles, so there are 7 favourable outcomes.
  The total number of marbles is:

  $5 + 6 + 7 + 7 = 25$

  So, there are 25 possible outcomes.
  The theoretical probability of picking a green marble is $\frac{7}{25}$.

Practice

1. A paper bag contains 2 green tiles, 4 yellow tiles, and 1 blue tile. Liz draws a tile without looking.
   a) List the possible outcomes.
   b) What is the theoretical probability that the tile is:
      i) green?   ii) yellow?   iii) blue?

2. There are 13 girls and 17 boys in a Grade 6 class. The teacher puts each student's name into a hat, then draws one name. The student whose name is drawn will be the first to present her or his speech. What is the theoretical probability that a girl will present first?

3. Jade spins the pointer on this spinner.
   a) List the possible outcomes.
   b) What is the theoretical probability of each outcome?
      i) The pointer lands on black.
      ii) The pointer lands on red.
      iii) The pointer lands on yellow or white.
      iv) The pointer does not land on yellow.

4. Shen rolls a die labelled 1 to 6.
   a) List the possible outcomes.
   b) What is the probability of rolling a 1?
      An even number? A number greater than 4?

We usually say *probability* instead of theoretical probability.

5. A jar contains 9 black, 22 red, 26 orange, and 13 green marbles. A marble is picked at random.
   a) List the possible outcomes.
   b) What is the probability of each outcome?
      i) A black marble is picked.
      ii) A green marble is picked.
      iii) A red or an orange marble is picked.

6. A letter is chosen at random from each word listed below. In each case, what is the probability that the letter chosen is a vowel?
   a) Yukon   b) Saskatchewan   c) Nunavut   d) Manitoba

7. An object with 10 congruent faces is a regular decahedron. Shannon and Joshua roll a decahedron labelled 1 to 10.
   a) List the possible outcomes.
   b) What is the probability Shannon rolls an odd number?
   c) Joshua says there is a probability of $\frac{1}{5}$ for rolling a number with a certain digit. What is the digit?

8. At a carnival, you can choose one of these wheels to spin.
   To win a prize on the first wheel, the pointer must land on a star.
   To win a prize on the second wheel, the pointer must land on a happy face.
   Which wheel would you choose to spin?
   Use words and numbers to explain your answer.

9. This table shows the number of birthdays each month for a Grade 6 class.
   A student is picked at random.
   What is the probability of each event?
   a) The student has a birthday in March.
   b) The student has a birthday in October.
   c) The student has a birthday in June, July, or August.
   d) The student does not have a birthday in December.

Month	Jan.	Feb.	Mar.	Apr.	May	June	July	Aug.	Sept.	Oct.	Nov.	Dec.
Number of Students	2	4	3	1	5	3	2	3	3	1	1	2

10. A bag contains 6 cubes.
    The cubes are coloured blue and yellow.
    Draw and colour the cubes in the bag for each probability:
    a) The probability of picking a yellow cube is $\frac{1}{6}$.
    b) The probability of picking a blue cube is $\frac{3}{6}$.

Math Link

Your World

Carnival games often involve probability.
You may make a prediction or perform a task
to win a prize. But the prize you are most
likely to win is usually worth less than what
you pay to play the game. To win a large
prize, you have to play several times and
trade up, or be very lucky.

Reflect

Where is theoretical probability used in real life?
Find 2 examples where it helps people make decisions.

Experimental Probability

A die labelled 1 to 6 is rolled.
What is the theoretical probability of rolling a 3?
How do you know?

Explore

Your teacher will give you a large copy of this spinner.
You will need an open paper clip as a pointer and a sharp pencil
to keep it in place.

➤ Suppose the pointer is spun.
What is the theoretical probability of the pointer
landing on Wolf? Landing on Bear? Landing on Moose?
Order these probabilities from greatest to least.

➤ Conduct the experiment 50 times.
Record your results in a tally chart.
In the last column, write the total as a fraction of 50.

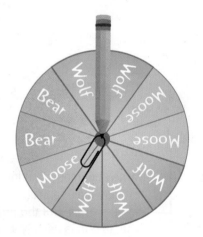

Sector	Tally	Total	$\frac{\text{Total}}{50}$
Wolf			
Bear			
Moose			

➤ Order the fractions from greatest to least.
How does this order compare with the order of the theoretical probabilities?

Show and Share

Combine your results with those of another pair of students to get 100 trials.
How do the experimental results compare with the theoretical probabilities now?

Connect

Jenny and Morningstar put coloured cubes into a bag.
They used 4 blue, 2 red, 2 green, and 2 yellow cubes.
A cube is picked from the bag at random.
The theoretical probability that a blue cube
is picked is $\frac{4}{10}$, or $\frac{2}{5}$.

➤ Jenny and Morningstar planned an experiment
for the class.
Each student would pick a cube from the bag
without looking, then replace it.
She would do this 10 times.
Here are the results of one experiment.

Colour	Blue	Red	Green	Yellow
Number of Times	6	1	1	2

The blue cube was picked 6 times.
The **experimental probability** is the likelihood that something occurs
based on the results of an experiment.

$$\text{Experimental probability} = \frac{\text{Number of times an outcome occurs}}{\text{Number of times the experiment is conducted}}$$

So, the experimental probability of picking a blue cube is $\frac{6}{10}$, or $\frac{3}{5}$.
This is different from the theoretical probability.

➤ Jenny and Morningstar combined the results from 10 experiments.
Here are the results for 100 trials.

Colour	Blue	Red	Green	Yellow
Number of Times	43	22	18	17

The blue cube was picked 43 times.
So, the experimental probability of picking a blue cube is $\frac{43}{100}$.

The experimental probability is close to the theoretical probability of $\frac{4}{10}$.

The more trials we conduct, the closer
the experimental probability may come
to the theoretical probability.

$$\overset{\times 10}{\frac{4}{10}} = \frac{40}{100}$$
$$\underset{\times 10}{}$$

$\frac{40}{100}$ is close to $\frac{43}{100}$.

Practice

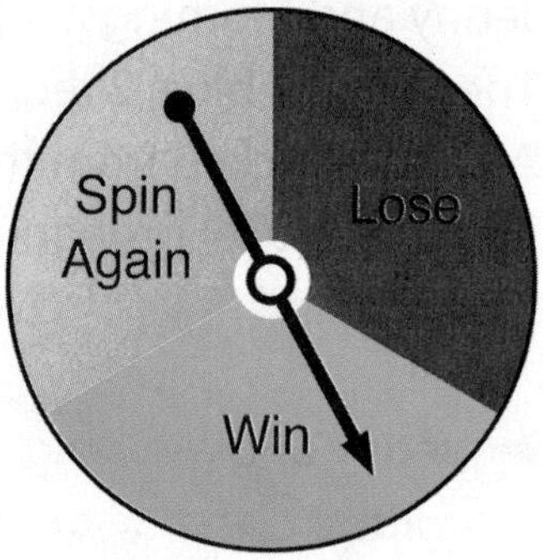

1. For each experiment, state the possible outcomes.
   a) The spinner has 3 equal sectors labelled Win, Lose, Spin Again. The pointer on a spinner is spun.
   b) A bag contains 6 marbles: 3 red, 2 black, and 1 blue. One marble is picked at random.
   c) A regular tetrahedron has 4 faces labelled 1, 2, 2, 3. The tetrahedron is rolled.

2. Dave tossed a coin 20 times. Heads showed 12 times.
   a) How many times did tails show?
   b) What fraction of the tosses showed heads? Tails?
   c) Are these results what you would expect? Explain.
   d) Dave tosses the coin 100 times. What would you expect the results to be? Explain.

3. Avril spins the pointer on this spinner several times. Here are her results.

Blue	Orange
卌 卌 卌 ||	卌 ||

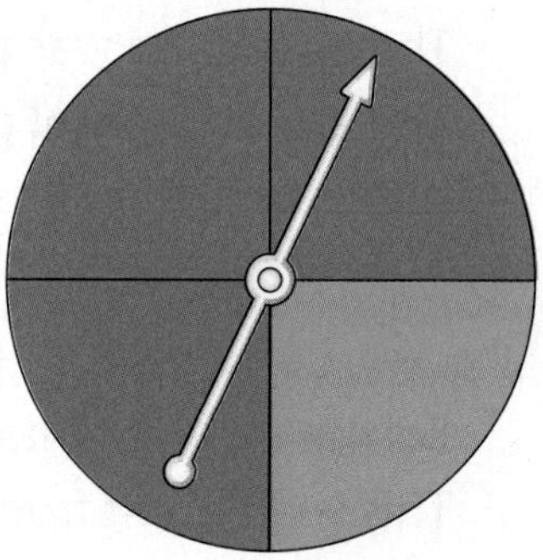

   a) How many times did Avril spin the pointer? How do you know?
   b) What fraction of the spins were blue? Orange?
   c) Were Avril's results what you would have expected? Explain.

4. Nina and Allegra placed 35 red tiles and 15 yellow tiles in a bag. At random, they picked a tile from the bag, recorded its colour, and replaced it. They did this 100 times.
   a) What is the theoretical probability of picking a red tile?
   b) Predict how many times Nina and Allegra should get a red tile in 100 trials.
   c) Nina and Allegra picked a red tile from the bag 58 times. What is the experimental probability of picking a red tile?
   d) Nina said, "I think we did something wrong." Do you agree? Why?
   e) Work with a partner. Try the experiment. Record your results. What is your experimental probability of picking a red tile?

5. A die labelled 1 to 6 is rolled.
   a) What are the possible outcomes?
   b) What is the theoretical probability of
      each outcome?
      i) rolling a 6
      ii) rolling an even number
      iii) rolling a 2 or a 4
      iv) rolling a number greater than 4
   c) Work with a partner. Roll a die 20 times.
      Record your results.
      What is the experimental probability of
      each outcome in part b?
      How do these probabilities compare with
      the theoretical probabilities? Explain.
   d) Combine your results with those of 4 other groups.
      What is the experimental probability of
      each outcome in part b?
      How do these probabilities compare with
      the theoretical probabilities? Explain.
      What do you think might happen if you rolled the die 500 times?

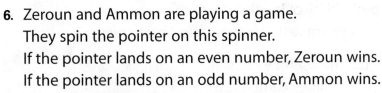

6. Zeroun and Ammon are playing a game.
   They spin the pointer on this spinner.
   If the pointer lands on an even number, Zeroun wins.
   If the pointer lands on an odd number, Ammon wins.
   a) Is this a fair game? How do you know?
   b) What is the theoretical probability of the pointer
      landing on an even number?
   c) Use a spinner like this one.
      Play the game at least 30 times.
      Record your results.
      Were the results what you expected? Explain.
   d) What results would you expect if you played the game
      100 times? Explain how you made your prediction.

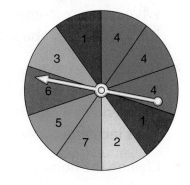

Reflect

What is the difference between experimental and theoretical probability?
Are they ever equal? Sometimes equal? Never equal?
Use examples to explain.

Investigating Probability

We can use technology to explore probability.
Use virtual manipulatives.
This software has an adjustable spinner that spins a pointer randomly.
You can use this spinner to conduct many trials quickly.

Use the spinner to conduct this experiment.

➤ Create a spinner with 4 equal sectors.
  Each sector should be coloured differently.
  What are the possible outcomes when the pointer is spun?

➤ What is the theoretical probability of landing on each colour?
  Write each probability as a fraction.

➤ Conduct the experiment 10 times.
  How many times did the pointer land on each colour?
  What is the experimental probability of landing on each colour?
  How do these probabilities compare with the theoretical probabilities?

➤ Repeat the experiment for 100, 1000, and 9999 spins.
  How do the experimental probabilities compare with
  the theoretical probabilities as the number of
  spins increases?

About how long did it take to
make 9999 spins?

➤ Change the number of sectors
  on the spinner.
  This time have at least 2 sectors
  the same colour.
  Experiment with different
  numbers of spins.
  What do you notice?

Game of Pig

You will need 2 dice, each labelled from 1 to 6.

➤ Players take turns to roll both dice.

➤ On your turn, roll the dice as many times as you want.
Keep track of the sum of all numbers rolled.
The total is your score for that round.

➤ If either die shows a 1 before you decide to stop rolling,
your score for the round is 0.

➤ If you roll double 1s before you decide to stop rolling,
you lose all points earned so far in the game.

➤ The first player to score 100 or more points wins.

➤ What strategies did you use?

➤ List the possible outcomes.
What is the theoretical probability of rolling a sum of 1?
Of rolling a sum of 2?

Strategies Toolkit

Explore

You will need a copy of this spinner.
Suppose you spin the pointer 24 times.
How many times do you think the pointer will land
on each colour? Explain your thinking.
Spin the pointer and record the results.
Explain what you found out.

Show *and* Share

Share your explanation with a classmate.
If your classmate does not understand your explanation,
what can you do to make it clearer?

Connect

Here are some ways to explain your thinking.

**Strategies
for Success**

- **Check and reflect.**
- **Focus on the problem.**
- **Represent your thinking.**
- **Explain your thinking.**

Make sure you clearly understand the problem you are solving:

Think about how to explain the problem to someone
who has never seen it before. Include details.
Use the language of the problem. Use thinking words
such as *I noticed, I was surprised, I think/thought, I wondered.*

Justify your thinking:

Tell **how** you know something is true.
Defend your thoughts.
Prove your statements.
Use thinking words and cause and effect phrases like: *I know…,*
because …, so that means …, as a result, if you … then …

Include examples:

Use examples to make your thoughts clear.
Include labelled sketches or diagrams.
If you have made tables or done calculations,
put those in, too.

Practice

1. **a)** Make a three-part spinner that is different
   from that in *Explore*.
   Colour the sectors red, blue, and yellow.
   Repeat the activity from *Explore* using your spinner.

   b) Compare your spinner to a classmate's spinner.
   Predict what will happen if both of you spin
   your pointers once.
   Explain your prediction. Spin the pointer to check it.

Reflect

Describe two things that are important when you are explaining
your thinking to someone who has not done the question.

LESSON

1

1. Suppose you want to find out about your classmates' favourite sports team.
   a) Design a questionnaire.
   b) Ask the question.
      Record the results.
   c) What did you find out from your classmates?

2

2. Predict how many times you can write the word "experiment" in one minute.
   Work with a partner.
   Take turns writing the word and timing one minute.
   Record your results. Compare your results with your prediction.
   What conclusions can you make?

3. For each question below, choose an appropriate method to collect data to answer the question. Explain your choice.
   a) What are the 5 largest countries by area in the world?
   b) What is the favourite summer activity of students in your class?
   c) How many steps does it take a Grade 6 student in your school to walk from one end of the hallway to the other?

3

4. Would you use a line graph or a series of points to display each set of data? Explain your choices.
   a) the number of DVDs sold by a store every day for 1 week
   b) the volume of water in a swimming pool as it fills
   c) the temperature of an oven as it heats up
   d) the population of Whitehorse from 2002–2006

4

5. Duncan brought 250 mL of water to a boil, then recorded the temperature of the water as it cooled.
   a) Draw a graph to display these data.
   b) Explain how you chose the scale on each axis.
   c) Did you join the points? Explain.
   d) Write 2 things you know from the graph.

Time (min)	Temperature (°C)
0	93
5	79
10	69
15	63
20	57
25	53
30	49

6. Trevor used the Statistics Canada Web site to find the number of Canadians who visited various destinations in 2006.
The table shows the data he collected.
a) Draw a graph to display these data.
Explain your choice of graph.
b) What conclusions can you make from the graph?

Destination	Canadian Visitors (thousands)
Hong Kong	150
China	250
Cuba	638
France	645
Germany	334
Mexico	841
United Kingdom	778

7. Find the theoretical probability of each outcome.
Order the outcomes from most likely to least likely.
a) the pointer on this spinner lands on red
b) tossing a coin and getting heads
c) rolling a die labelled 1 to 6 and getting 5
d) randomly picking a red marble from a bag that contains 3 green, 5 blue, and 1 red marble

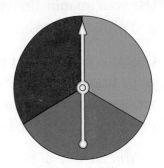

8. Nalren and Chris made up a game with a spinner.
It has 8 equal sectors labelled: 6, 24, 9, 29, 15, 7, 18, 12
Nalren wins if the pointer lands on a multiple of 2.
Chris wins if the pointer lands on a multiple of 3.
a) Is this a fair game?
Explain your thinking.
b) What is the theoretical probability that the pointer will land on a multiple of 3?
c) Work with a partner. Make the spinner.
Play the game 20 times and record the results.
What is the experimental probability of landing on a multiple of 3?
How do these probabilities compare? Explain.
d) Combine your results with those of 4 other groups.
How do the theoretical and experimental probabilities compare now? Explain.

UNIT
7 Learning Goals

☑ choose and justify an appropriate method to collect data
☑ construct and interpret line graphs to draw conclusions
☑ graph collected data to solve problems
☑ find theoretical and experimental probabilities
☑ compare theoretical and experimental probabilities

Alien Encounters!

Most Canadians believe that a visit from aliens is highly unlikely. However, each year some Canadians claim to have seen UFOs.

This table shows the number of UFO sightings reported in Canada from 2001–2006.

Year	Number of Sightings
2001	374
2002	483
2003	673
2004	882
2005	763
2006	738

1. a) Draw a graph to display these data. Explain your choice of graph.
   b) What conclusions can you make from the graph?

Use your imagination and your knowledge of data and probability to answer these questions.

One afternoon, a fleet of spaceships lands in your schoolyard. You see green faces and purple faces peering out of the spaceships' windows.

2. You are one of the 40 students and 10 teachers who rush out to greet the aliens. Who will approach the spaceships? To decide, names are put in a hat. One name will be drawn. What is the probability of each outcome?
   a) A student will be chosen.
   b) You will be chosen.

The aliens are playing a game with a spinner like this.

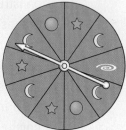

To win, the pointer must land on a green planet.

3. **a)** What is the theoretical probability of winning a point?
    b) How many points would you expect to win in 20 spins? Explain.

4. Work with a partner.
    Make a spinner to match the aliens' spinner.
    Use a pencil and paper clip as the pointer.
    Take turns spinning 20 times each.
    Record the number of times you win a point.
    How do your experimental results compare with the prediction you made in question 3?

5. The aliens invite you to predict how many times you will win in 100 spins.
    You will then spin 100 times.
    If your results are within 5 points of your prediction, you will win a trip to their planet.
    a) Suppose you want to win the trip. What prediction would you make? Why?
    b) Suppose you do not want to win the trip. What prediction would you make? Why?

Reflect on Your Learning

Think of times when you might use data and probability outside the classroom.
What have you learned in this unit that will help you?

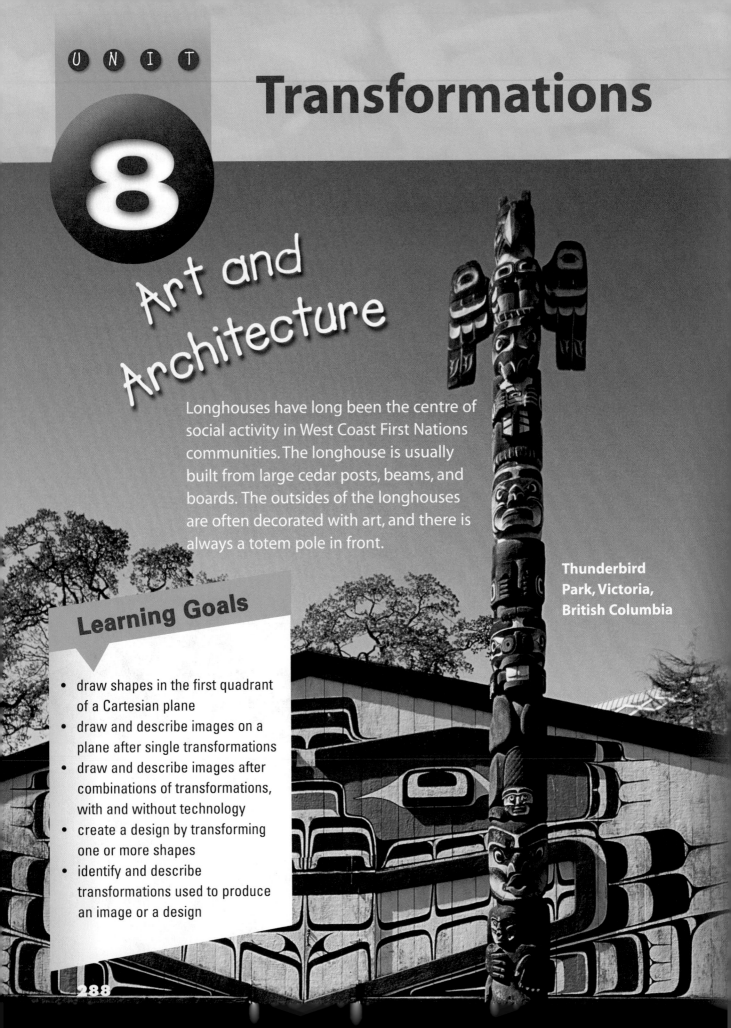

Transformations

Art and Architecture

Longhouses have long been the centre of social activity in West Coast First Nations communities. The longhouse is usually built from large cedar posts, beams, and boards. The outsides of the longhouses are often decorated with art, and there is always a totem pole in front.

Thunderbird Park, Victoria, British Columbia

Learning Goals

- draw shapes in the first quadrant of a Cartesian plane
- draw and describe images on a plane after single transformations
- draw and describe images after combinations of transformations, with and without technology
- create a design by transforming one or more shapes
- identify and describe transformations used to produce an image or a design

K'san Village, Hazelton, British Columbia

In 1993, the University of British Columbia opened The First Nations Longhouse. It is a meeting place and library for First Nations students.
The construction was overseen by First Nations elders and it reflects the architectural traditions of the Northwest Coast.

First Nations Longhouse, University of British Columbia

• Describe the photographs you see.
• Which transformations are shown in the photographs?
• How did you identify the transformations?

Drawing Shapes on a Coordinate Grid

Here is a plan for an amusement park drawn on a coordinate grid.

What are the coordinates of the water ride?
The swinging ship?

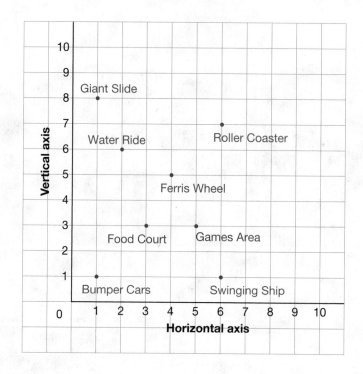

Explore

You will need 1-cm grid paper and a ruler.
Copy this grid.

Take turns.
Draw a shape on the grid.
Do not show your partner the shape.
Describe the shape you drew and its position to your partner.
Your partner draws the shape as you describe it.
Compare shapes. What do you notice?

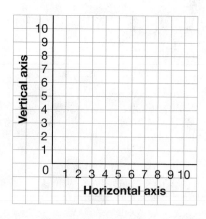

Show and Share

Talk with another pair of classmates.
Trade ideas for describing the position of a shape on a grid.
Did your shapes match exactly?
If not, how could you have improved your description?
How can you tell that two shapes match exactly?

We can use ordered pairs to describe the position
of a shape on a Cartesian plane.

> Recall that the Cartesian plane is often called a coordinate grid.

➤ Aria is designing a rectangular playground
for a local park in Victoria.

To help plan the playground, Aria drew a rectangle on a coordinate grid.
She used the scale 1 square represents 2 m.

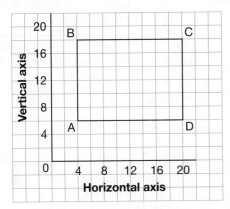

To describe the rectangle, we label its vertices with letters.
The letters are written in order as you move around the
perimeter of the shape.

We then use coordinates to describe the locations of the vertices.
Point A has coordinates (4, 6).
Point B has coordinates (4, 18).
Point C has coordinates (20, 18).
Point D has coordinates (20, 6).

➤ Here are 2 strategies students used to find the length
and width of the playground.

- Gwen counted squares.

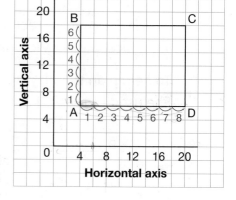

There are 8 squares along the horizontal segment AD.
The side length of each square represents 2 m.
So, the playground has length:
$8 \times 2\ m = 16\ m$

There are 6 squares along the vertical segment AB.
The side length of each square represents 2 m.
So, the playground has width:
$6 \times 2\ m = 12\ m$

- Jarrod used the coordinates of the points.

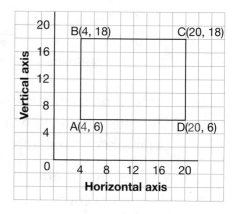

The first coordinate of an ordered pair tells
how far you move right.

The horizontal distance between D and A is:
$20 - 4 = 16$
So, the playground has length 16 m.

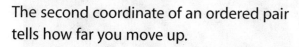

I could count
squares to check.

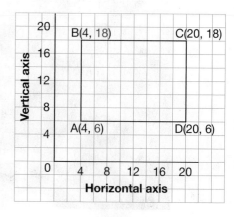

The second coordinate of an ordered pair
tells how far you move up.

The vertical distance between B and A is:
$18 - 6 = 12$
So, the playground has width 12 m.

1. Write the coordinates of the vertices of each shape.

a)
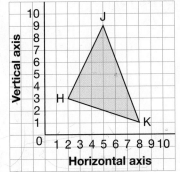

b)
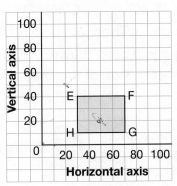

c)
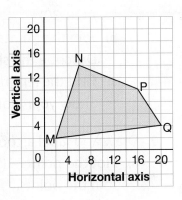

2. Find the length of each line segment on this coordinate grid.
   Describe the strategy you used.

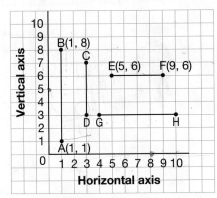

3. Copy this grid.
   a) Plot each point on the grid.

   A(10, 5)   B(5, 15)   C(10, 25)
   D(20, 25)   E(25, 15)   F(20, 5)

   b) Join the points in order. Then join F to A.
   c) Describe the shape you have drawn.

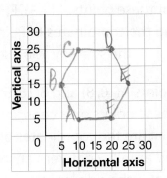

4. Draw and label a coordinate grid.
   a) Plot each point on the grid.
      What scale will you use? Explain your choice.

      J(4, 2)   K(4, 10)   L(10, 12)   M(10, 4)

   b) Join the points in order. Then join M to J.
      Describe the shape you have drawn.

5. Draw a shape on a coordinate grid.
   Each vertex should be at a point where grid lines meet.
   List the vertices of the shape, in order.
   Trade lists with a classmate. Use the list to draw your classmate's shape.

6. Draw and label a coordinate grid.
   a) Plot each point on the grid.
   What scale will you use?
   Explain your choice.
   A(10, 30)   B(35, 30)   C(35, 15)   D(10, 15)
   b) Join the points in order. Then join D to A.
   Describe the shape you have drawn.
   c) Find the length of each side of the shape.
   Show your work.

7. Draw and label a coordinate grid.
   a) Plot the points A(5, 1) and B(5, 5).
   Join the points.
   b) Find point C so that △ABC is isosceles.
   How many different ways can you do this?
   Draw each way you find.
   Write the coordinates of C.
   How do you know each triangle is isosceles?
   c) Find point D so that △ABD is scalene.
   Show 3 different scalene triangles.
   Write the coordinates of D.
   How do you know each triangle is scalene?

8. Draw and label a coordinate grid.
   a) Plot these points: E(5, 1), F(3, 3), G(5, 6)
   b) Find the coordinates of Point H that forms Kite EFGH.
   Explain the strategy you used.

9. The points A(10, 8) and B(16, 8) are two vertices of a square.
   Plot these points on a coordinate grid.
   a) What are the coordinates of the other two vertices?
   Find as many different answers as you can.
   b) What is the side length of each square you drew?

Reflect

How do you decide which scale to use when plotting a
set of points on a grid?
Is more than one scale sometimes possible? Explain.

Transformations on a Coordinate Grid

Translations, rotations, and reflections are transformations.

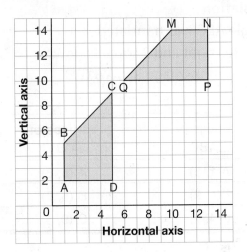

- Which transformation moves Quadrilateral ABCD to its image, Quadrilateral NMQP?

- What are the coordinates of the vertices of the quadrilateral and its image?

Explore

👥 **Game**

You will need:
- scissors
- Shape Cards
- coordinate grids
- tracing paper
- Transformation Cards

It's a Transforming Experience!

➤ Cut out the Transformation Cards and the Shape Cards. Shuffle each set of cards. Place the cards face down in separate piles.

➤ Player A takes one card from each pile. On the grid, Player A:
  – draws and labels the shape described on the Shape Card
  – draws and labels the image of the shape after the transformation described on the Transformation Card

➤ If you are able to draw the image of the shape, you score 2 points. If you are not able to draw the image, you score no points.

➤ Switch roles. Continue to play until each player has had 4 turns. The player with more points wins.

Show *and* Share

Share your work with another pair of students.
What strategies did you use to draw the images?

Translation

Triangle ABC was translated
5 squares right and 2 squares down.
Its translation image is △A'B'C'.

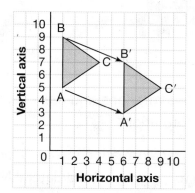

Vertices of △ABC	Vertices of △A'B'C'
A(1, 5)	A'(6, 3)
B(1, 9)	B'(6, 7)
C(4, 7)	C'(9, 5)

Each vertex moved 5 squares right and
2 squares down to its image position.

Point A' is the image
of point A.
We write: A'
We say: "A prime"

After a translation, a shape and its image
face the same way.
The shape and its image are congruent.
That is, corresponding sides and corresponding
angles are equal.
We can show this by measuring.

Reflection

Quadrilateral JKLM was reflected in a vertical
line through the horizontal axis at 5.
Its reflection image is Quadrilateral J'K'L'M'.

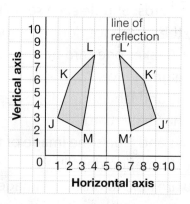

Vertices of Quadrilateral JKLM	Vertices of Quadrilateral J'K'L'M'
J(1, 3)	J'(9, 3)
K(2, 6)	K'(8, 6)
L(4, 8)	L'(6, 8)
M(3, 2)	M'(7, 2)

Each vertex moved horizontally so the distance between
the vertex and the line of reflection is equal to the distance
between its image and the line of reflection.

After a reflection, a shape and its image face opposite ways.
The shape and its image are congruent.
We can show this by tracing the shape, then flipping the tracing.
The tracing and its image match exactly.

Rotation
When a shape is turned about a point, it is rotated.
A complete turn measures 360°.

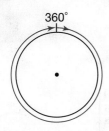

So, we can name fractions of turns in degrees.

A rotation can be clockwise or counterclockwise.

A $\frac{1}{4}$ turn is
a 90° rotation.

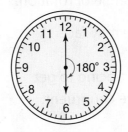

A $\frac{1}{2}$ turn is
a 180° rotation.

A $\frac{3}{4}$ turn is
a 270° rotation.

Trapezoid PQRS was rotated a $\frac{3}{4}$ turn clockwise about vertex R.
Its rotation image is Trapezoid P'Q'RS'.

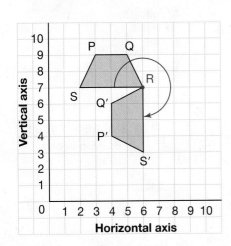

After a $\frac{3}{4}$ turn clockwise, the reflex angle between RS and RS' is **270°**.

Vertices of Trapezoid PQRS	Vertices of Trapezoid P'Q'RS'
P(3, 9)	P'(4, 4)
Q(5, 9)	Q'(4, 6)
R(6, 7)	R(6, 7)
S(2, 7)	S'(6, 3)

Since R is a vertex on the trapezoid and its image, we do not label the image vertex R'.

The sides and their images are related.
For example,

- The distances of S and S' from the point of rotation, R, are equal; that is, SR = RS'.
- Reflex ∠SRS' = 270°, which is the angle of rotation.

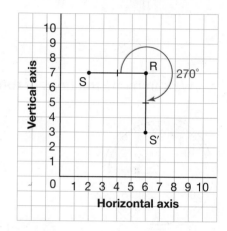

After a rotation, a shape and its image may face different ways.
Since we trace the shape and use the tracing to get the image, the shape and its image are congruent.

Practice

Use tracing paper or a Mira when it helps.

1. Copy this triangle on a grid.
   a) Draw the image of △DEF after the translation 6 squares left and 1 square down.
   b) Write the coordinates of the vertices of the triangle and its image. How are the coordinates related?
   c) Another point on this grid is G(10, 2). Use your answer to part b to predict the coordinates of point G' after the same translation.

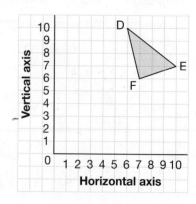

2. Copy this triangle on a coordinate grid.

   a) Draw the image of △STU after a reflection in the line of reflection.

   b) Write the coordinates of the vertices of the triangle and its image. Describe how the positions of the vertices of the shape have changed.

   c) Another point on this grid is V(4, 3). Predict the location of point V′ after a reflection in the same line. How did you make your prediction?

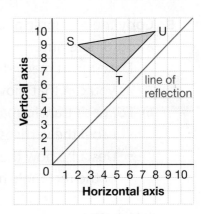

3. This diagram shows a shape and its image after 3 different transformations.

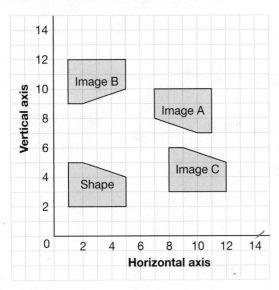

Identify each transformation.
Explain how you know.

   a) the shape to Image A

   b) the shape to Image B

   c) the shape to Image C

4. Copy this quadrilateral on a coordinate grid. Trace the quadrilateral on tracing paper. Draw the image of the quadrilateral after each rotation below. Write the coordinates of the vertices.

   a) 90° clockwise about vertex B

   b) 270° clockwise about vertex B

   c) 270° counterclockwise about vertex B

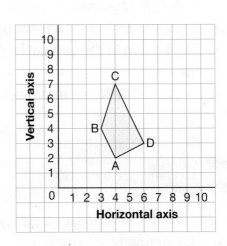

5. Copy the rectangle and its image on a coordinate grid.
   a) Describe as many different transformations as you can that move the rectangle to its image.
   b) For each transformation:
      • Label the vertices of the image.
      • Describe how the positions of the vertices of the rectangle have changed.

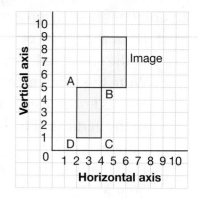

6. A quadrilateral has these vertices:
   Q(5, 2), R(4, 5), S(9, 4), T(6, 3)
   Draw the quadrilateral on a coordinate grid.
   For each transformation below:
   • Draw the image.
   • Write the coordinates of the vertices of the image.
   • Describe how the positions of the vertices of the quadrilateral have changed.
   a) a translation of 3 squares left and 1 square down
   b) a rotation of 90° clockwise about vertex S
   c) a reflection in the horizontal line through the vertical axis at 6

7. Copy this pentagon on a coordinate grid.
   Write the coordinates of each vertex.
   For each transformation below:
   • Draw the image.
   • Write the coordinates of the vertices of the image.
   • Describe how the positions of the vertices of the pentagon have changed.
   a) a translation 2 units right and 3 units up
   b) a reflection in the vertical line through the horizontal axis at 5
   c) a rotation of 90° counterclockwise about P

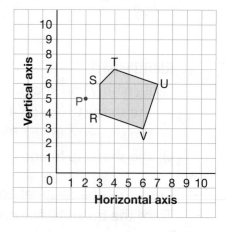

Reflect

How does a coordinate grid help you describe a transformation of a shape?

Using Technology to Perform Transformations

We can use geometry software to transform shapes.

Use dynamic geometry software.
Open a new sketch.
Display a coordinate grid.
Move the origin to the bottom left of the screen.
Check that the distance units are centimetres.
If you need help at any time, use the Help menu.

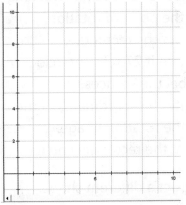

Translating a Shape

- Construct Quadrilateral ABCD.
  Record the coordinates of each vertex.
- Select the quadrilateral.
- Translate the quadrilateral 5 squares right and 3 squares down.
- Label the vertices.
- Write the coordinates of the vertices of the translation image.
- Print the quadrilateral and its image.

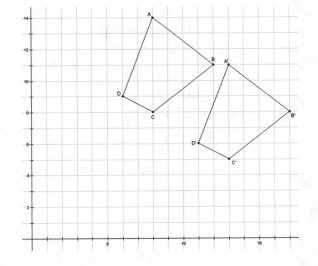

Reflecting a Shape

- Construct △EFG.
  Record the coordinates of each vertex.
- Select one side of the triangle as the line of reflection.
- Select the triangle.
- Reflect it in the line of reflection.
- Label the vertices.
- Write the coordinates of the vertices of the reflection image.
- Print the triangle and its image.

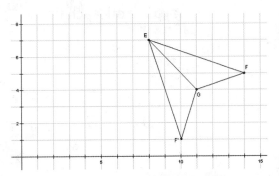

Rotating a Shape

- Construct Rectangle JKLM.
  Record the coordinates of each vertex.
- Select a vertex of the rectangle
  as the point of rotation.
- Select the rectangle.
- Rotate it 270° counterclockwise.
- Label the vertices.
- Write the coordinates of the vertices
  of the rotation image.
- Print the rectangle and its image.

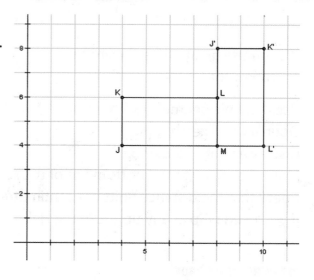

1. Construct a different shape.
   Label its vertices.
   Record the coordinates of each vertex.
   a) Choose a translation.
      Translate the shape.
   b) Choose a reflection.
      Reflect the shape.
   c) Choose a rotation.
      Rotate the shape.

   For each transformation image:
   - Label, then write the coordinates
     of the vertices.
   - Describe how the positions of the
     vertices of the shape have changed.
   - Print your work each time.

Reflect

Do you prefer to transform a shape using geometry software
or using paper and pencil? Explain your choice.

Successive Transformations

3

Which type of transformation does this diagram show?
Describe a transformation that moves the shape directly to Image C.

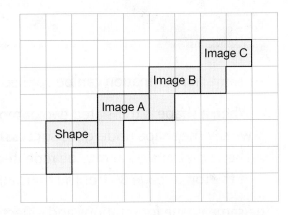

Explore ·· 👥 **Game**

You will need an 11 by 11 geoboard, 3 colours of geobands, a Mira, tracing paper, and grid paper.

Transformation Challenge

➤ Player 1 uses a geoband to make a shape.
Player 2 names a transformation.
Player 1 uses the transformation to make Image A.
With Image A as the shape, he then uses the same transformation to make Image B.
If the transformation cannot be done twice, Player 2 loses 1 point.

➤ Player 1 draws the shape and its images on grid paper.
He then names a single transformation that would move the shape directly to Image B.
Player 1 scores 1 point for each correct transformation he names.
Player 2 uses the geoboard to check.

➤ Players switch roles and repeat.

➤ The first player to get 10 points wins.

LESSON FOCUS | Draw and describe the image of a shape after repeated transformations.   **303**

Show *and* Share

Share your transformations with another pair of students.
What strategies did you use to identify the single transformations?
What do you know about a shape and each of its images?
How can you show this?

Connect •••

The same transformation can be applied to a shape more than once.

➤ When a shape is translated two or more times,
we say the shape undergoes **successive translations**.
The same translation may be repeated, as shown
at the top of page 303, or the translations may be different.

The same is true for rotations and reflections.

➤ Trapezoid PQRS undergoes **successive rotations**:
  • It is rotated 180° about vertex R.
  • Then, its image is rotated 90° clockwise about
    its top right vertex.

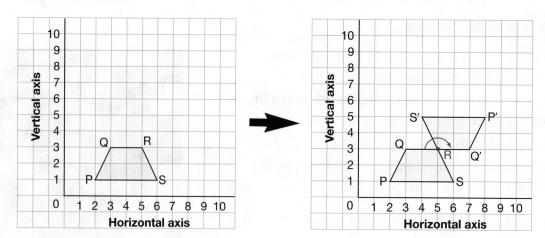

To find the image after the first rotation:

  • Trace Trapezoid PQRS on tracing paper.
  • Rotate the tracing 180° about R.
  • Mark the positions of the vertices of the image.
  • Draw the rotation image.
  • Label the vertices P'Q'RS'.

To find the final image:

- Trace Trapezoid P'Q'RS'.
- Rotate the tracing 90° clockwise about its top right vertex, P'.
- Mark the positions of the vertices of the image.
- Draw the rotation image.
- Label the vertices P'Q"R"S".

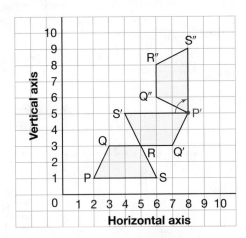

Read Q" as "Q double prime."

The trapezoid and both its images are congruent.
That is, corresponding sides and
corresponding angles are equal.
We know this because we traced the
trapezoid each time.

➤ Hexagon A"B"C"D"E"F" is the image
of Hexagon ABCDEF after two
successive reflections.

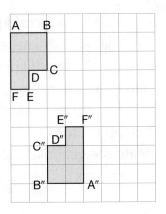

To identify the reflections:

- Reflect the original hexagon so that the image of
AF is on the same grid line as A"F".
The line of reflection passes through side BC.
- Draw the reflection image of Hexagon ABCDEF.
This is Image A'BCD'E'F'.

You might need to use guess
and test or a Mira to find the
lines of reflection.

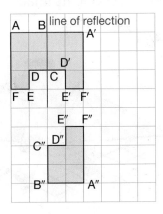

A′BCD′E′F′ and A″B″C″D″E″F″ face opposite ways and are equal distances from the horizontal line halfway between E′F′ and E″F″.
So, this is the line of reflection.

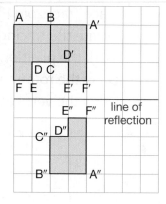

Hexagon A″B″C″D″E″F″ is the image of Hexagon ABCDEF after a reflection in the line through BC, followed by a reflection in the horizontal line halfway between E′F′ and E″F″.

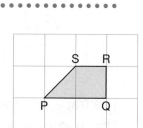

If we trace the hexagon and superimpose it on each image, we see that they match exactly.
The original hexagon and both its images are congruent.

Practice

You will need grid paper, tracing paper, and a Mira.

1. Copy this quadrilateral on grid paper. Make:
   a) 3 successive translations of 1 square right and 2 squares up
   b) 3 successive reflections in the line through SR
   c) 3 successive rotations of 180° about vertex R

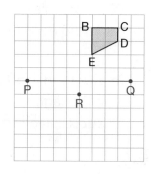

2. Copy this diagram on grid paper.
   Draw and label both images each time.
   a) Translate the quadrilateral 3 squares left and 2 squares down.
      Then translate the image 1 square right and 3 squares down.
   b) Reflect the quadrilateral in a line through BE.
      Then reflect the image in the line PQ.
   c) Rotate the quadrilateral 90° counterclockwise
      about vertex E. Then rotate the image 180° about point R.

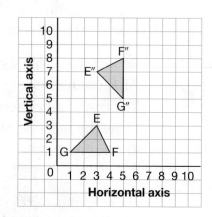

3. Describe two successive transformations that
   move △EFG to its image, △E″F″G″.
   Show your work.

306

4. Draw a triangle on grid paper.
   a) Choose two successive translations, reflections, or rotations.
      Apply the first transformation to the triangle.
      Then apply the second transformation to the image.
   b) Label the vertices of each image.
   c) What can you say about the triangle and the images?
      How could you check this?
   d) Describe a single transformation that would move
      the triangle directly to its final image.

5. a) Describe two successive transformations that move the octagon
   to its image.

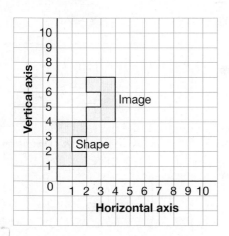

   b) Can you find two other successive transformations?
      Explain.

6. The coordinates of a shape are:

   A(3, 2)   B(3, 6)   C(5, 6)
   D(6, 4)   E(5, 3)   F(5, 2)
   • The shape is translated 3 squares right and 1 square up.
   • Then, the image is translated 2 squares left and 2 squares up.
   • Then, the image is translated 1 square left and 3 squares down.
   What are the coordinates of the final image?
   How have the positions of the vertices of the shape changed?
   Explain.

Reflect

Give a real-world example of successive:
   • translations   • reflections   • rotations

Combining Transformations

Explore .... **Game**

You will need grid paper, scissors, and tracing paper.
Your teacher will give you a large copy of these pentominoes.
Cut out the pentominoes.

What's My Move?

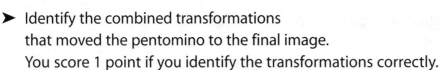

➤ Each of you chooses 1 pentomino.
Draw or trace your pentomino
on the grid paper.
Trade grids and pentominoes with your partner.

➤ Select and record 2 different transformations.
Keep the transformations secret
from your partner.
Apply one transformation to your
partner's pentomino.
Then apply the second transformation
to the image.
Draw only the second image.
Return the grid to your partner.

➤ Identify the combined transformations
that moved the pentomino to the final image.
You score 1 point if you identify the transformations correctly.

➤ Repeat the game as many times as you can.
The person with more points wins.

Show *and* Share

Share your transformations with another pair of students.
What strategies did you use to identify your partner's transformations?
In each case, are the pentomino and each of its images congruent?
How can you tell?

A combination of 2 or 3 different types of transformations can be applied to a shape.

➤ To find the final image of Rectangle ABCD after a rotation of 180° about C, followed by a reflection in a vertical line through 6 on the horizontal axis:

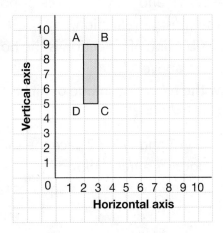

Trace Rectangle ABCD on tracing paper.
Rotate the tracing 180° about C.
Mark the positions of the vertices of the rotation image.
Draw the rotation image.
Label the vertices A'B'CD'.

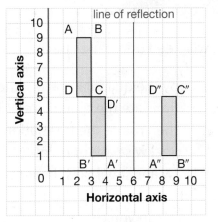

Draw the line of reflection through 6 on the horizontal axis. Reflect the rotation image in the line of reflection.
Each vertex of the reflection image is the same distance from the line of reflection as the corresponding vertex on the rotation image.
The shape and both images are congruent.

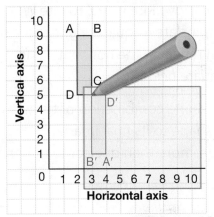

➤ Kite W"X"Y"Z" is the image of Kite WXYZ after two transformations.

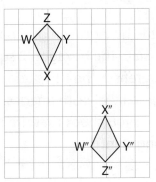

To identify the transformations:
Work backward.
Kites WXYZ and W"X"Y"Z" face opposite ways.
This suggests a reflection.
A possible line of reflection is the horizontal line
1 square above X".
Draw the reflection image of Kite W"X"Y"Z".
This is Kite W'X'Y'Z'.

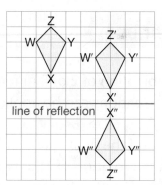

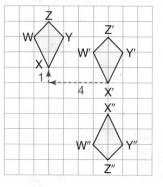

Kites WXYZ and W'X'Y'Z' face the same way.
This suggests a translation.
To go from X' to X, move 4 squares left
and 1 square up.

So, to move Kite WXYZ to Kite W"X"Y"Z"
we translate 4 squares *right* and 1 square *down*,
then reflect in the horizontal line
1 square *below* X'.

This is one combination of transformations that moves
the shape to its final image.
Often, more than one combination is possible.

Practice

You will need grid paper, tracing paper, and a Mira.

1. **a)** Copy the quadrilateral on grid paper.
   - Translate the quadrilateral 3 squares right.
   - Then rotate the translation image 90°
     clockwise about point Q.
   b) Draw and label both images.
   c) What can you say about the quadrilateral and its final image?
   How can you check?

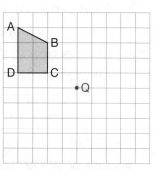

2. **a)** Copy the hexagon on grid paper.
   - Translate the hexagon 2 squares left and 3 squares down.
   - Then reflect the translation image in the line of reflection.
   b) Draw and label both images.
   c) How can you check that the hexagon and both images
   are congruent?

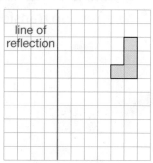

3. **a)** Copy the octagon on a coordinate grid.
   - Reflect the octagon in the line of reflection.
   - Then rotate the reflection image 270°
     counterclockwise about P.

   b) Draw and label both images.

   c) What are the coordinates of the vertices
   of the final image?

   d) Are the octagon and its final image congruent?
   How do you know?

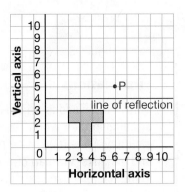

4. Draw and label a quadrilateral on grid paper.
   a) Choose two different transformations.
   - Apply the first transformation to the quadrilateral.
   - Then apply the second transformation to the image.
   What can you say about the quadrilateral and its images?
   How can you check?

   b) Use a different colour.
   Apply the transformations from part a in the reverse order.

   c) Compare the final images from parts a and b.
   Does the order in which transformations
   are applied matter? Explain.

5. Triangle A″B″C″ is the image of △ABC
   after 2 transformations.
   a) Describe a pair of transformations that move
   the triangle to its final image.
   Show your work.

   b) Can you find another pair of transformations?
   If your answer is yes, describe the transformations.
   If your answer is no, explain why not.

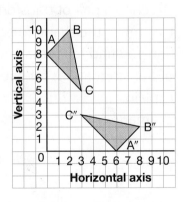

6. Describe a pair of transformations that move
   the shape to its image.
   Find as many pairs of transformations as you can.

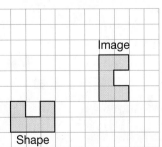

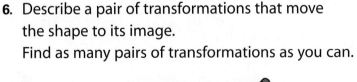

First Nations Art

Many First Nations artists use beads and braiding in their work. They produce many items, including jewellery, belts, purses, moccasins, and mukluks. We can often see transformations in the designs used by these artists.
What transformations do you see in the beading on these mukluks?

7. The coordinates of the vertices of a pentagon are:

    A(7, 3)   B(6, 4)   C(6, 5)   D(7, 6)   E(8, 5)

    The pentagon is translated 5 squares left and 3 squares up.
    Then, it is reflected in a horizontal line through (0, 5) and (10, 5).
    Then, it is translated 2 squares right and 2 squares up.

    a) What are the coordinates of the final image?

    b) What do you notice about the pentagon and its final image?

8. Describe a pair of transformations that move the shape to each image. Can you find more than one pair of transformations for each image? Explain.

    a) Image A
    b) Image B
    c) Image C

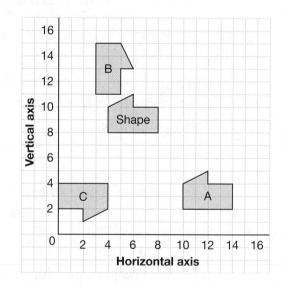

Reflect

Suppose you know the location of a shape and its final image after 2 transformations.
What strategies can you use to identify the transformations?

Creating Designs

You will need tracing paper and scissors.
Your teacher will give you a large copy of these shapes.

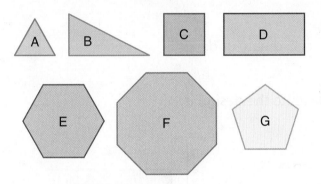

Cut out the shapes.

➤ Choose one shape. Make sure it is different
from the shapes chosen by others in your group.
Trace copies of the shape to make a design.
Think about translations, rotations, and reflections.
Colour your design.
Write to explain how your design can be created
by repeatedly transforming the shape.

➤ Repeat the activity.
This time, try to make a design using 2 different shapes.
Write to explain how your design can be created by repeatedly
transforming the 2 shapes.

Show and Share

Compare your designs with those of a classmate who used the same shapes.
Did you use the same types of transformations? Explain.
Do your designs look the same? Why or why not?

We can use transformations of one or more shapes to create a design.

➤ Calum designed this logo for his local cycling club in Comox Valley, BC.

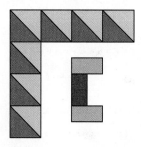

When creating the logo, Calum worked on a coordinate grid.

There are many transformations in his design.
One possible set of transformations used to create the design is:

Start with Triangle A.
Reflect the triangle in its sloping side to get Image B.
Translate Triangle A two squares up to get Image C.
Reflect Image C in its sloping side to get Image D.
Continue to translate and reflect in this way
to get Images E, F, G, and H.
Or, translate C and D together 2 squares up, twice.

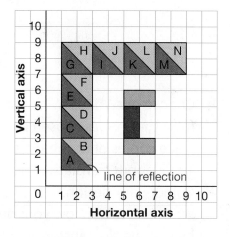

Translate Image G two squares right to get Image I.
Reflect Image I in its sloping side to get Image J.
Continue to translate and reflect in this way to get
Images K, L, M, and N.
Or, translate G and H together 2 squares right, 3 times.

To create the letter C:

Start with the red rectangle.
Rotate the rectangle 90° counterclockwise about point (5, 5) to get Image P.

Rotate the red rectangle 90° clockwise about point (5, 3) to get Image Q.

Calum may have used other possible sets of transformations to create his design.

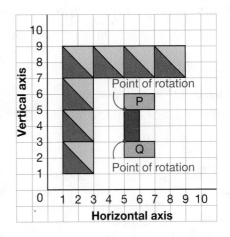

Practice

1. Explain how you could use transformations to make each design.

a)

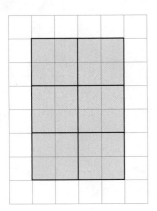

b)

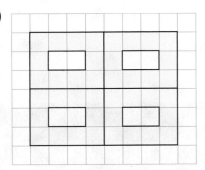

c)

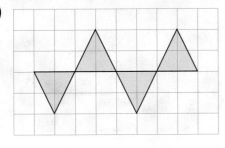

2. Draw a shape on grid paper.
   Transform copies of the shape to create a design.
   Describe the transformations you used.

3. Recreate this design.
   Identify the original shapes.
   Describe a set of transformations that could be used to
   create the design.

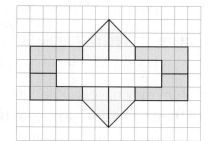

4. a) Plot these points on a coordinate grid.

A(2, 0)	B(2, 2)	C(0, 2)	D(0, 4)
E(2, 4)	F(2, 6)	G(4, 6)	H(4, 4)
I(6, 4)	J(6, 2)	K(4, 2)	L(4, 0)

   Join the vertices in order. Then join L to A.
   b) Translate the shape different ways to make a design.
      Describe the translations you used.
   c) Use a different transformation to make a design.
      Describe the transformations you used.

5. Wahaba designed this logo for her canoe club's trip
   to Bowron Lake Provincial Park.

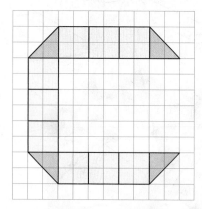

She transformed copies of 2 shapes to create
the letter C. The letter C looks like it is made
from 3 overlapping canoe-like shapes.
a) What were the original shapes?
b) Describe the transformations that could
   have been used to create the logo.
c) Is another set of transformations possible?
   If your answer is yes, describe
   the transformations.

6. Suppose you have been hired to create a logo for a rock-climbing club in Squamish, BC.

   a) Choose two or more shapes for your logo.
      Create the logo by transforming copies of your shapes on grid paper.
      Colour your logo to make it attractive.

   b) Identify the original shapes.
      Describe the transformations you used.

   c) Describe how your logo represents the rock-climbing club.

7. This is the Bear Paw quilt block.

   a) Draw a coordinate grid.
      Label the axes from 0 to 7.

   b) Copy the quilt block onto the grid.

   c) The block can be made by transforming shapes.
      • Identify the original shapes.
      • Describe a set of transformations that can be used to create the block.

Reflect

When you see a design with congruent shapes, how do you decide which transformations could have been used to create it?
Use an example to explain.

At Home

Look for designs at home that can be described using transformations. Copy each design. Share the designs with your classmates. Describe a possible set of transformations for each design.

Strategies Toolkit

Explore

You will need Pattern Blocks and a Mira.

Choose 3 Pattern Blocks, 2 the same and 1 different.
Arrange the 3 blocks to make a shape with exactly
1 line of symmetry.
Each block must touch at least one other block.
Trace the shape.
Draw a dotted line to show the line of symmetry.

Show and Share

Describe the strategy you used to solve the problem.
Could you make more than one shape? Explain.

Connect

You will need pentominoes, grid paper, and a Mira.
Choose 2 different pentominoes.
Arrange the pentominoes to create a shape
with exactly 1 line of symmetry.
Trace the shape and show the line of symmetry.

Strategies

- Make a table.
- Solve a simpler problem.
- Guess and test.
- Make an organized list.
- Use a pattern.

What do you know?
- Use 2 different pentominoes.
- Arrange the pentominoes to make a shape.
- The shape must have exactly 1 line of symmetry.

Think of a strategy to help you solve this problem.
- You can use **guess and test** to find a shape with exactly 1 line of symmetry.

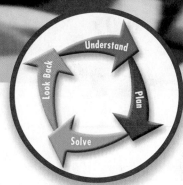

Arrange the pentominoes to make a shape.
Use a Mira to check for lines of symmetry.
If the shape has no lines of symmetry
or more than 1 line of symmetry,
try a different arrangement to make a new shape.

Check your work.
Does your shape have exactly 1 line of symmetry?
How do you know?

Practice

Choose one of the

Strategies

1. Draw lines of reflection to divide a piece of grid paper
   into 4 congruent sections.
   a) Draw Shape A in one section.
      Reflect Shape A in one of the lines of reflection.
      Label the image B.
   b) Reflect Image B in the other line of reflection.
      Label the image C.
   c) Describe a transformation that would
      move Shape A directly to Image C.
      How many different transformations can you find?

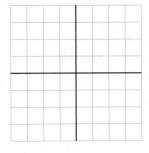

2. Repeat question 1.
   This time divide the grid paper into 3 congruent
   sections.

Reflect

How does guess and test help you solve a problem?
Use pictures and words to explain.

We can use geometry software and transformations to make designs.

Use dynamic geometry software.
Open a new sketch.
Display a coordinate grid.
Move the origin to the bottom left of the screen.
Check that the distance units are centimetres.

> To create a design:
> Construct a rectangle.
>
> Use the software to translate, reflect, or rotate the rectangle.
>
> Continue to transform the rectangle or an image rectangle to create a design.
> Colour, then print your design.

If you need help at any time, use the Help menu.

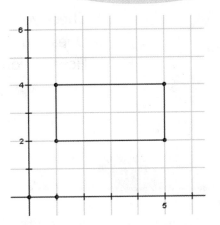

1. Construct two shapes.
   Use transformations to create a design using the two shapes.
   Colour your design.
   Identify and describe the transformations used to make the design.

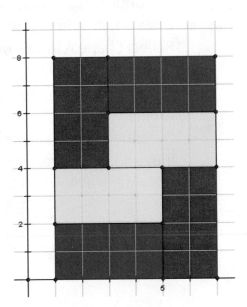

Reflect

What are the advantages of using a computer to create a design?
Are there any disadvantages? Explain.

Unscramble the Puzzle

In this game, you use transformations to put a puzzle together.

You will need 1-cm grid paper, scissors, a ruler, and a pencil.
Your teacher will give you a copy of a mixed-up puzzle.

Work with a partner.

➤ Use and describe transformations to move each
piece to its correct spot.
After you describe the transformation, cut out
the puzzle piece.
Write the transformation on the back of the piece.
Place the piece on the puzzle below.

➤ The game is over when the puzzle is complete.

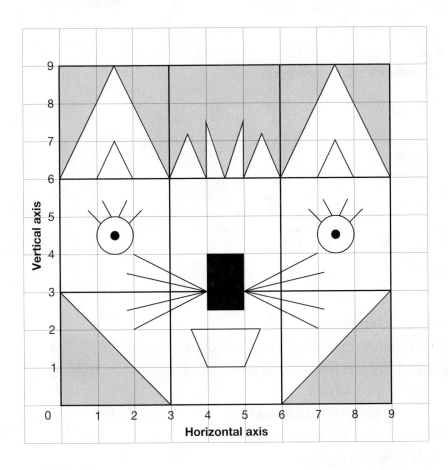

LESSON

1

1. Draw and label a coordinate grid.

   a) Plot each point on the grid.
   What scale will you use? Explain your choice.

   A(2, 6)   B(4, 14)   C(12, 14)   D(8, 10)   E(10, 2)

   Use tracing paper when it helps.

   b) Join the points in order. Then join E to A.
   Describe the shape you have drawn.

   c) Find the length of the horizontal side of the shape.

2

2. Copy △DEF on a coordinate grid.
   For each transformation below:
   • Draw the image after the transformation.
   • Write the coordinates of the vertices of the image.
   • Describe how the positions of the vertices
     of the triangle have changed.

   a) a translation of 4 squares left and 1 square down

   b) a reflection in the vertical line through
      the horizontal axis at 5

   c) a 90° counterclockwise rotation about vertex E

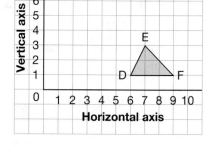

3. Copy octagon PQRSTUVW and its
   image on grid paper.

   a) Describe as many different
      single transformations as you
      can that move the octagon
      to its image.

   b) For each transformation, label
      the vertices of the image.

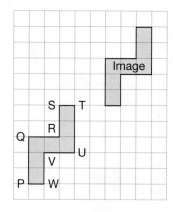

3

4. Copy this octagon on grid paper.
   Draw and label both images each time.

   a) Translate the octagon 2 squares right and 3 squares down.
      Then translate the image 4 squares left and 4 squares up.

   b) Reflect the octagon in a line through DE.
      Then reflect the image in the given line of reflection.

   c) Rotate the octagon 90° clockwise about point F.
      Then rotate the image 180° about point J.

   d) What can you say about the octagon and all its images?

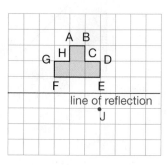

5. a) Copy this hexagon on a coordinate grid.
   - Rotate the hexagon 180° about (4, 7).
   - Then, reflect the rotation image in a line through FE.
   Draw and label both images.
   b) What are the coordinates of the vertices
   of the final image?

6. a) Describe two successive transformations
   that move the shape to its image.
   b) Find as many pairs of transformations as you can.

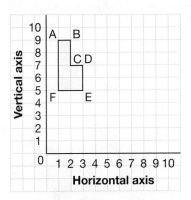

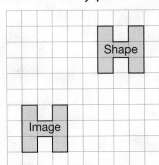

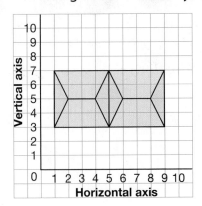

7. This design was formed by repeatedly transforming 2 shapes.

a) Copy the design.
   Identify the 2 original shapes.
b) Describe the transformations that could have
   been used to create the design.
c) Is another set of transformations possible?
   If your answer is yes, describe the transformations.
d) Use the 2 original shapes and transformations
   to make a different design.
   Describe the transformations you used.

UNIT

8 Learning Goals

- ☑ draw shapes in the first
  quadrant of a Cartesian plane
- ☑ draw and describe images
  on a plane after single
  transformations
- ☑ draw and describe images
  after combinations of
  transformations, with and
  without technology
- ☑ create a design by transforming
  one or more shapes
- ☑ identify and describe
  transformations used to
  produce an image or a design

Art and Architecture

Hatley Castle, Victoria, British Columbia

Many buildings have interesting designs that show transformations.

Part 1

These patterns are found on buildings in Saskatchewan.
Identify the transformations in each pattern.

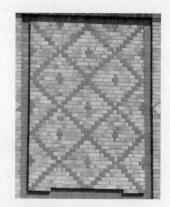

Brick pattern on the Performing
Arts Centre in Moose Jaw

Pattern on Bellamy Block in
Moose Jaw

Herringbone brick pattern on former
Bank of Toronto, in Assiniboia

Part 2

Suppose a new building is to be constructed
in your city.
Design a pattern for the outside of the building.
Sketch some shapes you could use in the pattern.
Use the shapes you sketched.
Use transformations to create a pattern.
Colour your pattern.

Part 3

Describe your pattern.
Describe the transformations you used
to create your pattern.
Give the building a name.
Where on the building will this pattern be found? Explain.

Check List

Your work should show
☑ accurate identification
of transformations
☑ a building pattern that uses
transformations
☑ a clear explanation of how
you constructed your pattern
☑ correct use of geometric
language

Reflect on Your Learning

How do you think transformations could be used by an architect,
a clothing designer, a bricklayer, or a landscaper?

Investigation

The Domino Effect

You will need dominoes, a metre stick, a stopwatch, and grid paper.

Part 1

➤ Begin with 20 dominoes.
   Stand them on end, 3 cm apart. Use a stopwatch.
   Push one domino at one end, so all the dominoes fall.
   Time how long it takes them to fall.
   Record the number of dominoes and the time in a table.

➤ Repeat with 30 dominoes, 40 dominoes, 50 dominoes,
   up to 80 dominoes.

➤ Describe any patterns you see in the table.

➤ Predict how long it would take 120 dominoes to fall.
   How did you make your prediction?

Part 2

Draw a graph to display the data in your table.
Explain your choice of graph.
Describe the graph.
About how long would it take 35 dominoes to topple?
What strategy did you use to find out?

Display Your Work

Report your findings using pictures, numbers, and words.

Take It Further

Investigate different arrangements of dominoes.
What effect does placing the dominoes closer together
have on the time it takes them to topple? Explain.
Arrange the dominoes in a curve.
How long does it take them to topple?

Unit

1

1. Mrs. Tetrault wants the students
   in her Grade 6 class to read each
   night. She said they should start at
   5 min and add 3 min each night
   until they reach 50 min.

   a) Make a table to show the time spent
      reading for each of the first 4 nights.

   b) Write a pattern rule that relates
      the night to the time spent reading.

   c) Write an expression to represent
      the pattern.

   d) On which night will the students read
      for 50 min?

2

2. In the 2006–2007 season, the Western Hockey League had a total attendance
   of 3 519 007. Write this number in a place-value chart, then in expanded form
   and in word form.

3

3. Multiply or divide. Which strategies did you use?
   a) 2.737 × 5   b) 0.463 × 3   c) 14.025 × 4
   d) 16.488 ÷ 6   e) $18.37 ÷ 3   f) 0.133 ÷ 7

4. Sidney and his friends save money to go skiing
   at Grouse Mountain. A daily lift ticket costs $37.00.
   Sidney saves $5.45 each week for 7 weeks.
   Does Sidney have enough money to buy a lift ticket?
   How do you know?

4

5. a) Use a ruler and a protractor. Draw a 35° angle.
      Which type of angle did you draw?

   b) What is the measure of the outside angle
      in part a? How do you know?
      How would you classify this angle?

   c) Use tracing paper to copy the angle in part a.
      Rotate the angle $\frac{1}{4}$ turn counterclockwise about its vertex.
      Measure the angle. What do you notice?

6. Find the measure of each unknown angle without measuring.

a)
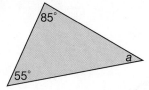
85°
a
55°

b)
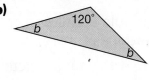
120°
b
b

c)
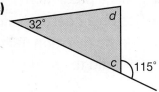
32°
d
c
115°

7. Write each mixed number as an improper fraction.

a) $2\frac{4}{9}$ b) $4\frac{1}{7}$ c) $3\frac{3}{8}$ d) $1\frac{2}{5}$

8. Write each ratio in as many ways as you can.
  a) snowshoes to snowboards
  b) snowboards to snowshoes
  c) snowboards to snowshoes and snowboards
  d) snowshoes to snowshoes and snowboards

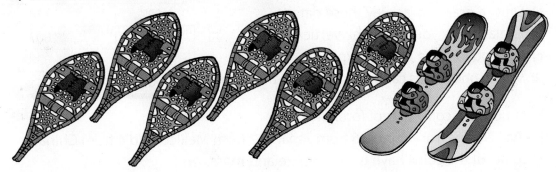

9. Write 2 equivalent ratios for each ratio.
  a) 5 : 3   **b)** 1 : 6   **c)** 4 : 7   **d)** 1 : 5

10. Use a ruler and plain paper to draw 6 different triangles.
  Measure each angle.
  a) Classify each triangle as acute, right, or obtuse.
    Explain how you know.
  b) Is any triangle isosceles or equilateral?
    How do you know?

11. Bethany sent her pen pal in Baker Lake,
  Nunavut, a stuffed animal. She packed the
  stuffed animal into a box that measured
  22 cm by 12 cm by 15 cm.
  What was the volume of the box?

12. What is your classmates' favourite winter activity?

a) Make a prediction.

b) Design a questionnaire you could use to find out.

c) Ask the question. Tally the results.

d) How did the results compare with your prediction?

13. Would you use a line graph or a series of points to display each set of data? Explain your choices.

a) the height of a corn plant as it grows

b) the life left in a light bulb as it burns

c) the population of your school over the last 10 years

14. This table shows the estimated grizzly bear population on Alberta provincial land (excluding national parks) from 1996 to 2000.

a) Draw a graph to display these data.

b) Explain how you chose the vertical scale.

c) Did you join the points? Explain.

d) What conclusions can you make from the graph?

Year	Estimated Number of Grizzly Bears
1996	765
1997	776
1998	807
1999	833
2000	841

15. Étienne has a collection of foreign coins.

He has 2 coins from Britain, 6 from Japan, 12 from Mexico, and 4 from China.

Assume all the coins have the same size and mass.

Étienne places the coins in a bag and picks one without looking.

a) List the possible outcomes.

b) What is the theoretical probability of each outcome?

- Étienne picks a Chinese coin.
- Étienne picks a Canadian coin.
- Étienne picks a Mexican coin.
- Étienne picks a coin that is not British.

16. Olivie surveyed the Grade 6 students in her school to answer this question:

What do you use the Internet for most often?

The table shows the data she collected.

a) Draw a graph to display these data. Explain your choice of graph.

b) What do most students use the Internet for? How does the graph show this?

Use	Number of Students
E-mail	15
Chatting	18
Downloading Music	12
Homework	8
Other	7

17. Draw and label a coordinate grid.
   a) Plot each point on the grid.
   P(20, 20)   Q(20, 60)   R(40, 70)   S(60, 60)   T(50, 10)
   b) Join the points in order. Then join T to P.
   What scale did you use? Explain your choice.
   c) Describe the shape you have drawn.
   d) Find the length of the vertical side of the shape.

18. Copy this shape and its image on grid paper.
   a) Describe as many different single transformations
   as you can that move the shape to its image.
   b) For each transformation, label the vertices of
   the image.

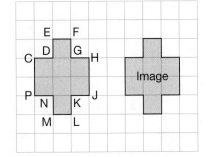

19. Copy the shape and the line of reflection
   onto a coordinate grid.
   Reflect the shape in the line of reflection.
   Then translate the reflection image 5 squares down.
   What are the coordinates of the final image?

20. Look at your answer to question 19.
   Suppose you translated the shape first, then reflected
   the translation image in the line of reflection.
   What would the coordinates of the final image be?

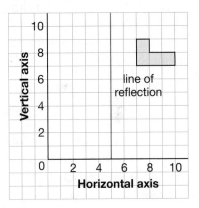

21. Rhiannon designed this logo for her
   gardening club in Strathcona, Alberta.
   She transformed copies of 2 shapes to
   make a flower-like shape.
   a) Copy the design.
   Identify the 2 original shapes.
   b) Describe the transformations that could
   have been used to create the logo.
   c) Is another set of transformations possible?
   If your answer is yes, describe the
   transformations.

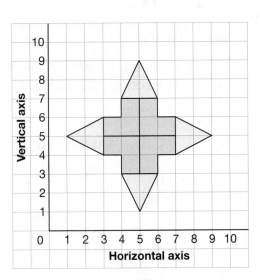

Illustrated Glossary

A.M.: A time between midnight and just before noon.

Acute angle: An angle that measures less than 90°.

Acute triangle: A triangle with all angles less than 90°. All angles are acute.

Angle: Two lines meet to form an angle. Each side of an angle is called an arm. We show an angle by drawing an arc.

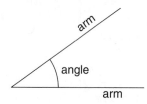

Area: The amount of surface a shape or region covers. We measure area in square units, such as square centimetres or square metres.

At random: In a probability experiment, when picking at random, each outcome has an equal chance of being picked.

Axis (plural: axes): A number line along the edge of a graph. We label each axis of a graph to tell what data it displays. The horizontal axis goes across the page. The vertical axis goes up the page.

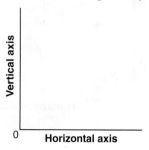

Bar graph: A graph that displays data by using bars of equal width on a grid. The bars may be vertical or horizontal.

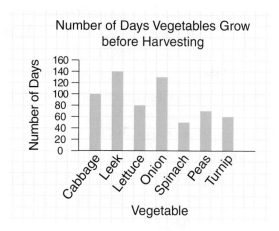

Base: The face that names an object. For example, in this triangular prism, the bases are triangles.

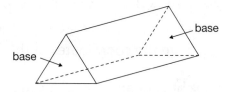

Benchmark: Used for estimating by writing a number to its closest benchmark; for example,

1. For whole numbers: 47 532 is closer to the benchmark 47 500 than to the benchmark 47 600.

2. For fractions: $\frac{1}{3}$ is closer to $\frac{1}{2}$ than to 0 or to 1.

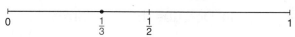

3. For decimals: 0.017 is closer to 0.020 than to 0.010.

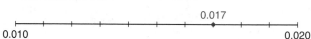

Biased question: In questionnaires, a question that might lead a person to answer a certain way; for example, *Is blue your favourite colour?*

Billion: One thousand million.

Capacity: A measure of how much a container holds. We measure capacity in litres (L) or millilitres (mL); for example, this carton has a capacity of 1 L.

Carroll diagram: A diagram used to sort numbers or attributes.

	Even		Odd	
Multiples of 3	6 36	12 42	9 21	27 39
Not multiples of 3	8 16	44 74	35 53	67 17

Cartesian plane: Another name for a coordinate grid.
See **Coordinate grid**.

Centimetre: A unit used to measure length. We write one centimetre as 1 cm.
1 cm = 0.01 m
1 cm = 10 mm
100 cm = 1 m

Certain event: An event that always happens; for example, the month that follows June is July.

Clockwise: The hands on a clock turn in a clockwise direction.

Clockwise

Common factor: A number that is a factor of each of the given numbers; for example, 3 is a common factor of 15, 9, and 21.

Common multiple: A number that is a multiple of two or more numbers; for example, 6 is a common multiple of 2 and 3.

Commutative property of addition: A property that states that numbers can be added in any order without affecting the sum; for example, $24 + 13 = 13 + 24$.

Commutative property of multiplication: A property that states that numbers can be multiplied in any order without affecting the product; for example, $7 \times 11 = 11 \times 7$.

Compatible numbers: Pairs of numbers that are easy to work with; for example,

1. The numbers $340 + 160$ are compatible for adding because $40 + 60 = 100$.
2. Multiples of 10 or 100 are compatible for estimating products because they are easy to multiply.

Compensation: A strategy for estimating; rounding one number up and rounding the other number down when the numbers are added. For example, to estimate $2180 + 3432$, round 2180 *up* to 2200 and 3432 *down* to 3400; $2200 + 3400 = 5600$

Composite number: A number with more than 2 factors; for example, 4, 6, 8, and 9 are composite numbers.

Concave polygon: A polygon that has at least one angle greater than 180°.

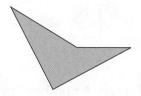

Congruent shapes: Two shapes that match exactly.

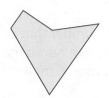

Consecutive numbers: Numbers that follow in order; for example, 4, 5, 6, 7, …

Continuous data: Data that can include any value between data points; for example, time, temperature, and mass are continuous.

Convex polygon: A polygon that has all angles less than 180°.

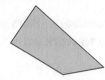

Coordinate grid: A two-dimensional surface on which a coordinate system has been set up.

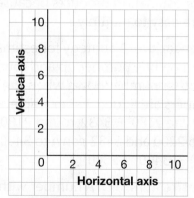

Coordinates: The numbers in an ordered pair that locate a point on the grid. See **Ordered pair**.

Core: See **Repeating pattern**.

Counterclockwise: A turn in the opposite direction to the direction the hands on a clock turn.

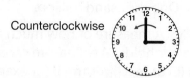

Counterclockwise

Cube: An object with 6 faces that are congruent squares. Two faces meet at an edge. Three or more edges meet at a vertex.

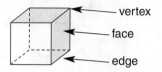

Cubic centimetre (cm³): A unit to measure volume. A centimetre cube has a volume of one cubic centimetre. We write one cubic centimetre as 1 cm³.

Cubic metre: A unit to measure volume. One cubic metre is the volume of a cube with edge length 1 m. We write one cubic metre as 1 m³.

Data: Information collected from a survey or experiment.

Database: An organized collection of data. There are two database formats: print and electronic.

Decagon: A polygon with 10 sides.

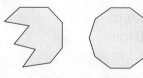

Decimal: A way to write a fraction. For example, the fraction $\frac{2}{10}$ can be written as the decimal 0.2.

Decimal point: Separates the whole number part and the fraction part in a decimal. We read the decimal point as "and." We say 3.2 as "three **and** two-tenths."

Degree:

1. A unit to measure temperature. We write one degree Celsius as 1°C.

2. A unit used to measure the size of an angle; the symbol for degree is °.

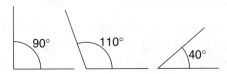

Denominator: The part of a fraction that tells how many equal parts are in one whole. The denominator is the bottom number in a fraction. For example, in the fraction $\frac{3}{5}$, the denominator is 5. There are 5 parts in one whole.

Diagonal: A line segment that joins 2 vertices of a shape, but is not a side.

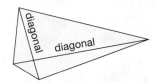

Difference: The result of a subtraction. For example, the difference of 3.5 and 2 is $3.5 - 2 = 1.5$

Dimensions:

1. The measurements of a shape or an object. A rectangle has 2 dimensions, length and width. A cube has 3 dimensions, length, width, and height.

2. For an array, the dimensions tell the number of rows and the number of columns.

Discrete data: Data that can be counted; for example, the number of students in a class.

Displacement: The volume of water moved or displaced by an object put in the water. The displacement of this cube is 50 mL or 50 cm³.

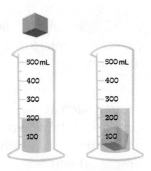

Dividend: The number to be divided. For example, in the division sentence $2.4 \div 6 = 0.4$, the dividend is 2.4.

Divisor: The number by which another number is divided. For example, in the division sentence $2.4 \div 6 = 0.4$, the divisor is 6.

Double bar graph: A graph that displays two sets of data at once.

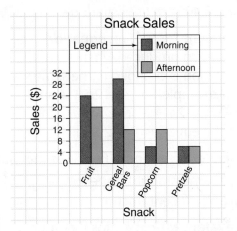

Edge: Two faces of an object meet at an edge. See also **Cube**, **Prism**, and **Pyramid**.

Equally likely events: Two or more events, each of which is as likely to happen as the other. For example, if you toss a coin, it is equally likely that the coin will land heads up as tails up.

Equally probable: See **Equally likely events**.

Equation:

1. Uses the = symbol to show two things that represent the same amount; for example, $5 + 2 = 7$ is an equation.

2. Uses the = symbol with a variable, an operation such as $+, -, \times,$ or $\div$, and numbers to show two things that represent the same amount; for example, $20 = p + 6$.
See **Solution of an equation**.

Equilateral triangle: A triangle with 3 equal sides and 3 equal angles.

Equivalent decimals: Decimals that name the same amount. For example, 0.4, 0.40, and 0.400 are equivalent decimals.

Equivalent form of an equation: The equation produced when each side of an equation is changed in the same way. For example, $8 + 4 = 2n + 4$ and $8 - 3 = 2n - 3$ are equivalent forms of the equation $8 = 2n$.

Equivalent fractions: Fractions that name the same amount; for example, $\frac{1}{3}, \frac{2}{6}, \frac{3}{9}, \frac{10}{30}$ are equivalent fractions.

Equivalent ratios: Ratios that represent the same comparison; for example, $2 : 3$ and $6 : 9$ are equivalent ratios.

Estimate: Close to an amount or value, but not exact.

Event: The outcomes or a set of outcomes from a probability experiment. For example, when a die labelled 1 to 6 is rolled, some events are: rolling a number greater than 3, rolling an even number, rolling a 6.

Expanded form: Shows a number as a sum of the values of its digits. For example,

1. For whole numbers:

    $123\,456 = 100\,000 + 20\,000 + 3000 + 400 + 50 + 6$

2. For decimals:

    $5.0713 = 5 + 0.07 + 0.001 + 0.0003$

Experiment: In probability, a test or trial used to investigate an idea.

Experimental probability: The likelihood that something occurs based on the results of an experiment.

Experimental probability =

$$\frac{\text{Number of times an outcome occurs}}{\text{Number of times the experiment is conducted}}$$

Expression:

1. A mathematical statement with numbers and operations; for example, $3 \times 4 - 2$ is an expression.

2. Uses a variable and numbers to represent a pattern; for example, $d + 2$ represents the number of dots on Figure d in the pattern shown in the table below.

Figure Number	Number of Dots
1	3
2	4
3	5
4	6
5	7

Face: Part of an object. See also **Cube**, **Prism**, and **Pyramid**.

Factor: Numbers that are multiplied to get a product are factors. For example, in the multiplication sentence $3 \times 7 = 21$, the factors of 21 are 3 and 7.

Factor tree: A diagram used to find factors of a number; for example, 3, 5, and 9 are factors of 45.

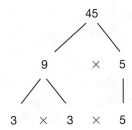

Fair game: A game where all players have the same chance of winning.

Fair question: In questionnaires, a question that does not influence a person's answer.

First-hand data: Data you collect yourself.

Formula: A short way to state a rule. For example, a formula for the area of a rectangle is $A = \ell \times w$, where ℓ represents the length of the rectangle and w represents its width.

Front-end estimation: Using only the first one or two digits of each number to get an estimate. For example,

1. For adding: 23 056 + 42 982 is about 23 000 + 42 000 = 65 000

2. For multiplying: 72 × 23 is about 70 × 20 = 1400

Gram: A unit to measure mass. We write one gram as 1 g. 1000 g = 1 kg

Hexagon: A polygon with 6 sides.

Horizontal axis: See **Axis.**

Horizontal line: A line that is parallel to the horizon.

Hundredth: A fraction that is one part of a whole when it is divided into 100 equal parts. We write one-hundredth as $\frac{1}{100}$, or 0.01.

Hundred-thousandth: A fraction that is one part of a whole when it is divided into 100 000 equal parts. We write one hundred-thousandth as $\frac{1}{100\,000}$, or 0.000 01.

Image: The shape that is the result of a transformation. For example, this is a rectangle and its image after a translation of 6 squares right and 1 square up.

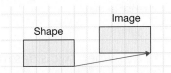

Impossible event: An event that cannot happen; for example, an earthworm can talk.

Improbable event: An event that is unlikely to happen, but not impossible. For example, you will go for a hot air balloon ride today.

Improper fraction: A fraction that shows an amount greater than one whole. The numerator is greater than the denominator. For example, $\frac{3}{2}$ is an improper fraction.

Increasing pattern: A pattern where each frame or term is greater than the previous frame or term.

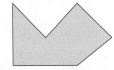

Frame 1   Frame 2   Frame 3

1, 3, 8, 10, 15, 17, 23, …

Input/Output machine: Performs operations on a number (the input) to produce another number (the output).

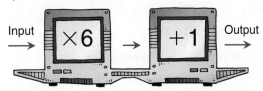

Inspection: To solve an equation by inspection, find the value of the unknown by using addition, subtraction, multiplication, and division facts.

Integers: The set of numbers
   ... −3, −2, −1, 0, +1, +2, +3, ...

Interior angle: An angle inside a triangle or other polygon.

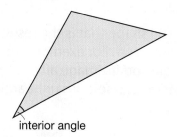

interior angle

Intersect:

1. For shapes, when two sides meet, they intersect at a point called the vertex.

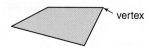

vertex

2. For objects, when three or more edges meet, they intersect at a point called the vertex. When two faces meet, they intersect at an edge. See **Cube**.

Irregular polygon: A polygon that does not have all sides equal or all angles equal. Here are two irregular hexagons.

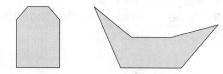

Isosceles triangle: A triangle with 2 equal sides and 2 equal angles.

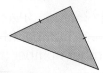

Key: See **Pictograph**.

Kilogram: A unit to measure mass. We write one kilogram as 1 kg. 1 kg = 1000 g

Kilometre: A unit to measure long distances. We write one kilometre as 1 km. 1 km = 1000 m

Kite: A quadrilateral with two pairs of adjacent sides equal.

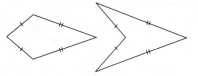

Legend: Tells the scale on a double bar graph and what each bar represents. See **Double bar graph**.

Likely event: An event that will probably happen; for example, you will talk to someone tomorrow.

Line graph: A graph used to show continuous data. Consecutive points are joined by line segments.

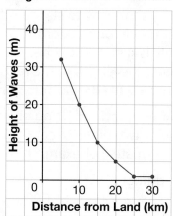

Line of reflection: A line in which a shape is reflected.
   See **Reflection**.

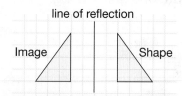

Line of symmetry: Divides a shape into two congruent parts. If we fold the shape along its line of symmetry, the parts match.

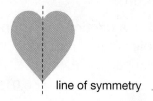

line of symmetry

Linear dimension: Length, width, depth, height, thickness.

Litre: A unit to measure the capacity of a container. We write one litre as 1 L.
1 L = 1000 mL

Mass: A unit to measure how much matter is in an object. We measure mass in grams or kilograms.

Metre: A unit to measure length.
We write one metre as 1 m.
1 m = 100 cm
1 m = 1000 mm

Milligram: A unit to measure mass.
We write one milligram as 1 mg.
1000 mg = 1 g

Millilitre: A unit to measure the capacity of a container. We write one millilitre as 1 mL.
1000 mL = 1 L
1 mL = 1 cm³

Millimetre: A unit to measure length.
We write one millimetre as 1 mm.
One millimetre is one-tenth of a centimetre:
1 mm = 0.1 cm
10 mm = 1 cm
One millimetre is one-thousandth of a metre:
1 mm = 0.001 m
1000 mm = 1 m

Millionth: A fraction that is one part of a whole when it is divided into 1 000 000 equal parts. We write one-millionth as $\frac{1}{1\,000\,000}$, or 0.000 001.

Mixed number: A number that has a whole number part and a fraction part; for example, $1\frac{1}{6}$ is a mixed number.

Multiple: Start at a number, then count on by that number to get the multiples of that number. For example, to get the multiples of 3, start at 3 and count on by 3:
3, 6, 9, 12, 15, …

Multiplication fact: A sentence that relates factors to a product. For example, $3 \times 7 = 21$ is a multiplication fact.

Negative integer: An integer less than 0; for example, -3 and -14 are negative integers.

Net: An arrangement that shows all the faces of an object, joined in one piece. It can be folded to form the object.

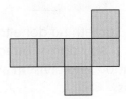

Number line: Has numbers in order from least to greatest. The spaces between pairs of consecutive numbers are equal.

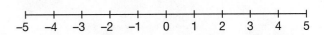

Numerator: The part of a fraction that tells how many equal parts to count. The numerator is the top number in a fraction. For example, in the fraction $\frac{2}{3}$, the numerator is 2. We count 2 thirds of the whole.

Object: Has length, width, and height. Objects have faces, edges, vertices, and bases. We name some objects by the number and shape of their bases.

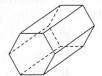

Pentagonal pyramid   Hexagonal prism

Obtuse angle: An angle that measures between 90° and 180°.

Obtuse triangle: A triangle with one angle greater than 90° and less than 180°.

Octagon: A polygon with 8 sides.

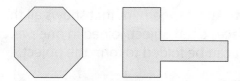

Operation: Something done to a number or quantity. Addition, subtraction, multiplication, and division are operations.

Opposite integers: Two integers that are the same distance from 0 but are on opposite sides of 0; for example, +2 and −2 are opposite integers.

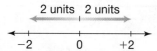

Order of operations: The rules that are followed when evaluating an expression.

- Do the operations in brackets.
- Multiply and divide, in order, from left to right.
- Then add and subtract, in order, from left to right.

Ordered pair: Two numbers that describe a point on a coordinate grid. The first number tells how far you move right from the origin. The second number tells how far you move up from the origin.

Origin: The point of intersection of the axes on a coordinate grid.

Outcome: One result of an event or experiment. Tossing a coin has two possible outcomes, heads or tails.

P.M.: A time between noon and just before midnight.

Palindrome: A word, phrase, or number that reads the same from both directions; for example, noon and 636 are palindromes.

Parallel:

1. Two lines that are always the same distance apart are parallel.

2. Two faces of an object that are always the same distance apart are parallel; for example, the shaded faces on the rectangular prism below are parallel.

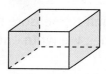

Parallelogram: A quadrilateral with 2 pairs of opposite sides parallel.

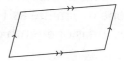

Partial products: Used as a strategy for multiplying 2-digit numbers; for example,

$$42 \times 57 = (40 + 2) \times (50 + 7)$$
$$= (40 \times 50) + (40 \times 7) + (2 \times 50) + (2 \times 7)$$
$$= 2000 + 280 + 100 + 14$$
$$= 2394$$

There are 4 partial products.

Part-to-part ratio: A ratio that compares a part of the whole to another part of the whole. For example, there are 11 boys and 14 girls in the class. The ratio of boys to girls is 11 : 14.

Part-to-whole ratio: A ratio that compares a part of the whole to the whole. For example, there are 11 boys and 14 girls in the class. The ratio of boys to students is 11 : 25.

Pattern rule: Describes how to make a pattern. For example, for the pattern 1, 2, 4, 8, 16, …, the pattern rule is: Start at 1. Multiply by 2 each time.

Percent: The number of parts per hundred. The numerator of a fraction with denominator 100; for example, $\frac{31}{100}$ is 31%.

Perimeter: The distance around a shape. It is the sum of the side lengths. For example, the perimeter of this rectangle is: 2 cm + 4 cm + 2 cm + 4 cm = 12 cm

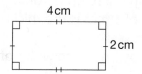

Perpendicular:

1. Two lines that intersect at a right angle are perpendicular.

2. Two faces that intersect on a rectangular prism or a cube are perpendicular.

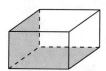

Pictograph: Uses pictures and symbols to display data. Each picture or symbol can represent more than one object. A key tells what each picture represents.

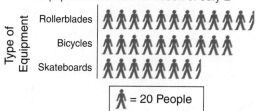

Equipment Rentals for Week of July 2

Place-value chart: It shows how the value of each digit in a number depends on its place in the number; see page 47 for whole numbers and page 89 for decimals.

Placeholder: A zero used to hold the place value of the digits in a number. For example, the number 603 has 0 tens. The digit 0 is a placeholder.

Point of rotation: The point about which a shape is rotated. See **Rotation**.

Polygon: A shape with three or more sides. We name a polygon by the number of its sides. For example, a five-sided polygon is a pentagon.

Positive integer: An integer greater than 0; for example, +2 and 17 are positive integers.

Possible event: An event that may happen; for example, rolling a 6 on a die labelled 1 to 6.

Prediction: You make a prediction when you decide how likely or unlikely it is that an event will happen.

Preservation of equality: When each side of an equation is changed in the same way, the values remain equal.

Prime number: A whole number with exactly 2 factors, 1 and itself; for example, 7, 13, 19, and 23 are prime numbers.

Prism: An object with 2 bases.

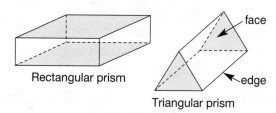

Rectangular prism   Triangular prism

Probability: Tells how likely it is that an event will occur.

Probable event: An event that is likely, but not certain to happen; for example, it will rain in April.

Product: The result of a multiplication. For example, the product of 1.5 and 2 is $1.5 \times 2 = 3$

Proper fraction: Describes an amount less than one. A proper fraction has a numerator that is less than its denominator. For example, $\frac{5}{7}$ is a proper fraction.

Protractor: An instrument used to measure the number of degrees in an angle.

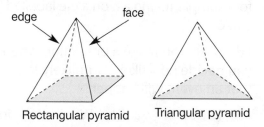

Pyramid: An object with 1 base.

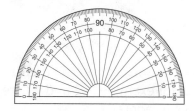

Rectangular pyramid Triangular pyramid

Quadrilateral: A shape with 4 sides.

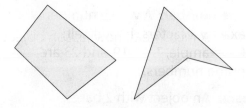

Quotient: The number obtained by dividing one number into another. For example, in the division sentence $2.4 \div 6 = 0.4$, the quotient is 0.4.

Ratio: A comparison of 2 quantities measured with the same unit.

Rectangle: A quadrilateral, where 2 pairs of opposite sides are equal and each angle is a right angle.

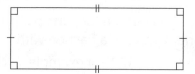

Rectangular prism: See **Prism**.

Rectangular pyramid: See **Pyramid**.

Referent: Used to estimate a measure; for example, a referent for:
a length of 1 mm is the thickness of a dime.
a length of 1 m is the width of a doorway.
a volume of 1 cm³ is the tip of a finger.
a volume of 1 m³ is the space taken up by a playpen.
a capacity of 1 L is a milk pitcher.
a capacity of 1 mL is an eyedropper.

Reflection: Reflects a shape in a line of reflection to create a reflection image. See **Line of reflection**.

Reflection image: The shape that results from a reflection.
See **Reflection**.

Reflex angle: An angle that measures between 180° and 360°.

Regular polygon: A regular polygon has all sides equal and all angles equal. Here is a regular hexagon.

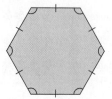

342

Regular shape: See **Regular polygon**.

Related facts: Sets of addition and subtraction facts or multiplication and division facts that have the same numbers. Here are two sets of related facts:

$2 + 3 = 5$	$5 \times 6 = 30$
$3 + 2 = 5$	$6 \times 5 = 30$
$5 - 3 = 2$	$30 \div 6 = 5$
$5 - 2 = 3$	$30 \div 5 = 6$

Remainder: What is left over when one number does not divide exactly into another number. For example, in the quotient $13 \div 5 = 2$ R3, the remainder is 3.

Repeating pattern: A pattern with a core that repeats. The core is the smallest part of the pattern that repeats. In the pattern: 1, 8, 2, 1, 8, 2, 1, 8, 2, ..., the core is 1, 8, 2.

Rhombus: A quadrilateral with all sides equal and 2 pairs of opposite sides parallel.

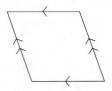

Right angle: An angle that measures 90°.

Right triangle: A triangle with one 90° angle.

Rotation: Turns a shape about a point of rotation in a given direction. For example, this is a triangle and its image after a rotation of 90° counterclockwise about one vertex:

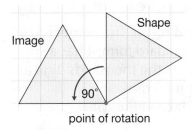

Rotation image: The shape that results from a rotation.
See **Rotation**.

Scale: The numbers on the axis of a graph show the scale.

Scalene triangle: A triangle with no equal sides and no equal angles.

Second: A small unit of time. There are 60 seconds in 1 minute.
60 s = 1 min

Second-hand data: Data collected by someone else.

Solution of an equation: The value of a variable that makes the equation true; for example, $p = 14$ is the solution of the equation $20 = p + 6$.

Speed: A measure of how fast an object is moving.

Square: A quadrilateral with all sides equal and 4 right angles.

343

Square centimetre: A unit of area that is a square with 1-cm sides. We write one square centimetre as 1 cm².

Square metre: A unit of area that is a square with 1-m sides. We write one square metre as 1 m².

Standard form: The number 579 328 is in standard form; it has a space between the thousands digit and the hundreds digit.
See **Place-value chart**.

Standard units: Metres, square metres, cubic metres, kilograms, and seconds are some standard units.

Straight angle: An angle that measures 180°.

Successive reflections: A shape that is reflected two or more times.

Successive rotations: A shape that is rotated two or more times.

Successive translations: A shape that is translated two or more times.

Sum: The result of addition. For example, the sum of 3.5 and 2 is $3.5 + 2 = 5.5$

Survey: Used to collect data. You can survey your classmates by asking them which is their favourite ice-cream flavour.

Symmetrical: A shape is symmetrical if it has one or more lines of symmetry. For example, an isosceles triangle has one line of symmetry, so it is symmetrical.

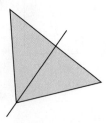

Tenth: A fraction that is one part of a whole when it is divided into 10 equal parts. We write one-tenth as $\frac{1}{10}$, or 0.1.

Ten-thousandth: A fraction that is one part of a whole when it is divided into 10 000 equal parts. We write one ten-thousandth as $\frac{1}{10\,000}$, or 0.0001.

Term: One number in a number pattern. For example, the number 4 is the third term in the pattern 1, 2, 4, 8, 16, …

Terms of a ratio: The quantities that make up a ratio; for example, in the ratio 2 : 3, 2 and 3 are the terms of the ratio.

Theoretical probability: The likelihood that an outcome will happen.
Theoretical probability =
$$\frac{\text{Number of favourable outcomes}}{\text{Number of possible outcomes}}$$

Thousandth: A fraction that is one part of a whole when it is divided into 1000 equal parts. We write one-thousandth as $\frac{1}{1000}$, or 0.001.

Tonne: A unit used to measure a very large mass. We write one tonne as 1 t. 1 t = 1000 kg

Transformation: A translation (slide), a reflection (flip), and a rotation (turn) are transformations.

Translation: Slides a shape from one location to another. A translation arrow joins matching points on the shape and its image. For example, this shape has been translated 6 squares left and 2 squares up.

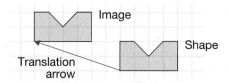

Translation arrow: See **Translation**.

Translation image: The shape that results from a translation.
See **Translation**.

Trapezoid: A quadrilateral with exactly 1 pair of sides parallel.

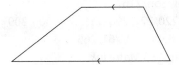

Triangular prism: See **Prism**.

Triangular pyramid: See **Pyramid**.

Trillion: One thousand billion.

Unlikely event: An event that will probably not happen; for example, you will win a trip to Australia.

Variable: A letter, in italics, that is used to represent a number in an equation, or a set of numbers in a pattern.
See **Equation** and **Expression**.

Venn diagram: A diagram that is used to sort numbers, shapes, or objects.

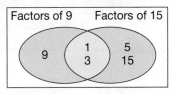

Vertex (plural: vertices):

1. The point where two sides of a shape meet.

2. The point where three or more edges of an object meet.

Vertical axis: See **Axis**.

Vertical line: A line that is perpendicular to the horizon.

Volume: The amount of space occupied by an object or the amount of space inside an object. Volume can be measured in cubic centimetres or in cubic metres.

Index

reflection, 296, 297, 301, 309, 310, 314
reflex angle, 127, 135, 140
regular polygon, 215
    congruence in, 219–221
right angle, 127, 135
right triangle, 206
rotation, 297, 298, 302, 309, 315

S

scalene triangle, 201, 210
standard form of numbers, 47, 89
standard protractor, 133–135, 140
    drawing triangles with, 209–211
straight angle, 127, 135
substitution, 228
    in order of operations, 70
successive reflections, 305, 306
successive rotations, 304, 305
successive transformations, 303–306
successive translations, 303, 304
superimposed, 220

T

tables,
    modelling patterns with, 30
    patterns from, 11–13, 21
Technologies:
    investigating probability, 280
    gathering data by databases and electronic
        media, 252–254
    making designs with geometry software, 320
    performing transformations with geometry
        software, 301, 302
temperature, 74
tens, 47, 48, 88, 89
ten-thousandths, 88–90
tenths, 88, 89, 96, 100, 104
terms of a ratio, 177
theoretical probability (*also* Probability), 271–273,
    276, 277
thousands, 47, 48
thousandths, 88–90, 96

tiles,
    modelling patterns with, 30
transformation, 312 *MathLink*
    performing with geometry software, 301, 302
        Technology
    combining, 308–310
    creating designs with, 313–315
    on coordinate grids, 295–298
    successive, 303–306
translation, 296, 301, 314
trapezoid, 297, 298
triangles, 200, 201
    acute, 206
    angles in, 146, 147
    equilateral, 201
    isosceles, 201
    naming and sorting by angles, 205, 206
    obtuse, 206
    right, 206
    scalene, 201, 210
trillions, 48

V

variables, 34
    describing patterns with, 19–21
Venn diagram, 63
    sorting triangles with, 206
vertex, 126, 131, 134
    of a polygon, 215
vertical axis, 25, 26, 264, 290–292
volume,
    of a rectangular prism, 235, 236

W

watts, 87
Weather Dancer, 87
William Big Bull, 87
word form of numbers, 47, 90

Z

ziggurat, 158 *Investigation*

Acknowledgments

Pearson Education would like to thank the Royal Canadian Mint for the illustrative use of Canadian coins in this textbook. In addition, the publisher wishes to thank the following sources for photographs, illustrations, and other materials used in this book. Care has been taken to determine and locate ownership of copyright material in this text. We will gladly receive information enabling us to rectify any errors or omissions in credits.

Photography

Cover: Thomas Kitchin and Victoria Hurst/firstlight.ca; p. 2 Ian Crysler; p. 3 Ian Crysler; p. 4 © Hulton-Deutsch Collection/CORBIS; p. 7 Ian Crysler; p. 13 Ian Crysler; p. 18 Ian Crysler; p. 19 © Barrett & MacKay Photo; p. 20 Michael Schmidt; p. 23 Tatiana Ivkovich/iStockphoto; p. 24 Brian Summers/firstlight.ca; p. 25 Leonard de Selva/CORBIS; p. 26 Ian Crysler; p. 27 Gunter Marx Photography/CORBIS; p. 28 (centre background) CP/Edmonton Sun/Darryl Dyck; p. 28 (centre inset) Michael Newman/Photo Edit Inc.; p. 28 (bottom) Ian Crysler; p. 29 Ian Crysler; p. 30 Ian Crysler; p. 40 © Paul A. Souders/CORBIS; p. 42 © David L. Moore – Lifestyle/Alamy; p. 43 Ian Crysler; p. 44–45 Photos.com; p. 44 (inset) Lynn M. Stone/Nature Picture Library; p. 45 (inset) Ablestock.com; p. 46 Courtesy Guinness World Records; p. 47 Ian Crysler; p. 48 CAMR/A.B. Dowsett/Photo Researchers; p. 49 (top) John Cancalosi/Nature Picture Library; p. 49 (bottom) CP PHOTO/Calgary Sun/Mike Drew; p. 50 (top) Michael Freeman/CORBIS; p. 50 (bottom) Ian Crysler; p. 52 Ian Crysler; p. 53 (top) Corel Collection Insects; p. 53 (bottom) CP PHOTO/Winnipeg Free Press – Jeff de Booy; p. 54 © Tony Kurdzuk/Star Ledger/Corbis; p. 55 design pics/firstlight.ca; p. 57 (centre left) Digital Vision/Getty Images; p. 57 (centre right) Valerie Giles/Photo Researchers Inc.; p. 57 (bottom) Lawrence Migdale Photography; p. 59 Ian Crysler; p. 63 © Clarence W. Norris/Lone Pine Photo; p. 66 Clyde H. Smith/© Peter Arnold, Inc./Alamy; p. 67 Ian Crysler; p. 69 © Calgary Zoo by Garth Irvine; p. 71 Ian Crysler; p. 73 Michelle D. Bridwell/Photo Edit, Inc.; p. 74 Elizabeth Quilliam/iStockphoto; p. 76 Corel Collections Divers and Diving; p. 77 (top) Don Tran/Shutterstock; p. 77 (bottom) Courtesy of Pier 21, National Historic Site; p. 78 Radius Images/Jupiter Images; p. 79 Gordon Wiltsie/National Geographic/Getty Images; p. 80 CP PHOTO/Chuck Stoody; p. 82 Franck Fife/AFP/Getty Images; p. 84 (main) Bach/zefa/CORBIS; p. 84 (inset) M. Jepp/zefa/Masterfile Corporation; p. 85 Ian Crysler; pp. 86–87 Janet Foster/Masterfile; p. 87 (inset) Used by permission of Canadian Environment Awards; p. 88 Vladyslav Morozov/iStockphoto; p. 89 (left) United States Department of Agriculture, http://www.ars.usda.gov/Wikipedia.com; p. 89 (right) Ian Crysler; p. 90 (top) Sebastian Duda/Shutterstock; p. 90 (bottom) S. Gschmeisser/SPL/PUBLIPHOTO; p. 91 Susan Trigg/iStockphoto; p. 94 (top) © Lksstock/Dreamstime.com; p. 94 (bottom) Ian Crysler; p. 95 Courtesy of Joe McIver, www.Joesworld.ca; p. 98 © Robert Shantz/Alamy; p. 99 © Clouds Hill Imaging Ltd./Comet/CORBIS; p. 100 Ian Crysler; p. 101 Ian Crysler; p. 102 CP PHOTO/Peterborough Examiner–Clifford Skarstedt; p. 103 (top) Canadian Press STRPA/Gareth Coplay; Canadian Press STRCOC/Jean Baptiste Benavent; p. 104 © Robert Holmes/CORBIS; p. 106 Courtesy of © VANOC/COVAN

2008; p. 107 blickwinkel/Alamy; p. 108 Canadian Press/Jonathan Hayward; p. 113 Ian Crysler; p. 115 Ian Crysler; p. 116 Ian Crysler; p. 117 (top) Ian Crysler; p. 117 (bottom) AP Photo/Rick Rycroft; p. 118 (top) Michael R. Clapp; p. 118 (bottom) Eric Hosking/Photo Researchers, Inc.; p. 119 AP Photo/Rick Rycroft/CP; p. 120 Canadian Press/Adrian Wyld; p. 121 CP Photo/Adrian Wyld; p. 123 Vladimir Rys/Bongarts/Getty Images; pp. 124–125 Courtesy of Festival of Quilts Heritage Park Historical Village, Calgary, AB; p. 124 (inset) Religion News Service photo, from "Fabric of Faith: A Guide to the Prayer Quilt Ministry" by Kimberly Winston, courtesy of Morehouse Publishing/CP; p. 127 Martha Berry, www.berrybeadwork.com; p. 128 BC & SK: Image Club/Fotosearch; Nunavut: Flags courtesy of www.theodora.com/flags used with permission; Canada: Darren Whitt/Shutterstock; p. 129 © Paul A. Souders/CORBIS; p. 130 Ian Crysler; p. 138 (top) Ron Zmiri/Shutterstock; p. 138 (bottom) Ian Crysler; p. 139 Ian Crysler; p. 142 Ralf Kraft/Fotolia; p. 143 Ian Crysler; p. 144 Ian Crysler; p. 145 Ian Crysler; p. 147 Ian Crysler; p. 148 Barrett & MacKay/© All Canada Photos/Alamy; p. 150 Ian Crysler; p. 151 Ian Crysler; p. 154 (left) Peter Ryan/National Geographic/Getty Images; p. 154 (centre) T. Parker/IVY IMAGES; p. 154 (right) Keith Levit Photography/World of Stock; p. 157 Ian Crysler; p. 158 (top) © Christopher Boisvieux/CORBIS; p. 158 (bottom) Ian Crysler; p. 159 Ian Crysler; pp. 160–161 © Allan Baxter/Digital Vision/Maxx Images; p. 162 Ian Crysler; p. 163 Ian Crysler; p. 165 Myrleen Ferguson Cate/PhotoEdit, Inc.; p. 166 Ian Crysler; p. 167 Ian Crysler; p. 168 Ian Crysler; p. 169 © Richard Hutchings/Photo Edit; p. 170 Ian Crysler; p. 171 Ian Crysler; p. 172 Ian Crysler; p. 173 Ian Crysler; p. 175 Village of McCreary/Courtesy of Nancy Buchanan; p. 176 Ian Crysler; p. 180 Willi Schmitz/iStockphoto; p. 181 Ian Crysler; p. 182 © Gunter Marx/Alamy; p. 183 (top) Ian Crysler; p. 183 (bottom) © Laura Norris/Lone Pine Photo; p. 185 Ian Crysler; p. 186 B. Lowry/Ivy Images; p. 187 Ian Crysler; p. 189 (top) Mike Agliolo/Photo Researchers, Inc.; p. 189 (bottom) Ian Crysler; p. 190 Ian Crysler; p. 194 Brandon Blinkenberg/Shutterstock; p. 196 sculpies/Shutterstock; p. 197 © LWA-Dann Tardif/CORBIS; pp. 198–199 Volker Kreinacke/iStockphoto; p. 198 (inset) Scala/Art Resource, NY; p. 200 Ian Crysler; p. 202 CP PHOTO/Jonathan Hayward; p. 204 © Roger Ressmeyer/CORBIS; p. 207 Ian Crysler; p. 209 Ian Crysler; p. 213 Ian Crysler; p. 215 Marilyn Angel Wynn/Nativestock.com; p. 217 Dainis Derics/iStockphoto; p. 218 (top left) PNC/© Photodisc/Alamy; p. 218 (top centre) Harris Shiffman/iStockphoto; p. 218 (top right) © Cphoto/Dreamstime.com; p. 218 (bottom left) Michael Tupy/iStockphoto; p. 218 (bottom centre) US FHWA Manual on Uniform Traffic Control Devices, sign number R5-6, retrieved from http://commons.wikimedia.org; p. 218 (bottom right) fritzkocher/Shutterstock; p. 226 Ian Crysler; p. 227 Ian Crysler; p. 228 Ian Crysler; p. 229 Keith Srakocic/Associated Press; p. 231 Ian Crysler; p. 233 Jim Larson/iStockphoto; p. 234 (top) © Gunter Marx/Alamy; p. 234 (bottom) Courtesy of Festival du Voyageur, www.festivalvoyageur.mb.ca; p. 235 Ian Crysler; p. 236 Ian Crysler; p. 237 (top) Courtesy of Owen Products, Inc., www.owens-pro.com; p. 237 (bottom) Grant Dougall/iStockphoto.com; p. 239 Ian Crysler; p. 241 (top) Sandra Tatsuko Kadowaki, www.tatsuko.etsy.com; p. 241 (bottom) Courtesy of Winipedia Commons; p. 244 Marco Rametta/iStockphoto; p. 245 Angelo Gilardelli/iStockphoto;

Illustrations